The Sacred Art of Dying

How World Religions Understand Death

Kenneth Paul Kramer

PAULIST PRESS
NEW YORK/MAHWAH

ACKNOWLEDGEMENTS

The Publisher gratefully acknowledges the use of the *Jesus* graphic in chapter 9 used by permission of Franciscan Herald Press, Illinois. The graphic originally appeared in their publication, THE WAY OF THE CROSS by Fr. Humbert Randag.

Library of Congress Cataloging-in-Publication Data

Kramer, Kenneth, 1941–
    The sacred art of dying.

    Bibliography: p.
    Includes index.
    1. Death—Religious aspects.   I. Title.
BL504.K73   1988   291.2'3   87–25854
ISBN 0-8091-2942-6 (pbk.)

Published by Paulist Press
997 Macarthur Boulevard
Mahwah, New Jersey 07430

Printed and bound in the United States of America

CONTENTS

Contents

To my "only" daughters

YVONNE ROSE
and
LEILA ANN

who know already that somewhere
in the distance lies the
soft spread of Heaven

I have already died all deaths,
And I am going to die all deaths again,
Die the death of the wood in the tree,
Die the stone death in the mountain,
Earth death in the sand,
Leaf death in the crackling summer grass
And the poor bloody human death.

H. Hesse, "All Deaths" in *Poems*

PREFACE

What is the purpose of death? Does existence end at death? If not, what happens after death? Are we reembodied in a similar or in a different form? Is there a final judgment? And how are we to prepare for our own dying? Answers to questions like these not only bring meaning into life but also suggest the value of bringing the experience of death into life. In fact, one of our major themes is what can be called spiritual death—a dying before dying. Unlike physical and psychological forms of dying, which have potentially negative implications, spiritual death evokes the experience of rebirth.

The title, *The Sacred Art of Dying,* was selected for two fundamental reasons. First, I want to highlight the fact that from a world religious perspective, dying is a *sacred* art, the final ritual, the last opportunity we have to discover life's ultimate meaning and purpose. Therefore, religious traditions ritualize the death process to remind us of the impermanence of life, and that whatever lies on the other side of death is as real, if not infinitely more so, than life itself. These rituals offer mourners a sense of victory over death, a way to dance on the dome of death.

Second, I want to emphasize that dying is a sacred *art*. Speaking about loving in theory and practice, Erich Fromm in *The Art of Loving* writes that living itself is an art, and that if we want to learn how to live and love we should proceed in the same way we would if we wanted to learn any other art. In this text we will speak in a similar fashion about death, for to see death as a sacred art involves both dying and being reborn together, and in an altogether new way. As the reader will discover, each of the sacred traditions represented in this text teach practitioners how to die artfully, not only before dying, but at death. Each tradition affirms that one must discover how to outlive the end of the world, while yet alive, so that all fears of death die. In this sense, dying becomes one of the greatest arts of life, and one of the most difficult to cultivate.

Distinct from most books in the field, *The Sacred Art of Dying* presents the story of death in its comparative religious context. Whereas many texts focus on psychological questions, sociological case studies, health care systems, medical ethics, the structure of wills, and sundry death issues (e.g., suicide, abortion, the death penalty, and the nuclear shadow), this text focuses primarily on religious attitudes toward death, dying and afterlife. What

1

do Hindus, Buddhists and the Chinese do about death? What do they believe happens after death? How do Jews, Christians and Muslims approach death? How do they prepare for death?

To address these questions, I introduce primary source materials and pertinent sacred texts from each tradition studied. In Chapter 1, images of physical, psychological and spiritual death are explored in literature and scripture. In Chapters 2-12, comparative religious attitudes toward death and dying are set forth. Each chapter in this cluster includes a story or *stories* which are central to each tradition, *conceptual teachings* about spiritual death and afterlife, and death *rituals*. Together, these three form a dynamic constellation which crystallizes each tradition's views. In Chapter 13, eastern and western viewpoints on death are presented through their creation stories. The eastern view of reincarnation is juxtaposed with the western view of the resurrection of the body. Chapter 14 then explores a common factor in each tradition studied—a self-surpassing death-and-rebirth experience. This chapter is especially significant for those who seek to be freed from the fear of dying.

Emerging from this structure is a fundamental assumption of the text— to be fully ready to die, a person must develop firm convictions about the dying process as well as practical methods for dying in a sacred way. Whereas culturally death is perceived as an anxiety-producing threat to human existence, it will be our purpose to demonstrate that the sacred traditions view death transformationally. At the same time, it is my hope that readers will become better prepared to face their own death experience and perhaps begin to develop a fearlessness in its face.

When asked for whom the book was written, I have typically replied that I had in mind at least two audiences: the university student who is probably taking a course in Death and Dying, and the non-matriculated student who for various personal reasons is seeking answers to death-related questions. It occurs to me now that there is also a third audience, anyone who experiences the inevitable vicissitudes of grief in response to loss (e.g., of a relationship, or of a job) and who wishes to be free from its associated fears and anxieties.

I have written therefore as simply as I possibly could while yet at the same time preserving the structural integrity and cultural pluralities endemic to the subject. This explains why there is no attempt here to be pedantically comprehensive. Rather, I have chosen a more evocative style to help readers become more deeply involved with the text.

I am aware that for some readers my method of re-presenting the central stories, teachings and rituals of the so-called world religions (drawn from their sacred texts) may appear, from a social-scientific point of view, naive, or, from a phenomenological point of view, overly-Western and idiosyncratic. At the same time I am aware that from the students' point of view, the method of narratively and textually introducing comparative world views on the death process is educationally catalytic. And it is for students that this book is written, for the student in all of us who still has much more to learn and who, therefore, is now eager to proceed.

I would like to acknowledge the following people for their invaluable help along the way: my father who says, "Why death? I'd rather live" and my mother who continues to smile within in spite of it all; my teachers, especially Bernard Phillips who first sensitized me to the integral and necessary connection between the sacred and the creative, Maurice Friedman who first introduced me to the connection between personal life and the life of dialogue, the Community of the Holy Trinity who first exposed me to monastic contemplation and whose on-going trinitarian brotherliness inspires me as I am brought face-to-face with death, and Elisabeth Kübler-Ross who reawakened for me the transcendent significance of the dying process in a presentation at Monterey, California entitled "Life and Transitions"; Professor J. Benton White, Coordinator, Department of Religious Studies, San Jose State University, for hiring me in the first place and for reading a portion of the manuscript; Professor Richard Keady who initiated the "Death, Dying and Religions" course at San Jose State and who first introduced me to the caring work done by the "Center for Living with the Dying"; my students whose questions and challenges help sharpen hazy expressions and who make me laugh at myself in the process; all who read portions of the manuscript including Stephen Voss, Ved Sharma, George Moore, Christian Jochim, Mishael M. Caspi, Noel King and Alan Leventhal; Earl Leeke Jr. and Brother William McKinley who made many stylistic suggestions from which the reader will necessarily benefit; Maria Mendenhall whose diligent and creative editing of the entire manuscript renewed the face of the text; Nora Jamison-Danko who diligently prepared the index; Kathy Cohen, Project Director of the "Paths to the Present" Program at San Jose State, who invited me to assemble a slide-illustrated module "Creation and Death: Eastern and Western Traditions" which became Chapter 13; the "International Society for Philosophy and Psychotherapy" at whose first annual meeting in October of 1986 I presented the material in Chapter 14; the American Academy of Religion at whose Western Regional Convention in April 1987 I presented "The Three Faces of Death" which became Chapter 1; Geoff Norman for his sensitive graphics; Douglas Fisher, my editor, and Paulist Press for their support; and the anonymous student who looked into my eyes and said: "Thanks for teaching me how to die!"

Most treasured is the woman who, like death, prefers to remain a mystery but who, like stars, outshines the night. For her, "life is eternal, love is immortal and death is only a horizon."

Kenneth Paul Kramer
Santa Cruz, California
Ash Wednesday, 1987

BEGINNING: DIALOGUE WITH DEATH

> Every phrase and every sentence
> is an end and a beginning,
> Every poem an epitaph[1]
>
> T.S. Eliot, *Four Quartets*

I can imagine no better place to begin this journey than with these lines from T.S. Eliot's "Little Gidding." Every sentence is an end and a beginning, for with each sentence the writer brings the experience of that sentence to a close, before beginning the next one. As the Zen monk Basho wrote: since "every moment of life is the last, every poem is a death poem."[2] Similarly, as we begin each new thought in this text, express each new feeling, the death of that thought and of that feeling is already present within our expression of it. Thus, as Eliot writes, the end of all human exploration, to arrive where we began and "to know that place for the first time," involves a "condition of complete simplicity (costing not less than everything)." We begin with these lines because they reinforce the central theme of each chapter, namely that dying, from the religious point of view, is a sacred art.

Given the complexity of the subject and the emotions which are likely to be raised as a result of this study, what would be the best way to approach the book?

The easiest and most helpful way for the reader to understand this text is to enter into a mutually reciprocal dialogue with its chapters. Each reader is in some sense a pilgrim making a ritual journey (i.e., leave-taking, journeying, arriving, and returning) always going toward the goal of death, for clearly death has its own unique mythos. Each traveler reaches this goal to the extent that death and the reader become dialogical partners. Though it may be necessary for you first to dialogue with your inability to accept any kind of afterlife before you can begin your dialogue with the stories of the dying process, it is the dialogue itself which opens reader and text to one another.

The goal of dialogue, Martin Buber writes, is to bring persons into true being, or what has been called authentic existence. "According to the logical conception of truth," Buber suggests, "only one of two contraries can be true, but in the reality of life as one lives it they are inseparable" and later he adds that "the unity of the contraries is the mystery at the innermost core of the dialogue."[3] For Buber, "genuine dialogue" differs from "technical dialogue"

5

(prompted solely by the need for objective understanding), and "monologue" (prompted solely by the need for self-gratification), in that each participant must be fully present to the other, and must respond to the other as a unique thou. From this perspective, a person's "true concern is not *gnosis*—unraveling the divine mysteries—but *devotio*—the way of (persons) in partnership with creation."[4]

To better understand this method, let me refer to an internal dialogue in which death is given a voice of its own. In T.S. Eliot's *Four Quartets,* the poet, during a Second World War air raid in England meets a stranger, a "compound ghost," who has the features of "some dead master."

> So I assumed a double part,
> and cried
> And heard another's voice cry:
> 'What! are *you* here?'
> Although we were not.[5]

Because he allows himself to become the other, the poet gives that other—death—a voice which speaks back. The dead master indicates that he is not anxious to rehearse old theories, and says to the poet that he should pray that he will be forgiven: "For last year's words belong to last year's language and next year's words await another voice." Death then reveals three gifts reserved for age, "expiring sense, impotent rage at human folly, and the shame of life-long motives exposed," and reveals that the aging spirit is bound to exasperation unless restored by a pentecostal fire.

Eliot's persona is able to look back at himself from the future because he chose death as a temporary companion. Eliot provides us here with a death-defying clue for facing the experience of dying: conversing with death brings the death-experience into life and thereby begins to prepare one to face death's inevitable claim. Eliot's protagonist is able to pass beyond the normal fear and disgust associated with death in order to listen to what death might have to say, and he is thereby awakened both intellectually and spiritually. The reader too, by virtue of a give-and-take discussion with the text, will become more cognizant of its content.

More specifically, to facilitate dialogue with the sacred art of dying you may wish to consider a journal keeping process, one which is certainly not a requirement for readers of this book.[6] I am aware that many will have neither the inclination, nor the time, to keep a journal. But for those who desire to deepen their dialogue with the death experience, a record of one's responses to the readings may be significantly revealing. Whether a sentence, a paragraph or a page, entries can be responses to, and developments of, text-related themes and ideas, as well as to ideas found in other readings (e.g., media, magazines, dreams, conversations, and private reflections). Journals usually contain insights and discoveries, disagreements and questions, comparisons and inner-reflections, comments on accompanying media excerpts or responses to the variety of human losses as experienced by the one who grieves. Journal responses are dated, even titled and occasionally reread. This enables journal-keepers to reflect more integrally on the process of death, dying and afterlife, and on the spiritual art of preparing for death.

The following student responses to the process of keeping a journal illustrate the journal's value:

I

It has taken me an entire semester to actually sit down and work this out—*my death*. I've made plenty of journal entries for certain. . . . But I wanted to examine my own views on death and I finally worked them out. I just ended up where I started from—dead is dead.

But now I have an understanding as to why. I don't fear death—not when I was a soldier and not now. Because it is a part of life. There is no sense in preparing for it because it will come regardless—and then I will cease to exist.

II

I have found that the use of a journal has helped me to explore these experiences more fully, and has helped me to discover the life in death and the death in life. The journal process has become a sort of confessional prayer for me: in writing I find myself, and myself sees itself in relation to God. It is a humbling experience.[7]

As these student writings indicate, in terms of initiating an ongoing dialogue with the text it is impossible not to, at the same time, enter into a dialogue with yourself. But what if, as we asked before, the reader does not like to write, or has no time to write? At the end of each chapter there will be a brief list of journal writing suggestions which can also be used as discussion-starters, as topics for short papers, or as chapter reflections to deepen the reader's understanding. Sample student journal writings are included in the Appendix and the reader may wish to peruse them before beginning the text.

As you begin to read, you will begin to discover your own way to navigate the stories, teachings and ritual practices of the world's sacred traditions, hopefully without turning back or becoming sidetracked by any of the exotic ports along the way. Our goal is to remain thoroughly open to each tradition's convictions about death so that we will be better able to develop our own attitudes and beliefs, dialogically, and in a holistic and global context. So, welcome to death!

NOTES

[1]T.S. Eliot, *Four Quartets* (New York: Harcourt, Brace & World, 1943), 58. In an unpublished dissertation "The Waiting Self: A Study of Eliot's *Quartets* as Meditative Poetry" (Temple University, 1971), I developed Eliot's thematic process of waiting meditatively, prayerfully and poetically. Now I see the dynamics of waiting as an expression of Eliot's dialogue with death.

[2]Quoted in Philip Kapleau's *The Wheel of Death* (New York: Harper Colophon Books, 1971), 65.

[3]Martin Buber, *Israel and the World: Essays in a Time of Crises* (New York: Schocken Books, 1963), 17.

[4]Maurice Friedman, *To Deny Our Nothingness* (New York: Delacorte Press, 1967), 288. I am deeply indebted in this section to Professor Friedman for his interdisciplinary insistence on the art of human dialogue in all of its nuances.

[5]Eliot, 53.

[6]I have discussed the pedagogical (and I could add existential) appropriateness of journal-keeping in the introduction to *World Scriptures* (New Jersey: Paulist Press, 1986).

[7]Jeffrey Reid and David Brooks, student journal papers, Fall 1985, San Jose State University.

Chapter 1   THE THREE FACES OF DEATH

> He searched for his former habitual
> fear of death and did not find it.
> 'Were was it? What death?'
>
> Tolstoy, *The Death of Ivan Ilych*

It began inauspiciously when Betty Maltz went on a vacation with her family near Clearwater, Florida. In hindsight, she describes herself at that time as a person who was stuck within biased, prejudicial, status-oriented living patterns, a person who only gave love to those who could help her further her wealth or her name. "I was stuck," she says, "and it took death to bring me back to life."

One night she experienced a pain in her right side which was so extreme that she had to be rushed to the hospital. She was told by a doctor in the small beach-town facility that she must have her appendix removed or it would burst. Since there were no beds or doctors available, she was rushed to the hospital where, before they could operate, her swelling disappeared.

Seven days later she was sent home; eleven days later she awakened blind, in pain, her body swollen with a 105-degree fever. She was immediately operated on for a ruptured appendix. The surgeons told her later that they removed a mass of gangrene the size of a man's head, and that she would not live. She passed the next forty-four days in a coma.

When she awoke, the gangrene had eaten so much of her blood that she needed massive transfusions of B-negative, more than was available. Once, when only several minutes from death, her uncle arrived who happened to have B-negative blood. He was hooked up directly to her arm, and with this injection she revived briefly, but then began failing again. Finally, a nurse entered the room, tried to take her pulse, checked for vital signs, found none, and pulled a sheet over her head. She was pronounced dead.

Just before sunrise, her father, a minister, visited her room. He had not been informed that she had died. He was so shocked when he saw her sheet-covered body that he could only repeat the name "Jesus, Jesus."

"I heard my father," she says, "and at the same time I heard echoes of more melodious voices. I was climbing a velvet green hill, where each blade of grass was vibrantly alive. The climb was effortless. A person in white

11

opened pearl gates and invited me to join a heavenly chorus but I said I wanted to return to my family. I will never forget the experience of the majesty of the presence of God throughout heaven.

"As I climbed down the hill, I witnessed the most glorious sunset I have ever seen. Just at that time, the sun was entering my hospital room through the window and its rays penetrated my sheets. I looked up and saw, dancing like dust particles in the sunbeams, two-inch-high ivory letters. They were Jesus' words from John 11:25: 'I am the resurrection and the life.' I reached up to touch each word that I saw in the sunbeam. When I touched them, warmth and healing entered my body and filled me with life. As I sat up to touch the words, my father was speechless. A nurse's aide ran out screaming: 'There's a ghost in there!' She never returned while I was in the room."

Days later, when Betty was about to leave the hospital, a doctor told her that if she were ever to have a child it would probably be mongoloid, that she would be blind, and would probably suffer morphine withdrawal symptoms. "I am thankful to report to people who hear this story today," she says, "that I have a perfect child, 20-20 vision, and have never had any drug problems. Rather, my life has been changed by God's gift, not by anything that I could do. With God's help I was able to drop my old prejudices. I can truly say now that every day is Easter!"[1]

Betty Maltz speaks with authority about her initial shock and fear of physical death, of her suffering and pain, of the emotional numbness which kept her from being able to respect other people and of her afterlife experience through which she was reborn with a new fervor for life. Through her near-physical death, her psychologically-numbed identity died, and spiritually she became a new person. She was able to shed the cocoon of self-doubt and self-uncertainty, of negative judgments and selfish expectations, and was able to emerge with a new attitude toward life and death.

Let us now shift our attention to a more structured look at the meaning of death and dying, for how we perceive death affects the way we live, how we live affects the way we die, and how we die gives new meaning to the way others can live.

In what follows, we will suggest that death may be viewed through at least three faces: *physical* (the irreversible loss of brain waves, central nervous system, heart and breath functions); *psychological* (the life of quasi-consciousness, living, as if having already died); and *spiritual* (the death or transformation of old patterns, habits, roles, identities and the birth of a new person). While in the remainder of the chapter we will elaborate each of these faces, our focus throughout the text will be on the third, spiritual death, since in one way or another each of the traditions studied emphasizes its necessity if fear of death is to be overcome.

Physical Death

What happens at death? That is, what is the physical process which occurs when a person reverses the process of being born? The following account vividly dramatizes one possibility:

> At sometime between 1:00 a.m. and 2:30 a.m., while asleep I felt overwhelmed by a force which sought to consume my very being. I began breathing with great difficulty (as if asthmatic) and sought to sit up but I only gasped faster, faster and though in desperation, I could not sit up. My chest tightened and I began choking and was near to suffocating. I struggled to rise but the force which was greater than me held me tightly to the bed—nor could I lift my arm, it was as lead. If only I could speak, perhaps my voice would frighten death away, but no, no utterance would come. My thought was, "no, death! you shall not have me." Alas! Now it was as if death embraced me. All was dark, my legs were heavy as well as my arms, suddenly I felt very tired. I wanted to sleep and sleep forever. Then I experienced nothingness and a feeling of falling. I looked and there was no bottom—only endless darkness. The darkness cloaked me but I did not welcome it. Where am I? The temperature increased as I continued to fall. Perspiration covered my body and though I felt a chill there was no wind. This is not for me—"death you will not have me," but I was not speaking for my throat was dry and only a hoarse croak resounded from the shadows. I tumbled—would it ever end?
>
> And as I laid in bed, I watched myself in the black hole. Was there no hope? Was there no escape? There I was falling perhaps doomed to do so for all eternity. Then I felt a pain in my chest, it tightened, and my body hurled even faster—and then my entire life flashed before my eyes.
>
> No, no this cannot and will not be! I must defy the force—it shall not have me! And with all my physical strength I put forth my last and perhaps my final effort and pushed the bed linen from my nostrils and breathed the cool night air. I awakened and sat upright—what a relief it was all a dream—thank God![2]

Traditionally, physical death has meant the loss of brain functions, heartbeat, pulse and breath. The Harvard Medical School Ad Hoc Committee to Examine the Definition of Brain Death identified four essential criteria: lack of receptivity and response to external stimuli; absence of spontaneous

muscular movement and spontaneous breathing; absence of observable reflexes, including brain and spinal reflexes; absence of brain activity, signified by a flat electroencephalogram (EEG).

Death then, we can say, is the irreversible termination of all essential
bodily functions. Statistically speaking, the number of deaths per 1,000 U.S.
population has dropped from 18 in 1920 to 8.6 in 1980. At the same time, life
expectancy in America rose from 55 for whites, and 45 for blacks in 1920, to
77 for white females, 72 for black females, 70 for white males, and 65 for
black males in 1980. Yet, despite a longer life expectancy, American culture
has turned its back on death, a fact made evident by our frequent use of
euphemisms for death.

Euphemisms Table[3]

Passed on	Made the change
Croaked	Got mertelized
Kicked the bucket	On the other side
Gone to heaven	God took him/her
Gone home	Asleep in Christ
Expired	Departed
Breathed the last	Transcended
Succumbed	Bought the farm
Left us	With the angels
Went to his/her eternal reward	Feeling no pain
Lost	Lost the race
Met his/her Maker	His/her time was up
Wasted	Cashed in
Checked out	Crossed over Jordan
Eternal rest	Perished
Laid to rest	Lost it
Pushing up daisies	Was done in
Called home	Translated into glory
Was a goner	Returned to dust
Came to an end	Withered away
Bit the dust	In the arms of the Father
Annihilated	Gave it up
Liquidated	It was curtains
Terminated	A long sleep
Gave up the ghost	On the heavenly shores
Left this world	Out of his/her misery
Rubbed out	Ended it all
Snuffed	Angels carried him/her away

Six feet under	Resting in peace
Consumed	Changed his/her form
Found everlasting peace	Dropped the body
Went to a new life	Rode into the sunset
In the great beyond	That was all she wrote
No longer with us	

These euphemisms substitute an inoffensive or less offensive expression for one that may offend or suggest something unpleasant. In our culture, individuals fear physical death because it is not understood and because it appears to be a final termination of life.

Beyond its physiological aspects, thinking about physical death produces internalized anxiety and fear, or, as Kierkegaard writes, the dread of dying. Historically speaking, this fear of death is as ancient as human self-reflective consciousness itself. Ernest Becker writes:

> The fear of death must be present behind all our normal functioning in order for the organism to be armed toward self-preservation. But the fear of death cannot be present constantly in one's mental functioning, else the organism could not function.[4]

It is as if humans are *a part of* the death process (and therefore afraid) and yet *apart from* it (and therefore function in spite of fears). Becker's point is that the inevitability of death forces everyone to explore its meaning in and for life. In fact, this raises three questions: What happens at death? What happens after death? And how should I prepare for my own dying?

Few have written more convincingly about the vicissitudes of physical death than Leo Tolstoy (1819-80). In his *Confession* he describes a conversion experience which was crystallized by a sudden, unpredictable reaction to a spiritual fable about the certainty of death. In this tale, the human condition is portrayed like that of a person who, fleeing from a furious beast, falls into a well and is held from dropping into the jaws of a devouring dragon below by clinging to a branch. The branch will inevitably give way, however, since two mice are gnawing at its roots. There is no escape; death is imminent.[5]

The power of this story led Tolstoy to the central question of his life: "Is there any meaning in life that the inevitability of death does not negate?" In *The Death of Ivan Ilych* (1886), Tolstoy narrated his answer.

The story begins with an obituary in the local "Gazette" which announces that the main character, Ivan Ilych, has died, and with responses to his death by family, friends and colleagues. The rest of the short novel is a flashback to Ivan's life, marriage, illness and death.

A public prosecutor and magistrate, Ivan was a person who judged and condemned others without being aware of them as people. When it is his turn to be sick and to suffer, he experiences the same indifference from others that he was once so proud of in himself. No one in his family tells him the truth. Doctors lie and provide false hopes. Their diagnosis is that it may be a floating kidney or chronic catarrh, or appendicitis. His wife grows increasingly distant and remains cold and uncaring. The judge is now the supplicant. His children ignore him, leaving him alone with his pain and fear. They deny the seriousness of his condition. Only Gerasim, his self-sacrificing servant who props up Ivan's legs, both pities him and does not lie to him. When the minor pain in his side progresses to a foul taste in his mouth and constant, debilitating pain, when he finally realizes that the doctors are lying when they tell him he will recover, Ivan admits:

> "It's not a question of appendix or kidney, but of life . . . and death. Yes, life was there and now it is going, going and I cannot stop it. Yes. Why deceive myself? Isn't it obvious to everyone but me that I'm dying, and that it's only a question of weeks, days . . . it may happen this moment."[6]

When finally Ivan accepts his death with all its dreadful implications, he asks a question which will reverberate throughout the text: "So where shall I be when I am no more?"[7]

Ivan experiences a complex nexus of *responses* to the inevitability of his death. He:

- questions where he will be when he is no more;
- feels choked with anger at everyone (except his servant Gerasim);
- refuses to accept his death;
- impersonalizes death as an "it" to keep it away from consciousness;
- understands that he is participating in a lie (since no one admits that he is dying);
- suffers incredible and unceasing pain;
- dreads being alone;
- feels helpless in face of the irreversibility of death;
- feels the absence of God;
- hears an inner voice, for the first time (the voice of death);
- feels guilty;
- vacillates between despair and hope;
- recalls a chain of memories, of recollections and flashbacks;
- confesses his guilt to a priest;

- discovers the Light;
- realizes that his life can be rectified;
- overcomes his fear of dying.

Ivan begins to experience a major shift in his attitude toward dying when one day he comes face-to-face with the dreaded, hateful reality of death. First he "hears" not an audible voice, but the voice of his soul say: "What is it you want?" "To live and not to suffer," Ivan replies. "To live? How?" his soul asks. Ivan answers: "As I used to—well and pleasantly." When Ivan again hears this inner voice, he asks: "Can it be that it is Death?" And his inner voice answers: "Yes, it is Death." Then Ivan asks the most crucial question: "Why do I have to endure sufferings?" And Death poignantly answers: "For no reason—they just are so." Beyond this, the author recounts, there was nothing.

Ivan's final response, which transformed his dread into triumphant acceptance, comes in the midst of terrible pain. As Ivan flares his arms about, screaming desperately, his son catches his father's hand and presses it to his lips. In this loving gesture lies Ivan's turning point, for by kissing his father's hand, the son shows Ivan, by example, how to reverse fear, doubt and mistrust into loving confidence. By reaching his father's heart and so rectifying their relationship, he inspires a parallel transformation of consciousness in his father.

At that crucial moment, simultaneously, Ivan catches sight of a light at the bottom of the black hole into which he falls. He discovers that when he lets go of pain and suffering, he has the sensation of reversing his direction. Suddenly, struck by a force, he falls through the hole. It is as if he is in a train moving forward but thinking he is going in reverse. He realizes that life's true direction is through death into unending life. Discovering that life can be rectified, it grows clear to him, as the sides of all previous restrictions fall away, that he is being born. He lets death go. He lets his pain be. He lets fear go. He feels sorry for his son and his wife but no longer for himself. The fear of death disappears—what oppressed him and would not leave suddenly vanishes. Where is death? What death? He feels no fear because there is no death, only light. He draws in a breath, breaks off in the middle of it, stretches out, and greets death peacefully.

We can see how profound these realizations are when we juxtapose them against other responses to Ivan's death with which the novel begins:

- Who cares?
- Who will get his job?
- Who will inherit his holdings?
- Thank God it's him who died, and not me!
- Now we'll have to fulfill the drudging demand of propriety!
- How much will it cost for the burial?

- Does his wife feel grief? Is she looking for distraction?
- Remember his pain and his suffering?
- It's God's will!

In place of these shallow considerations, Tolstoy leaves us with Ivan's final realization:

> In place of death there was light. "So that's what it is!" he suddenly exclaimed aloud. "What joy!" To him all this happened in a single instant, and the meaning of that instant did not change. For those present his agony continued for another two hours. Something rattled in his throat, his emaciated body twitched, then the gasping and rattle became less and less frequent. "It is finished!" said someone near him.
>
> He heard these words and repeated them in his soul. "Death is finished," he said to himself. "It is no more!" He drew in a breath, stopped in the midst of a sigh, stretched out, and died.[8]

In place of fear there arose certainty, in place of darkness, light, in place of suffering and pain, none, in place of anger, peace, and in place of death, a stretching out into an unknown future. For Tolstoi, it is at the point of death that rebirth occurs.

Psychological Death

Death is not just a biological cessation of the heart and electrical activity of the central nervous system and brain, for it reaches into everyone's life either threateningly (e.g., psychological death, when the anxiety of facing death threatens personal identity and creativity), or fulfillingly (e.g., spiritual death, when the anxiety of facing death catalyzes a transformative relationship toward the purpose of life and death).

If physical death is the irreversible termination of bodily functions, psychological death is the reversible termination of one's personal aliveness. It is rooted in a paralyzing bifurcation of the self, what William James calls the "divided self" or "heterogeneous personality," what Carl Jung calls a "split consciousness," and what a Zen Buddhist would call "dualistic consciousness." It manifests itself as habitual behavior, or an emotional deadening which results when normal psychic and volitional responses are shut down or suppressed.

A dramatic, even shocking example of psychological death is illustrated by Viktor Frankl's description of his concentration camp experiences. Frankl relates that prisoners, shortly after entering the camps, passed from their initial reaction of shock and outrage to a second response of apathy in which they achieved "a kind of emotional death" where feelings were blunted and it was easy to cease caring about being alive. Seeing inmates die became a commonplace, almost daily occurrence, and quickly was accepted as such. It was almost necessary, Frankl suggests, to stop caring in order to survive.

In modern cultures, psychological death manifests itself as habitual behavior, such as taking one's partner for granted. It appears as an emotional deadening, which occurs when normal psychic and volitional responses are suppressed or shut down. It also occurs as a psychic numbing, a necessity to some extent for all of us living under the nuclear shadow, in which fear of and anxiety about death are repressed. In each case the result is the same—a lessening of aliveness. As T.S. Eliot wrote: "I had not thought death had undone so many."

Samuel Beckett's tragicomedy, *Waiting for Godot,* perfectly demonstrates what is meant by psychological death. It takes place largely between two characters, Vladimir (Didi) and Estragon (Gogo), who are waiting for the arrival of Godot, who they hope will save them from their absurd situation. Whoever Godot is, and several interpretations have been suggested (e.g., God, death, Christ), Godot never comes. Instead, the practical, persistent, intellectual Vladimir badgers the volatile, forgetful, lethargic Estragon. Just as they are tied to waiting for Godot, they are tied to each other. They cannot stand to be without each other, yet, at the same time, they cannot stand to be together. Because of these opposites, there is an endless bickering which produces a series of threatened departures. Each character needs the other and yet, because of their uncomplementary natures, each annoys the other "to death." Each carries on a perpetual monologue. Their relationship has reached an impasse which they hope will be resolved if and when Godot arrives. And in the midst of this hell, they constantly experience pain, numbness and hopelessness, and they constantly frustrate each other.

Although suffering, they take no action, but just wait. This repetitive waiting is punctuated by Pozzo, the sadistic, attention-seeking master of Lucky, his slavish, luggage-bearer. Just as Vladimir and Estragon are psychologically tied to waiting for Godot, Lucky is tied to Pozzo by a rope around his neck which Pozzo controls. Ultimately, what can be said about one can be said about all four: each is afflicted with pain, physical as well as psychological; each is a social outcast and a vagabond, each fails to relate to the others because of fear and mistrust, each is caught in meaningless activity, and each struggles to achieve an identity through the quiet despair of waiting.

The play dramatizes the long, slow, often agonizingly, lonely process of dying both physically and psychologically. Pozzo compares human life to the passage of a day in which the morning light inevitably loses its effulgence and grows "pale (gesture of the two hands lapsing by stages) pale, ever a little paler until (dramatic pause, ample gesture of the two hands flung wide apart) pppfff! finished! it comes to rest." But, he continues, death is ever charging and bursts upon us when we least expect it. "That's how it is on this bitch of an earth."⁹

In what is perhaps the most revealing, as well as the most difficult speech to comprehend, Lucky, in his mechanical fashion, when ordered by Pozzo to think, offers a cosmological tirade. God, who is personal and outside of time, is impotent since he is without extension back into time. God is characterized as apathetic, as lacking the capacity for amazement and as speechless. Humans, for their part, despite nutritional advances and the varieties of physical culture, waste and pine, waste and pine in what Lucky calls the "great cold the great dark." All of this, he intones frantically, happens, what is more, "for reasons unknown." The utter absurdity of the human condition becomes in Lucky's imagination like an abandoned, unfinished skull.

The second act repeats the first; there is "nothing to be done," nothing happens and nothing is certain. It begins with an absurd nursery rhyme:

> A dog came in the kitchen
> And stole a crust of bread.
> Then cook up with a ladle
> And beat him till he was dead.
>
> Then all the dogs came running
> And dug the dog a tomb—

At this Vladimir pauses, ruminates and then resumes:

> And wrote upon the
> tombstone
> For the eyes of dogs to come . . . ¹⁰

He then repeats the whole lyric until it becomes like the picture of a picture within the picture, that is, an internalized repetition of itself.

As absurd as their situation becomes, Vladimir and Estragon still keep up the pretense of having a conversation:

ESTRAGON: In the meantime let us try to converse calmly, since we are incapable of keeping silent.
VLADIMIR: You're right, we're inexhaustible.
ESTRAGON: It's so we won't think.
VLADIMIR: We have that excuse.
ESTRAGON: It's so we won't hear.

VLADIMIR: We have our reasons.
ESTRAGON: All the dead voices.
VLADIMIR: They make a noise like wings.
ESTRAGON: Like leaves.
VLADIMIR: Like sand.
ESTRAGON: Like leaves.
                        Silence.
VLADIMIR: They all speak at once.
ESTRAGON: Each one to itself.[11]

The dead voices are not only in nature, but also are the voices of the living who live "as if" already dead, the voices of those who are bored to death, the voices of those who need something to give them the impression they exist, the voices of those born in the grave-digger's forceps. In perhaps the most telling lines of the play, Vladimir penetrates toward the heart of his absurd predicament:

VLADIMIR: Was I sleeping, while the others suffered? Am I sleeping now? To-morrow, when I wake, or think I do, what shall I say of to-day? That with Estragon my friend, at this place, until the fall of night, I waited for Godot? That Pozzo passed, with his carrier, and that he spoke to us? Probably. But in all that what truth will there be?

(Estragon, having struggled with his boots in vain, is dozing off again. Vladimir looks at him.)

He'll know nothing. He'll tell me about the blows he received and I'll give him a carrot. (Pause.) Astride of a grave and a difficult birth. Down in the hole, lingeringly, the grave-digger puts on the forceps. We have time to grow old. The air is full of our cries. (He listens.) But habit is a great deadener. (He looks again at Estragon.) At me too someone is looking, of me too someone is saying, He is sleeping, he knows nothing, let him sleep on. (Pause.) I can't go on! (Pause.) What have I said?[12]

What he has said, the insight into his condition which comes through his words, is not heard because Vladimir, like Estragon, Pozzo and Lucky, has died psychologically to his own aliveness. They are all in the chorus of the "dead voices." Each are victimizers and the victimized. All joy, expectation, hopefulness and excitement have been numbed by the enslaving habit of lives empty of meaning. Vladimir says to Estragon "Shall we go?" Estragon says, "Yes, let's go." They do not move. They cannot escape.

Spiritual Death

While it seems at times as if Bob Dylan is correct when he sings "He who isn't busy being born is busy dying," there is also a sense in which a person can accomplish both, together. Being born and dying, and vice versa, is a self-transformational experience, one which overcomes the fear of dying. Spiritual death is a process whereby one experiences salvation (western), or self-awakening (eastern), and by which the fear of death is de-repressed. Because the old self dies and a new self emerges, spiritual death transforms one's attitudes both toward life and in the face of death. The point is that spiritual death triggers awakening or rebirth.

Since we will be using this term "spiritual death" in a special way, let us be clear that it is not used here to mean a subjective loss of faith or the objective loss of the sacred.[13] In place of these meanings, spiritual death refers here to a death/rebirth experience which is necessary for one's well-being and personal wholeness.

Spiritual Death East and West

	EASTERN RELIGIONS	WESTERN RELIGIONS
TRADITION	Hindu Buddhist Chinese Tibetan Japanese	Egyptian Mesopotamian Jewish Christian Islamic
GOAL	Realization of Self Enlightenment Actualization of One's "True Self" (an inner-subjective realization of True Nature)	Salvation from Self Rebirth Participation in the Presence and Power of the Transcendent One
SOURCE	Immanent The Impersonal Within The "True Self" The Silence at the Center	Transcendent The Personal Without The "Wholly Other" The Word of God
METHOD	Self-Sacrifice Self-Surrender Spiritual Death/Rebirth	Self-Sacrifice Self-Surrender Spiritual Death/Rebirth

As the comparative outline indicates, spiritual death refers to dying while still alive, what Hindus call *moksha,* what Buddhists call *nirvana,* what Taoists call *wu wei,* what Zen calls *satori,* what Jews call living the Torah, what Christians call *kenosis,* and what Muslims call *fana.* In each instance spiritual death is a rebirth in which fear of physical dying is overcome, in which internalized anxieties and doubts are de-repressed, in which a deathless spirit is realized.

Though woven softly into its fabric, a major theme that emerges in this text is what Karl Rahner has called the "axiological presence of death." The word "axiological" literally means the axis of the "logos," the heart of wisdom. Here its use suggests both that death can be expressed in life in an anticipatory way, and that the presence of death in life creates the possibility of a spiritual rebirth or awakening to deathlessness. Each of the religious traditions teaches, in one way or another, that the best way to prepare for one's own death is to anticipate the death experience while yet alive. We shall speak, therefore, of the transformational presence of death in life, that is, of the de-repression of anxieties and a connatural liberation from fears associated with death.

While this experience of dying to separatistic I-consciousness is spoken of in multifarious images, there is cross-cultural testimony that in a special sense nothing happens, and nothing is done. Spiritual death is neither subjective activity nor objective forgetfulness. Rather, the isolated ego dissolves spontaneously only when the practitioner surrenders, or lets go, or gives up. In a special sense this complete sacrifice of any attempt to control or influence what happens next, this self-sacrifice is life-giving. Expressed in a Buddhist metaphor, self-negation is true self-affirmation. Expressed in a Christian metaphor, dying with Christ is also rising with him.

Self-Sacrifice

While there are innumerable examples of spiritual death, we will end this chapter with a brief review of the Hebrew story of the binding of Isaac (the Akedah). It is written that God one day decided to test Abraham, the first patriarch of the Jewish people. Totally unexpectedly, God asked him to sacrifice his son Isaac. Although explicitly God tested Abraham's faith, the story is also about Isaac's faith, for it is Isaac who was to be sacrificed. The story is all the more gripping since Isaac was Sarah's only son, born even though she was considered barren and beyond child-bearing age, and because it was through Isaac that God's covenantal promise was to be continued.

As the two men approached the sacrificial location, Isaac asked his father, "Here is the fire and the wood, but where is the lamb for the burnt offering?" Abraham replied: "God will provide the lamb for the burnt offering, my son." When they arrived, Abraham constructed a sacrificial altar, and tied his son Isaac on top of the wood. Abraham lifted his knife, and just as he was about to thrust it down, an angel of God stopped him. Abraham's faith had been proved. "You have not refused me your son, your only son," Abraham was told. Then, looking up, Abraham saw a ram caught in a thicket and offered it as a sacrifice in place of Isaac. And he called the place: "YHWH provides."[14]

In this story, there are in fact three self-sacrifices made. Sarah and Abraham are called upon to sacrifice their "only" son who is to father the nation of Israel, and Isaac of course is called upon to sacrifice his life. Abraham and Sarah had to die to their doubts about God's will and to their desires to preserve their son's life, and Isaac had to die to his own life-preserving instincts. All three sacrificed themselves and each experienced a spiritual death or in this case a willingness to surrender to God's will. Abraham and Isaac were of course in some sense reborn to one another in the process.

While one could say that the actions of both Abraham and Isaac were illogical and psychologically improbable, from the standpoint of faith God's demand for unconditional surrender makes perfect sense. Abraham, having already surrendered everything to God by following God's voice out into the desert, simply obeyed. Isaac, having already surrendered his life to the God of Abraham, simply obeyed. Each had already died to anything that was not God's will, and each had been reborn, in faith, to whatever God instructed.

As we shall see, to die spiritually before dying is to be reborn, fearless in the face of death. A spiritual death is self-transcendence, is getting outside prior confines of the self or, as it is analogously expressed in many traditions, is like falling unreservedly and compassionately in love. It is not a matter of choice.

NOTES

[1]From a taped talk by Betty Maltz. For a fuller account see her book *My Glimpse of Eternity* (Waco, Texas: Chosen Books, 1977). Raymond Moody, in *Life After Life* (Harrisburg, Pa: Stackpole Books, 1976), reports on some 150 cases like that of Betty Maltz which he characterizes as resuscitation or near death experiences.

[2]From class journal of Amtia Habteyes, Fall 1986, "Death, Dying and Religions," San Jose State University.

[3]Taken from Lynne De Spelder and Albert Strickland's, *The Last Dance* (Palo Alto: Mayfield Publishing Co., 1983), 19.

[4]Ernest Becker, *The Denial of Death* (New York: The Free Press, 1973), 16.

[5]Quoted in W.C. Smith, *Towards a World Theology* (Philadelphia: Westminster Press, 1981), 7.

[6]*Ibid.,* 129–30.

[7]Leo Tolstoy, *The Death of Ivan Ilych* (New York: New American Library, 1960), 130.

[8]*Ibid.,* 156.

[9]Samuel Beckett, *Waiting for Godot* (New York: Grove Press, 1954), 25.

[10]*Ibid.,* 37.

[11]*Ibid.,* 40–44.

[12]*Ibid.,* 58. What Vladimir has said is that habitual behavior deadens; what the sacred traditions teach is that spiritual death enlivens.

[13]In the 1960s, the latest theological current was called the "death of God." Theologians proposed that Christians act as if God did not exist (Bonhoeffer), as if the word "God" was dead (Van Buren), as if God died in Jesus (Altizer), as if God died in his absence (Hamilton), or as if God died when humans killed him (Nietzsche).

[14]This story is discussed in more detail in a forthcoming book by Mishael M. Caspi, Kenneth P. Kramer and Brent Walters called *Isaac, the Sacrifice: Jesus, the Sacrificed.*

JOURNAL EXERCISES

Physical Death

1. Recall your first encounter with death. Perhaps it was a childhood or early adolescent experience. Imaginatively relive it as if it is happening again, as if you are there again in that time-frame. In what ways did that earliest encounter with death influence the way you currently view death?

2. What does Ivan Ilych discover *about* physical death? What does Ivan discover *as he* actually dies? Do you accept or question his insight(s)?

Psychological Death

3. Think of your daily life as a series of habitual reactions by, and projections of, your personality. What is the biggest rut in which you always find yourself stuck? Discuss the last time that you did something spontaneously and broke out of your normal patterns.

4. What would happen if Godot showed up? If Godot's coming would save Vladimir and Estragon, could/would Godot ever come? If so, describe the way you think it would occur in Act III.

Spiritual Death

5. Imagine a situation in which you are converted/awakened to a new way of thinking, a new way of viewing yourself, a new way of understanding human problems. Is this new view worth dying for? If not, are there any principles or teachings or insights for which you would die?

6. Imagine that in a dream you are in a small East European village about to be beheaded. It is the custom in this village for the victim to call out one word which signals the victim's readiness to die. Only then does the executioner swing the blade. Putting yourself in that situation and thinking as spontaneously as you can, what would your last words be?

   After you have written your last words, ruminate upon them. What meaning do they have for your life?

Chapter 2 HINDU ATTITUDES
TOWARD DEATH

Die before dying,
die living.

Gopal, *Songs of the Bards of Bengal*

Mahatma Gandhi's last days were full of tension. Attempts at Hindu-Muslim unity and peaceful co-existence had collapsed into bloody riots. In January of 1948, there was an explosion at a prayer meeting where he was to speak. At later prayer meetings in New Delhi, there were occasional cries of "Death to Gandhi!" Shortly before he died, Gandhi told Manubehn, a close follower: "I wish I might face the assassin's bullets while lying on your lap and repeating the name of Rama with a smile on my face."[1]

As he moved into a crowd where he was to speak on the morning of January 29, 1948, it happened. A man brusquely pushed his way past Manubehn and fired three shots at Mahatma. "Sri Ram! Sri Ram!" Gandhi said, as he tumbled to the ground.

Death is, at most, minutes from any airport, train or bus station in any large city in India. Along the Ganges river bodies are regularly cremated, and the odor of burning flesh fills the air. On the streets of Calcutta, dead bodies become a nuisance to those responsible for keeping the streets clean. South, in Pondicherry, at the Bay of Bengal, followers of Sri Aurobindo Ghose tell visitors that his dead body lay outside for fourteen days without putrefying. In Puttaparthi, near Madras, pilgrims witness Satya Sai Baba "materialize" from nowhere in the palm of his hand *vibhuti* (the incensed ash of cow dung), and watch followers eat the ash which signifies a death to the world. In Madras itself, Shiva Bali Yogi teaches his followers a form of meditation in which practitioners temporarily die into the inner light of Shiva. To the north, just west of Bombay, in the Elephanta caves, is one of the most ancient Indian symbols of divinity, the Shiva lingham, which symbolizes the interfusion of sex and death (for Shiva is the god of creation as well as destruction). And finally, just south of New Delhi, lies Agra, home of the Taj Mahal. This marble splendor, which took twenty thousand laborers twenty-two years to erect, is a mausoleum built by Shah Jahan for his wife Mumtaz-i-Mahal, who died bearing their fourteenth child.

Even more so, when we look beneath the outer surface of India and into her sacred texts and stories, we find a preoccupation with death and what

27

happens after death. Here we will explore two of these ancient, sacred stories. The first is found in the Katha Upanishad, one of the most powerful, mystical documents and formative scriptures on Hindu culture (800–500 BCE). It relates the visit of Nachiketas to the Land of Death, Yama's kingdom. The second is from the epic grandeur of the *Bhagavad Gita* (500–200 BCE). It takes place on a battlefield in Northern India where the avatar Krishna teaches Arjuna about the illusion of death and about the deathless Self. In each story, a teaching dialogue occurs between an archetypal seeker and an immortal teacher. Both Nachiketas and Arjuna ask the same question: What is the purpose of life given the certainty of death? And both discover freedom from the question, indeed from all separateness, by realizing Atman (the deathlessness Self).

Nachiketas and Yama

In its early phase, the Hindu religious system developed from rituals and myths associated with sacrifice (*yajna*). In fact the Sanscrit root "*yaj-*" means "to offer," and the function of sacrifice was to offer something of' worth or value. The ensuing story illustrates a sacrifice made with impure motives. It begins when Vajasravas, in order to gain religious merit, offered to Agni (god of fire) a portion of his possessions. But his teenage son, Nachiketas, full of faith and fervor, noticed that his father had only provided cows that were too weak and too old to give milk. To provoke his father, Nachiketas said: "I am your best; offer me." Vajasravas pretended not to hear his son. But Nachiketas raised the issue again.

Finally, his father yelled in frustration: "I'll give you to death." Calmly, Nachiketas thought about all those who had gone to death never to return and about the futility of the merits and possessions of this world. He resolved to visit death, but not as others had, for he intended to return when he had discovered death's meaning.

Hindu scriptures tell us that Yama (to restrain), the King of Death, was the first of the immortals to give up immortality in order to conquer death as a mortal. Yama is presented as the god of the dead, the ruler of the departed, and it is he who prepares a resting place for the dead. As the first man to reach the world beyond, Yama is referred to as the father of fathers, the lord of death who presides over the world of the dead. He is pictured with a fearful dark green skin and with glowing red eyes. Usually he carries an ax, a sword and a dagger. In the *Upanishads,* as in the *Mahabharata,* Yama appears as splendid like the sun, of faultless blackness with beautiful red eyes.

Nachiketas was not afraid for he was determined to learn the secret of death. He left his father's house and after a long and arduous journey arrived at Yama's house, only to find that Yama was away and would not be back for several days. Undeterred, Nachiketas quietly waited for three days. He neither ate nor drank, nor did he disturb the calm running of Yama's home.

When Yama returned he was so impressed by Nachiketas' fortitude and determination that he decided to reward him:

> Since for three nights, O Brahman, thou hast dwelt in [this] my house, an honoured guest, [yet] nothing eating, I now salute thee, Brahman, may it go well with me. Three boons [I grant] thee, choose [what thou wilt].[2]

Nachiketas' first wish was not for himself. Rather, as a good Hindu, he asked that his father would receive him back without anger or rancor, and that their relationship would be restored. Yama was even more impressed and he promised that all would be as it was between father and son.

Then Nachiketas asked Yama to teach him how to perform the fire sacrifice which leads one to the realm of immortality. In response, Yama taught Nachiketas how to build the altar, with what materials, and how high. To honor the selflessness he saw in Nachiketas, he named the fire sacrifice after him.

Nachiketas then made his third request—he asked Yama to tell him the secret of death and life. He placed his question as succinctly as he could:

> When a man is dead, this doubt remains
> Some say, 'He is' others again, 'He is not.'
> This would I know, by thee instructed,—
> This is the third of the boons [I crave].[3]

A profound subtlety is to be noted here. With the receipt of the second boon, Nachiketas has been assured of immortality. Having received the knowledge of the sacred flame which leads to true life and, indeed, already standing in that further world, the knowledge he now seeks goes deeper. His final question is not "Do I survive?" but "What survives?"

"Ask for some other boon!" Yama replied. "Ask for anything you like, anything, but don't ask about death." But Nachiketas would not be dissuaded. "Sensual pleasures do not last. They die as mortals must. Dispel my doubt. Does one live after death or not?"

In the face of Nachiketas' persistence Yama finally agreed to reveal what, until now, had remained a secret. After giving Nachiketas the mystic sound which all scriptures praise—*Om*—(the Absolute, Imperishable Brahman), Yama said:

> This wise one is not born nor dies;
> From nowhere has He [sprung] nor has He anyone become;

Unborn is he, eternal, everlasting and primeval,—
He is not slain when the body is slain.
Should the killer think 'I kill',
Or the killed 'I have been killed',
Both these have no [right] knowledge: — Both in Avidya
He kills not, is not killed.
More Subtile than the subtile (sic), greater than the great,
The Self is hidden in the heart of creatures [here]:
The man without desire [all] sorrow spent, beholds It,
The majesty of the Self, by the grace of the Ordainer.[4]

When the body dies, the Self (Atman) does not die! The secret of death
is to *realize* the Supreme Self hidden in the heart, not by preaching, not by
sacrifice, but through meditation and grace. It can be attained, finally, only
by those whom the Self chooses. "One who knows the Self," Yama said, "puts
death to death." This realization, called *moksha* (liberation), emancipates
one from the vagaries of life's *karma* (action) and from *samsara* (the endless
round of birth, death, and rebirth).

Yama then described this inmost secret through an extended metaphor
in which the Self is depicted as Lord of a chariot: one's body is the chariot;
the intellect is the charioteer; the mind is the reins; the senses are the horses;
and one's desires are the roads traveled. When a person lacks discrimination
and discipline, the horses run out of control. But when the mind rests in Atman, the charioteer reaches the supreme goal of life and will never again fall
into the jaws of death. Yama then became extremely explicit:

Lo! I will declare to thee this mystery.
    Of Brahman never-failing,
And of what the self becomes
When it comes to [the hour of] death.
Some to the womb return,—
Embodied souls, to receive another body;
Others pass into a lifeless stone
In accordance with their works,
In accordance with [the tradition] they had heard
When all things sleep, [that] Person is awake,
    Assessing all desires:
That is the Pure, that Brahman,
That the Immortal, so they say:
In It all the worlds are established;
Beyond it none can pass.[5]

Those who die unaware of the Self are either reborn, or return to a lower evolutionary state as determined by their *karmic* life-actions. Those who die aware of the Self are at last released from the cycle of birth and death—eternal peace is theirs. Thus realized, they become immortal.

> Of the measure of a thumb is [this] Person,
> The Inmost Self, in the heart of creatures abiding ever.
> Stand firm! and from thy body wrench Him out
> Like pith extracted from a reed.
> Pure and immortal He: so know Him!
> So know Him: pure and immortal He!
> So did Nachiketas learn this [holy] science
> By Death declared, and all the arts of Yoga:
> Immaculate, immortal, to Brahman he won through;
> And so shall all who know what appertains to Self.[6]

Freed from all illusions of separateness by Yama's teachings and through his own inner realization, Nachiketas attained immortality in Brahman (the Absolute Reality) while yet alive. In the process he learned:

1. that death is ever-present within the body and in the world at every moment;
2. that while the gross and the subtle bodies change and die, the True Self of each person is undying;
3. that in order to realize the True Self one must die to fears about living and dying;
4. that the only teacher about death is Death itself;
5. that through the art of wholehearted and disciplined surrender, one attains immortality while yet alive.

Arjuna and Krishna

The *Bhagavad Gita* (Song of the Lord) presents a dialogue between Krishna, the divine teacher, and Arjuna, the warrior disciple. The context for the dialogue is a battlefield in northern India where a civil war is about to begin between the Kauravas and the Pandavas, cousins by birth. The Kauravas have wrongly taken possession of land belonging to Pandavas. Arjuna, third of the five Pandavas, is despondent at the prospect of killing his relatives. The land seems less important to him than preserving the lives of his family and friends. Should he fight, or not? The emotional weight of this question immobolizes him.

Krishna, his charioteer, a direct manifestation of Vishnu (he, Brahma and Shiva comprise the Absolute Brahman), listens to Arjuna's despair. Arjuna refuses to fight because he does not wish to kill his kinsmen nor to destroy the social fabric in the kingdom. But then Krishna speaks: "All things born must die," and "out of death in truth comes life" (B.G. 2:27). Krishna tells Arjuna that he in fact has no alternative but to fight, since that is the *dharma* (duty). Furthermore, Krishna says, death is an illusion. Echoing Yama's words in the Katha Upanishad, Krishna begins:

> Who thinks that he can be a slayer,
> Who thinks that he is slain,
> Both these have no [right] knowledge:
>   He slays not, is not slain.
> Never is he born nor dies;
> Never did he come to be, nor will he ever come to be again:
> Unborn, eternal, everlasting he—primeval:
> He is not slain when the body is slain.
> If a man knows him as indestructible,
> Eternal, unborn, never to pass away,
> How and whom can he cause to be slain
>   Or slay?
> As a man casts off his worn-out clothes
> And takes on other new ones [in their place],
> So does the embodied soul cast off his worn-out bodies
>   And enters others new.[7]

Death therefore is natural and unavoidable. But it is not real. Only union with Brahman is real. Only identity with the True Self (Atman) is real. In fact, the focus of Hindu scriptures is upon the Eternal Self, how to recognize it and how to realize it. Krishna expounds at length on the Eternal Self and teaches Arjuna the yoga of devotion and surrender (*bhakti yoga*). He also tells Arjuna that he should fight yogically without considering the results of his action (*karma yoga*). Arjuna begins to understand here that by yoga Krishna means specific meditative practices intended to yoke the practitioner with the Highest Self.

This teaching both fascinates and disturbs Arjuna for he is aware of the difficulties involved in yogic practice. "What if one faithfully practiced yoga yet failed to reach the goal of yoga? What would become of such a person?" he asks. Krishna replies:

> Not in this world nor in the next
> Is such a man destroyed or lost:
> No doer of fair works will tread

An evil path, my friend, no, none whatever.
The worlds of doers of good works he'll win,
And dwell there endless years;
And then will he be born again, this man who failed in Yoga,
In the house of pious men by fortune blest.
Or else he will be born in a family
Of real Yogins possessed of insight;
But such a birth as this on earth
  Is yet harder to win.
There is he united with the soul
(*Buddhi*)
As it had matured in his former body;
And once again he [girds his loins,]
Struggling for [Yoga's] highest Prize.[8]

Like those of the *Katha Upanishad,* Krishna's teachings on death argue four basic attitudes:

1. the death of one's physical body is inevitable and is not to cause prolonged grief;
2. the subtle dimension of the person (*jiva*) does not die at death, rather takes on a new body;
3. the Eternal Self (Atman) is birthless and deathless, and cannot be destroyed;
4. one who realizes the Eternal Self while yet alive, will not be reborn but, at death, will merge with Brahman.

Still, however, a large question arises: How does one realize Atman? It is one thing to theoretically acknowledge the Eternal Self and quite another to actualize it. It is the answer to this question that constitutes the sacred art of dying for the Hindu.

To this most crucial question, Krishna provides three clues, each in the form of a spiritual practice or yoga which, when mastered, prepares one for death.

The first, called *jnana yoga* (intellectual, intuitive, metaphysical meditation), is the way of knowledge, the single-minded awareness of the Eternal Self. Through meditational disciplines and ascetic austerities, one achieves a deathless identity in life. While the *Gita* acknowledges *jnana yoga,* which has its roots in the earlier *Upanishads,* Krishna emphasizes *karma yoga* (physical, self-sacrificial, detached activity) and *bhakti yoga* (emotional, self-surrendering devotion to the divine).

To live righteously, let alone to die artfully, one must act without possessing any attachments to that action. To be delivered from the fear of death and the certainty of rebirth, one must act without desire or purpose, independently of the results of the action. Here Krishna teaches one of the greatest insights of Hindu spirituality, what might be called the paradox of actionless action. To begin to understand this paradox one can think of long distance runners or swimmers who become so in tune with the rhythm of running or swimming that it moves them rather than the other way round. When the dancer becomes the dance, the dancer is no longer merely dancing but rather being danced by the dance. By offering every activity as a sacrifice to Krishna and by becoming detached from its rewards, the performer dies into Krishna and becomes the True Self.

There is one activity, beyond all others, which Krishna says should be performed without any intellectual, psychological or emotional attachments. The one way to assure detachment is to surrender oneself wholly to the Divine. The *bhakta's* ultimate goal is to be single-heartedly devoted to God, to offer everything that one does as a sacrifice to God. This becomes radiantly clear when Krishna reveals the highest secret to Arjuna:

> Further, the highest secret of all,
> My supreme message, hear.
> Because thou art greatly loved of Me,
>
> Therefore I shall tell thee what is good for thee.
>
> Be Me-minded, devoted to Me;
> Worshiping Me, revere Me;
> And to Me alone shalt thou go; truly to thee
> I promise it—(because) thou art dear to Me.
>
> Abandoning all (other) duties,
> Go to Me as thy sole refuge;
> From all evils I thee
> Shall rescue; be not grieved![9]

Whereas the practice of sacrifice in the *Upanishads* referred to an external ritual which included fire, drink, chants, stories and a grain or animal offering, Krishna teaches devotional sacrifice. Performing all actions without attachment to gain or to the results, the devotee sacrifices attachments to the sacrificer. This self-sacrifice, doing everything for Krishna, becomes in Hindu terms our second birth. Actually, from the Hindu viewpoint we experience two births after our physical birth—first when we practice external sacrificial rituals and then when we die internally (and are born anew).

That the *Gita's* highest secret is most appropriately practiced at the time of death becomes clear when Krishna counsels Arjuna to follow a path which the *Vedic* seers call Eternal:

> Let a man close up all [the body's] gates,
> Stem his mind within his heart,
> Fix his breath within his head,
> Engrossed in Yogic concentration.
> Let him utter [the word] Om, Brahman in one syllable,
> Keeping Me in mind;
> Then when his time is come to leave aside the body,
> He'll tread the highest Way.
> How easily am I won by him
> Who bears Me in mind unceasingly,
> Thinking of nothing else at all,—
> A Yogin integrated ever.[10]

Many traditions, east and west, stress the significance of a person's last words, last thoughts, last prayers, last meditation. Krishna reveals that one may be liberated from rebirth by being wholly concentrated, by keeping mind and heart united, by deeply surrendering to Krishna and by uttering the *mantra Om* as one dies. At this, Arjuna realizes that final thoughts determine the first moments of after-death experience.

In Krishna's teaching, the art of dying, like *bhakti yoga,* requires self-surrender. From Krishna's viewpoint, one dies yogically (with mindful concentration and absorption into the Self) when one falls in love with Krishna and becomes devoted to him. At that point forms and rituals vanish, sacred texts are superseded, temples are transcended. Nothing remains to bind a person to this life. Whether through the recitation of *mantras* (sacred sounds) or through selfless acts of mercy, the *bhakta* welcomes everything that happens as a gift from the beloved. As the result of this intensely all-absorbing love, the *bhakta* is able to welcome death when it comes.

Reincarnation and Moksha

One of the most fundamental teachings of the Upanishads is the development of the idea of *samsara,* or reincarnation. Reincarnation, also called transmigration, refers to the successive life-embodiments of an individual soul (*jiva*). In India, the flux of all life is viewed as a continual series of births, deaths and rebirths. Reincarnation blends the natural law of evolution with the spiritual process toward awakening. At the sub-human level, growth is automatic and progresses toward ever increasing complexity, from

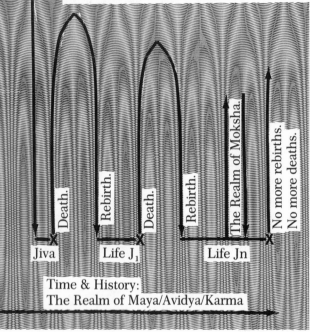

Hindu Cosmology

In the beginningless beginning Brahman-Atman "Breathed breathlessly" and emanated into all that is.

Death.
Rebirth.
Death.
Rebirth.
The Realm of Moksha.
No more rebirths.
No more deaths.

Jiva   Life J₁   Life Jn

Time & History:
The Realm of Maya/Avidya/Karma

inorganic to organic to vegetative to human levels. At the human level, the soul has the opportunity to break out of this cycle of births, deaths and rebirths. From the point at which each new self-consciousness begins, to the point of final awakening, each soul is *karmically* conditioned to choose rebirth. When a person awakes, and sees with a spiritual eye, reincarnation is no longer a necessity.

As the accompanying diagram illustrates, in the beginningless beginning the non-dual One became many. Each soul (*jiva*) lives, dies and is reborn many, many times. Finally, in one lifetime, the *jiva* or separated consciousness: wakes up from *avidya* (the ignorance of not knowing who the knower is), wakes up from *karma* (the impersonal law of causation in which action produces reactions), wakes up from *maya* (the illusion of separated identity), and realizes (Atman) True Self. When the Self-actualized *jiva* dies, he or she is not reborn except if that soul has a compassionate purpose.

While most people think of reincarnation as a unilateral progression of one's soul from life-form to life-form, in fact there are a variety of possibilities. Those who feel most comfortable in dimensions of time and space, who have created a lot of unfinished *karma* which needs to be completed, will choose to be reincarnated. Others may choose to leave the physical dimension altogether and to enter into an altogether different dimension. Still others, who are Self-realized in life, will not be reborn at all, but will be absorbed into the ground of Brahman.

But what happens to the person who chooses to be reborn in another human form?

To illustrate what happens at death from the Hindu standpoint, we will refer to the accompanying illustration. At death, the outer or gross body (skin, bones, muscles, nervous system and brain) falls away. The subtle body sheath (comprised of *karmic* tendencies, knowledge, breath and mind), which coats the *jiva*, or psychic sub-stratum begins to fall away. After death, the *jiva* at first continues to remain within or near the body. Soon, however, it shakes loose from the body and, for an appropriate period of time, enters a reality which is conditioned by its earthly life-cravings. When these cravings

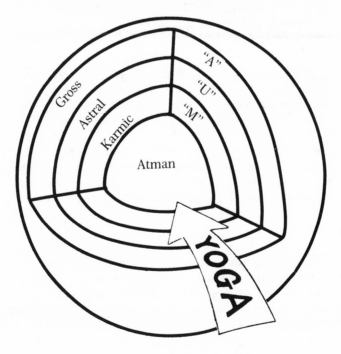

Hindu Psychology

have ceased, the *jiva* enters a temporally blissful existence until, at a *karmically* determined time, it takes on a new physical body and is reborn.

That one is reborn, what body one is reborn into, and at which level in the evolutionary scale, is solely determined by *karma*. According to the impersonal, cosmic law of *karma*, actions and reactions are equal, opposite, and other-initiating. *Karma* is the law of causation especially on the moral and spiritual sphere. It holds true regardless of time, place, person or events. While *karma* is individual (what I do) and collective (what happens to me), while it is fixed (sex and race) and variable (thoughts and attitudes), it is always either good or bad. Good *karma* for instance produces good effects both in this life and in the next. A person may be born in a higher caste or with higher spiritual realizations. *Karma* then is the force which determines one's next life-form. As long as life is *karmically* conditioned, rebirth is guaranteed. In light of this, we may ask, what hope is there?

In the *Upanishads*, it is said that the transmigration of the Self is conditioned upon a person's good or bad actions. The unliberated self passes from one life to another, but the person liberated from *maya, avidya and karma* is absorbed into the Real. Therein lies one's hope. The highest realization for Hindus is to actualize the Eternal Self while yet alive.

Almost all Hindu teachers agree that *moksha*, the final liberation from birth and death, is the goal of life. This final union with the Brahman, which takes place before death and which is described as a state of ecstasy, is a condition of pure joy (*ananda*). The early Hindu sages therefore taught *moksha* as the way to liberate the mind from fear of death. *Moksha* is a spiritual death which accentuates at least three consequences:

1. one's escape (liberation) from the endless cycle of birth and death and birth and death;
2. the activation of *samadhi* or emptiness, the void or nothingness which is also absolute fullness and compassion;
3. a liberation from the effects of the reincarnational cycle at death, and a return to full identification with Atman.

Death Ritual

As a Hindu approaches death, he or she is surrounded with religious rites and ceremonies which support the dying person throughout the death process. Here we will briefly consider two questions: What do Hindus do just before dying? And what is done with the physical body after death?

Before a Hindu dies, the son and relatives put water taken, if possible, from the Ganges into the dying person's mouth. While this relieves the pain of thirst, it also assures the family that the dying person will receive a blessing from the Ganges which will bring peace. At this time family and friends sing devotional prayers and chant *Vedic mantras*. More than the words, which are themselves comforting, the tone of the chanting soothes the dying person and comforts relatives in their time of stress and grief. If a monk is present, he recites *mantras* in order to revive the person; if unsuccessful, he will pronounce the person dead.

Prior to cremation, the body is washed, anointed, the hair (and beard) trimmed, and it is given new or clean clothes. During the procession relatives and mourners, who carry the body to the cremation ground, chant verses which invoke Yama's help. The body is then placed on a funeral pyre. If a man has died, the deceased's widow sits in vigil beside him and then is asked to rise up. The eldest son finally walks around the pyre three times, each time pouring sacred water on the deceased. He then sets fire to the wood with a torch that has been blessed. All the while relatives and mourners chant *Vedic mantras* to quicken the soul's release such as:

Let your eye go to the Sun; your life to the wind; by the meritorious acts that you have done, go to heaven, and then [for rebirth] to the earth again; or, resort to the Waters, if you feel at home there; remain in the herbs with the bodies you propose to take.[11]

Three fires ignite the body which is soon reduced to smoldering bones.

While three practices characterize the variety of death rituals in India—cremation, burial and outside disintegration—Hindus believe that cremation is most spiritually beneficial to the departed soul. It is believed that as long as the physical body remains visible, because of the astral body's lingering attachment, the soul remains nearby for days or months. The corpse is therefore burned so that the soul can begin its journey as soon as possible.

When the mourners return home they are obliged to ceremonially bathe themselves, again recite *mantras,* and offer a libation at the family altar, a practice which is continued for ten days. Three days after the death, the eldest son returns to the cremation spot, takes the remaining bones, and buries them or casts them into a river. These ceremonies support the soul in its journey into the next world, whether from one body to the next, or from this life to the Eternal Brahman.

Finally, we return to the death that conquers physical death, that death which is the birth of Self. Of the many schools and religious groups in India which practice anticipatory dying, none stands out more than the Bauls of Bengal. Poets, mystics, ecstatics, the Bauls were *bhaktas,* devotees of Vishnu or Krishna, who practiced meditating on their own death to become surrendered to God. Such devotees were willing to sacrifice their own desires for worldly possessions to be reborn in God—dead to self yet fully alive:

> Between the doors
> of birth and death,
> stands yet another door,
> wholly inexplicable.
>
> He who is able
> to be born
> at the door of death,
> is devoted eternally. . . .
>
> (Therefore)
>
> Die before dying,
> die living.[12]

NOTES

[1]M.V. Kamath, *Philosophy of Death and Dying* (Honesdale, Pa: Himalayan International Institute, 1978), 199.

[2]Katha Upanishad, I:9. This and the remaining quotations in this chapter are, unless otherwise indicated, from *Hindu Scriptures,* translated by R.C. Zaehner (New York: E.P. Dutton, 1966).

[3]Katha Upanishad, 1:20.

[4]Katha Upanishad, 11:18–20.

[5]Katha Upanishad, V:6–18.

[6]Katha Upanishad, VI: 17–18.

[7]Bhagavad Gita, 2:19–22. The following quotations are taken from *The Bhagavad Gita,* translated by Franklin Edgerton (New York: Harper Torchbooks, 1944).

[8]Bhagavad Gita, 6:40–43.

[9]Bhagavad Gita, 18:64–66.

[10]Bhagavad Gita, 8:12–14.

[11]Traditional *mantra* used at cremation.

[12]Gosain Gopal in *Songs of the Bards of Bengal* translated by Deben

Bhattacharya, (New York: Grove Press, 1969), 65. A discussion of Baul imagery is found in David Kinsley's " 'The Death That Conquers Death': Dying to the World in Medieval Hinduism," in *Religious Encounters with Death* (University Park, Pa.: The Pennsylvania State University Press; 1975), 97–108.

JOURNAL EXERCISES

1. Imagine, as best as you can, that you are Nachiketas and that you are able to travel to Yama's kingdom. Imagine the surroundings. Construct a conversation with Yama in which you ask Yama the most pressing questions you have about death.
2. Create a dialogue with Lord Krishna in which you ask him to explain what he means when he says: "When a person leaves the earthly body he should remember me. Those who are devoted to me will come to me." What might it be like to go to Krishna at death? Ask Krishna, and record his responses.
3. What do Nachiketas and Arjuna discover in common about the reality of death, and what does that realization allow them to understand about life?
4. What is your response to the Hindu teaching of *moksha*? Do you believe that it is possible to fully wake up in life, to experience the Eternal Self before you die? If so, explain what "Eternal Self" means to you. If not, explain why.
5. Restate in your own words the Hindu rationale for cremation. What is your response to this teaching. Would you want to be cremated? If not, explain your reasons for not wanting this done. What would you like done with your corpse?
6. How might an intelligent, practicing Hindu answer the following question: What does your tradition teach about how to die artfully? That is, what is the most sacred way of dying?

Chapter 3 BUDDHIST ATTITUDES TOWARD DEATH

> Of all mindfulness meditations,
> That on death is supreme.

Buddha, *The Sutra of Buddha's Entering into Parinirvana*

Buddha's teachings about death can be summed up as follows: all life is forever vulnerable to suffering; everything is constantly changing; while whatever is born must sooner or later die, there is no fixed self that dies; and as long as one is completely absorbed in grief there can be no release from the fear of death. All of these insights are contained in a brief story he once told his disciples about Kisa Gotami who had lost her only son.

Gotami was a frail, impoverished and unornamented woman. At that time, it was the custom that a woman upon her marriage would go live with her husband's family. Although Gotami came from a peasant background, his relatives never mistreated her. Due to her son's birth, Gotami gained the respect and her prosperity from her in-laws. However, when her child died, she was tormented by the fear that she would also lose the respect which she had gained for the first time in her life.

An immense sorrow welled up within her. She took her dead son on her hip and went from door to door throughout the village crying: "Give me medicine for my son." At this her neighbors laughed in derision: "Where did you ever find medicine for the dead!"

Now a certain wise man overheard her question and told her to go to a nearby monastery where the foremost individual in the whole world resided. "Ask him; he'll know." Recognizing the truth of what she heard, she traveled to the monastery. When she met the Buddha she said: "O Exalted One, give me medicine for my son!" The Buddha replied:

> You did well, Gotami, in coming hither for medicine. Go enter the city, make the rounds of the entire city, beginning at the beginning, and in whatever house no one has ever died, from that house fetch tiny grains of mustard seed.[1]

Full of hope, Gotami went from house to house asking for the mustard seeds but she could not find a house where death had not struck. Realizing this, she was overcome with Buddha's insightful compassion not only for her

43

but for the whole village. Awakened by this new awareness, she carried her son to the cremation grounds, and when she cast him in the fire, she said victoriously:

> No village law, no law of market town,
> No law of a single house is this—
> Of all the world and all the worlds of Gods,
> This only is the Law, that all things are impermanent.[2]

When Gotami returned to the Buddha, he asked if she had found any mustard seeds. "Done, reverend sir," she said, "is the business of the mustard seed." At that the awakened Teacher recited the following stanzas:

> Though one should live a hundred years,
> Not seeing the Region of the Deathless,
> Better were it for one to live a single day,
> The Region of the Deathless seeing. . . . [3]

By accomplishing the art of dying before dying, Gotami realized what Buddha calls the "Region of the Deathless." Of course this is to be taken as a symbolic, not literal, reference. Paradoxically speaking, the region of the Deathless is regionless.

When Buddha entered that regionless region he called it *Nirvana,* where one's individual identity has already been extinguished, and where there is no fear of death, only perfect mindfulness.

What Gotami learned from the master teacher was that her *passion* for her son had blinded her from experiencing a true *compassion* for all humanity. If one is passionately attached to the delights of this world, be they possessions or children, tragedy, even death can sweep them away. On the other hand, that person who experiences the unchangeable constant flux of life, the ever-changing reality of all phenomena, as Gotami did, is liberated from the sting of death.

We will now explore two related death-stories in Buddha's life, the first a spiritual death which prepared him for his own physical death. The first is the story of his awakening in which he died to his attachment to desire. As a result, he is liberated from fearing dying again. The second is the story of his actual death and of the unusual circumstances surrounding it.

Siddhartha's Awakening (560-480)

The Supreme Enlightenment begins with Siddhartha's Great Renunciation which is the culmination of the so-called Four Passing Sights. This Enlightenment, as we shall see, involved a spiritual death to Siddhartha's old self, and a rebirth or true awakening to the new. Since this experience stands behind Buddha's teaching about death, we will first briefly follow Siddhartha's journey toward his Great Enlightenment.

Siddhartha Gautama was born a prince. But before his death, it was prophesied that he would leave home. His father, not wanting to lose his son, kept the boy within the palace walls, indulging his every whim. Siddhartha grew up pampered, was taught by the finest teachers, but was utterly ignorant of the world outside his father's walls. He saw neither illness nor old age nor death; nothing unpleasant was allowed near him. Nevertheless, Siddhartha was bothered by a nagging feeling that something was missing. He was twenty-nine when he began to think seriously about his life, and at the same time he resolved to observe life outside the palace walls.

He rode out four times, driven in his father's chariot. The first time he saw an old, wrinkled woman—a crone. The sight disturbed him and he hurried home, thinking: Will I, too, become old? Again he went out again, driven by the same charioteer. This time he saw an old man suffering from a terrible illness, his skin infected and afflicted with festering sores. Deeply troubled he hurried back to the palace, wondering if such an illness could also strike him down. The third time when he went out the *sutra* says:

> He saw, as he was driving to the park, a great concourse of people clad in garments of different colors constructing a funeral pyre. And seeing them he asked his charioteer:
> "Why now are all those people come together in garments of different colors, and making that pile?"
> "It is because someone, my lord, has ended his days."
> "Then drive the carriage close to him who has ended his days."
> "Yea, my lord," answered the charioteer, and he did so. And Gotama saw the corpse of him who had ended his days and asked:
> "What, good charioteer, is ending one's days?"
> "It means, my lord, that neither mother, nor father, nor other kinsfolk will now see him, nor will he see them."
> "But am I too then subject to death, have I not got beyond reach of death? Will neither the raja, nor the ranee, nor any other of my kin see me more, or shall I again see them?"
> "You, my lord, and we too, we all are subject to death; we have not passed beyond the reach of death. Neither the raja, nor the ranee, nor any other of your kin will see you any more, nor will you see them."[4]

For the first time in Siddhartha's life, he faced head-on the inevitable limitations of physical life. Yet he rode out again. And it was in this confused state that he saw a shaven-headed recluse in a yellow robe. In response to Siddhartha's question about the spiritual recluse, his charioteer answered: "He is one who has gone forth." When Siddhartha asked: "What is the meaning of gone forth?" the charioteer answered:

> "To have gone forth, my lord, means being thorough in the religious life, thorough in the peaceful life, thorough in good actions, thorough in meritorious conduct, thorough in harmlessness, thorough in kindness to all creatures."[5]

After the fourth Passing Sight, while meditating, Siddhartha resolved that given the reality of old age, sickness and death, it would be better to live alone, away from the city. These human conditions raised questions in him for which he had no answers, and with which he was no longer able to continue to live. He left his father's palace (and his Hindu upbringing), and for six years he searched for an answer that would fully dissolve all his questions. He practiced yoga and austerities with the highest teachers, learned the stages of ecstatic meditation but perceived no one to be more on the road to enlightenment than he was.

Finally, with firm, deep resolve, he sat beneath a Bodhi Tree (tree of Wisdom), and resolved not to leave that seat until the insight of Supreme Enlightenment had been attained. As he sat Siddhartha became concentrated within his breath, within the rising of the abdomen and the falling of the abdomen. Immediately, he was tempted by Mara, the "one who causes death," the evil one, and by all his hosts. But centered in his meditation Siddhartha withstood the assaults and seductions, and then spoke to Mara:

> Pleasure is brief as a flash of lightning
> Or like an Autumn shower, only for a moment. . . .
> Why should I then covet the pleasures you speak of?
> I see your bodies are full of all impurity:
> Birth and death, sickness and age are yours.
> I see the highest prize, hard to attain by men—
> The true and constant wisdom of the wise.[6]

His tempter gone, Siddhartha sank into deeper and deeper dimensions of concentration. With mind purified, his supple body immovable, he recalled all his former modes of existence. At this, his omniscient (all knowing) eye opened and he saw the truth of the chain of causation (the inter-dependence of consciousness, body, mind, senses, contact, feeling, desires, attachments, old age, sickness, death). He entered the region of the Deathless and he proclaimed his song of victory:

Through many divers births I passed
Seeking in vain the builder of the house.
But O framer of houses, thou art found—
Never again shalt thou fashion a house for me!
Broken are all thy beams,
The king-post shattered!
My mind has passed into the stillness of Nibbana (Nirvana)
The ending of desire has been attained at last![7]

Buddha's Face

It is crucial to understand that Buddha died not to desire itself, for one cannot live without desires, but to his *attachment to desire*. Most especially, he died to his desire to be enlightened, for he realized that there was nothing to be realized, and no one to realize it. All ignorance dispelled, he realized that rebirth had been destroyed. Gone was his old identity; gone were his old desires and fears; gone were questions about the meaning of old age, sickness and death; gone was the one who searched. In their place was the Buddha, the one who was awake, the one who had ceased craving, who had ceased clinging, the one who died to the fear of death to become eternally present. Buddha had passed beyond the three states which keep humans unliberated, namely being attached, being unattached and being non-attached.

For the next forty years Buddha taught the wisdom of the Middle Way, of the Four Noble Truths (suffering, desire, liberation and the eightfold path), but he constantly reiterated that the religious life does not depend upon doctrines or formulations. In fact, he encouraged his followers to surrender their dependence on external teachings of any kind since views and theories only attract alternative views and lead to further confusion. The essence of Buddha's spiritual realization expressed itself as an unconditional, selfless compassion toward all creatures even at death. Dying while still alive, Buddha discovered the art of dying before dying, discovered the assurance that there is no reality in one's physical death.

Buddha's Death

According to the Buddhist legend, no sooner had Buddha eaten a meal prepared by his faithful follower Kunda than he began to suffer what he knew would be a sickness unto death. He immediately ate all of the food so that no one else would be poisoned. Then he called Ananda and asked to be

Buddha's
Face

taken to the Sala grove on the farther side of the river. There, Buddha lay down on his right side, one leg resting on the other, his head to the north, mindful, and self-possessed. "Be diligent in your practice, Ananda," Buddha said. "Be mindful of the teaching that all component things are imperma-nent." The Master then told Ananda of the four places that should be visited by pilgrims who wished to pay him reverence:

1. the place of his birth (as Siddhartha Gautama);
2. the place of his awakening (into Nirvana);
3. the place of his first sermon (the Middle or Way);
4. the place of his dying (*Parinirvana*).

To this Buddha added, "Do not honor my remains."

Despondently, Ananda, who was not yet fully awakened, went off to a nearby monastery where he wept at the thought of Buddha's passing away. "Who will teach the *dharma* (of suffering, of impermanence, of no-self) when Buddha dies?" he moaned. Hearing of this, Buddha called for Ananda and said: ~~Be own master~~

> Have I not already, on former occasions, told you that it is in the very nature of all things most near and dear unto us that we must divide ourselves from them, leave them, sever ourselves from them. How, then, Ananda, can this be possible—whereas anything what-ever born, brought into being, and organized, contains within itself the inherent necessity of dissolution—how, then, can this be pos-sible, that such a being should not be dissolved? No such condition can exist.[8]

His energy failing, Buddha sent messengers to the nearby villages to alert them that he was nearing death. At the same time a wandering seeker named Subhadda presented himself to the Buddha to have his doubt dissi-pated. At first he was refused access to the dying Master, but when Buddha overheard his request, he knew it was sincere. Subhadda's question, like that of many contemporary spiritual seekers, was: Which system or teaching is correct? When Buddha spoke of the eightfold path (Right Understanding, Right Resolve, Right Speech, Right Acts, Right Livelihood, Right Effort, Right Mindfulness, Right Concentration), Subhadda was awakened and be-came a monk (*arhat*).

Buddha then addressed all the brethren and three times asked if they had any questions or misgivings about his doctrine or method. There were none. Again he said: "Decay is inherent in all component things! Work out your salvation (awakening) with diligence!"[9]

These last words reminded them that to live is to be involved in an ines-capable process of decay and death, and that all reality is simply an ever-changing rearrangement of constituent elements and that each person is responsible for his own enlightenment. Buddha performed, therefore, in the midst of his pain, four acts of compassion as he died: he ate all the poisoned food so that no one else would die, he sent for the villagers so that they would not be kept from paying their last respects to him, he preached to Subhadda, and he gave Ananda the key teaching, that each person had to become aware by himself. Thereupon, he entered stages of rapture, infinite space and thought, emptiness and consciousness of sensations. All thoughts passed away.

For the next six days, lay followers and disciples paid honor to the body of the Exalted One. On the seventh day the body was carried to the burial grounds in the east. There, the monks wrapped his body and placed it on the funeral pyre. When the last pilgrim had arrived to pay respects, as the legend reports, the funeral pyre spontaneously combusted.

No-Self, Rebirth and Nirvana

Once when asked if he was a philosopher, a guru or just a man, Buddha rejected all three possibilities and simply said: "I am awake." He did not say what his Hindu tradition would have said (that he had realized Atman), for Buddha discovered that there was no Atman to realize. There was simply Awakening, awakening to itself. He called this insight *anatta* which literally means no-self (an-atman). Just as there is no fixed form, sensation, perception, volition, or consciousness, neither is there a soul that migrates from one life-form to another. Speaking about not having a self-identity, Buddha said to his disciples:

> Considering this, monks, the wise and noble disciple turns away from the body, turns away from sensation, turns away from perception, turns away from the synergies, turns away from body and mind.
>
> Turning away he loses passion, losing passion he is liberated, in being liberated the knowledge comes to him: "I am liberated," and he knows rebirth is exhausted, the holy life is completed, duty is fulfilled; there is no more living in these conditions.[10]

What did Buddha mean when he said that there is no permanent self to reincarnate?

The Hindus, as we have seen, rejected the immortality of the body but retained the immortality of the soul. Buddha denied both. He taught that all concepts and notions of "I" were in fact subtle projections of mind which were relative, conditioned and impermanent. Ultimately, there exists only an ever-changing combination of five aggregates—matter, sensations, perceptions, mental formations, consciousness—rhythmically forming a psychophysical configuration. Culturally and ordinarily, of course, we speak of "I," and "You," and "person" in order to acknowledge worldly conventions which are necessary for physical survival. What happens at death, according to Buddha, is the dissolution or the breaking apart of these temporally bonded aggregates. While the "person" dies, the life-stream continues, the five aggregates continue. While the Hindu sages asserted that the soul transmigrated from form to form, for Buddha there was no definite entity which receives a new cloak of flesh. Since there is no underlying self, no permanent entity, rebirth is sometimes described in early Buddhist texts as "redeath." Any particular so-called death is seen as one of a succession of deaths. One might say that at rebirth death is passed on, or at most the new person represents the recapitulation of the evolutionary process through its genetic configurations.

Buddhist thinkers, in order to explain this, have suggested various analogies. In one, a lit candle is touched to the wick of an unlighted one, and the light is carried from one candle to another. The actual flame of the first candle does not pass over, but it remains with the first candle. But light does transfer. In this sense, rebirth is the on-going process of the transmission of the entire evolutionary process in all its possibilities and probabilities.

A second analogy is that of two billiard balls. Consider what happens when a stationary ball is struck by a moving ball. The stationary ball immediately begins to move and the moving ball stops. While the balls are not the same, they enable energy to be transferred between them which is both old and new.

A third analogy used is of the impression of a seal in wax or mud. If our present condition is the seal, and our condition after death is the wax or mud, then the seal's design is the shape of human *karma* (action) which is precisely transposed. In this analogy it is *karmic*-tendencies, not character-traits, which are reborn.

A fourth, and perhaps the most satisfying analogy, is that of a motion picture. Just as each frame is similar to, yet slightly different from the one before it, and just as action occurs when the frames change rapidly, Buddhists believe in a moment-to-moment birth and death. Like the unrolling of a film, human life is seen as a continuous process of birth and death, birth and death, in every millionth of a second.

Teaching, as he did, the non-existence of the ego-I, it is easy to understand why Buddha consistently refused to talk about life after death. Buddha realized that whether he said there was life after death, or that there was not life after death, he would be wrong. Therefore, he said nothing.

Still, one day a follower came to the Buddha and asked if there was life after death, and he replied: Malunkyaputta, would a man who has been shot in the back with an arrow stop to wonder who could have shot him, or from what location the arrow was shot? No. He would immediately seek help to have the arrow removed. The point is that the question "Is there life after death?" is the wrong question to ask. It is a question which covers over the more vital one, namely "How can I become liberated from human suffering?" Buddha reminded Malunkyaputta not to depend on the dogma that there is or there is not eternal life.

> Accordingly, Malunkyaputta, bear always in mind what it is that I have not explained, and what it is that I have explained. And what, Malunkyaputta, have I not explained? I have not explained, Malunkyaputta, that the world is eternal; I have not explained that the world is not eternal; I have not explained that the world is finite; I have not explained that the world is infinite; I have not explained that the soul and the body are identical; I have not explained that the soul is one thing and the body another; I have not explained that the saint exists after death; I have not explained that the saint neither exists nor does not exist after death. And why, Malunkyaputta, have I not explained this? Because, Malunkyaputta, this profits not, nor has to do with the fundamentals of religion, nor tends to aversion, absence of passion, cessation, quiescence, the supernatural faculties, supreme wisdom, and Nirvana; therefore have I not explained it?[11]

Buddha implied that questions about life after death were the wrong questions to ask, especially before one is liberated. The goal of Buddha's teaching was human liberation, what has been called the Region of the Deathless which is perhaps explained best by this brief passage from the "Questions of King Menander":

> "Reverend Nagasena," said the King, "does the Buddha still exist?"
> "Yes, your Majesty, he does."
> "Then is it possible to point out the Buddha as being here or there?"
> "The Lord has passed completely away in Nirvana, so that nothing is left which could lead to the formation of another being. And so he cannot be pointed out as being here or there."
> "Give me an illustration."
> "What would your Majesty say—if a great fire were blazing, would it be possible to point to a flame which had gone out and say that it was here or there?"

"No, your Reverence, the flame is extinguished, it can't be detected."

"In just the same way, your Majesty, the Lord has passed away in Nirvana. . . . He can only be pointed out in the body of his doctrine, for it was he who taught it."

"Very good, Reverend Nagasena!"[12]

Of course, *nirvana* is not a state, not a place, not an idea, not a future promise, not being unconscious, asleep or merely dreaming. It is rather what is left when illusion and ignorance have passed away, when desire and attachments have fallen away. *Nirvana* is described as the "deathless place" which, like *moksha* for the Hindu, is the goal for all Buddhists. Here the liberated person is beyond death, his or her purification is completely self-surpassing. Such is the significance of Buddha's other title—Tathagata—the one who just comes, and just goes, the one who has thus attained, the one who goes nowhere, comes from nowhere, and who leaves no trace, the fully enlightened one.

Since, as Buddha taught, *nirvana* is unthinkable and incomprehensible, it can only be known mystically, by direct perception. As the profound antidote to death and dying, *nirvana* is liberation from suffering, extinction of desires, elimination of ignorance, absence of self, the abolition of all concepts including of *nirvana* itself, and the cessation of all desires to enter *nirvana*. The Buddha said:

"O bhikkhus (oh monks), what is the Absolute, (unconditioned)? It is, O bhikkhus, the extinction of desire, the extinction of hatred, The extinction of illusion, this, O bhikkhus, is called the Absolute."[13]

By entering Nirvana while yet alive, he negated any power that death might have held over him.

Death Ritual

The death practices among Buddhists vary greatly between countries and the various schools of Buddhism. In popular forms and practices, Buddhists generally agree that the thoughts and mental condition of a dying person are of primary importance. If a person dies in panic, fright, uncertainty or anxiety, it is believed that an unpleasant rebirth could result. I use the term rebirth here because it is popularly believed by many village Buddhists that the spirit of the dead person lives on. Therefore, while on one's deathbed, the person will be surrounded by family, relatives, friends and monks who recite Buddhist *sutras* (scriptures) and repeat *mantras* to help the dying person achieve a peaceful state of mind. This process continues until death, and even thereafter.

Looking more specifically at the practices of Burmese village Buddhists, when one dies the body is taken by the male members of the family and washed. The body is then wrapped in burial clothes, and the thumbs and big toes are tied together in hair from a deceased member of the family. A coin is placed inside the mouth and at the head; a vase is placed holding a flower so that the dead may still worship Buddha.

From the time of death until cremation, the body lies in state during which time family and friends come to pay respects to the deceased but without any outward signs of sympathy. The body is never left alone. Relatives do all the cooking and there will also be a group of men gambling in the room where the body lies.

Burmese Buddhists believe, for example, that the conscious soul remains in or around the body for up to three days, after which the body is cremated. On the seventh day after a person has died, monks are invited to the deceased's house to chant from the sacred texts. This has two functions: first, to drive away the ghost of the dead, and, second, to confer merit upon the soul of the dead person. This, it is believed, will make the dead person's passing from the material to the spiritual world easier. It also helps the living to be purged of any fear of the ghost or of personally dying. This ritual leads one to the awareness that human life will continue through myriad lifetimes until everyone reaches *nirvana.*

At the same time, it would be remiss to conclude this chapter without mentioning Buddhist monasticism and its great contribution to the sacred art of dying, especially the practice called "mindfulness of death." In the fifth century, the Indian scholar Buddhaghosa, compiler of the most ancient commentaries on the Pali Canon, authored *The Path of Purity.* The importance of this text for our study can be seen in the instructions on "the recollection of death" given to monks and novices. To develop full awareness of death, a monk is advised to be secluded and to pay attention to the words: "Death will take place, the life-force will be cut off," or simply "Death, death." When a certain facility for this was attained, the monk was directed to recall death from several different points of view: as a murderer standing in front of you, as the inevitable loss of all achievements, as the weakness of the stuff of life, and as the shortness of the moment.[14] These meditation devices are for achieving mindfulness of death in which the truth of death is brought forth in an anticipatory fashion. By contemplating each of these separately, the meditator, paradoxically, is liberated from the fear of dying by bringing death into life ahead of its time. Meditating on death in these ways provides a monk with practice in dying which can be gained in no other way. In this way the monk gains full familiarity with the reality of impermanence; the not-self arises. And, most significantly:

At the hour of death, beings who have not developed the recollection of death feel fear, fright and bewilderment, as if they were suddenly attacked by wild beasts, ghosts, snakes, robbers or murderers. He, on the contrary, dies without fear and bewilderment. If in this very life he does not win deathlessness, he is, on the dissolution of his body, bound for a happy destiny.[15]

NOTES

[1]E.A. Burtt, editor, *The Teachings of the Compassionate Buddha* (New York: New American Library, 1955), 45.

[2]*Ibid.*

[3]*Ibid.*, 46.

[4]Clarence Hamilton, editor, *Selections from Buddhist Literature* (New York: Bobbs-Merrill Company, 1952), 8–9.

[5]*Ibid.*, 9.

[6]Ananda Coomarasvamy, *Buddha and the Gospel of Buddhism* (New York: Harper & Row, 1916), 34.

[7]*Ibid.*, 35–36.

[8]*Ibid.*, 183.

[9]*Ibid.*, 86. Parentheses are mine.

[10]Hamilton, 33–34.

[11]Henry Clarke Warren, *Buddhism* (New York: Atheneum, 1969), 122.

[12]William Theodore de Bary, editor, *The Buddhist Tradition* (New York: Vintage Books, 1969), 30.

[13]Quoted in Walpola Rahula's *What the Buddha Taught* (New York: Grove Press, 1959), 36.

[14]From *The Path of Purity,* translated by Edward Conze, quoted in Roger Eastman's *The Ways of Religion* (San Francisco: Canfield Press, 1975), 112.

[15]*Ibid.*, 116. According to Buddhist tradition, Buddha practiced a form of meditation called Vipassana, (insight into the nature of things) which is

based on clear mindfulness, pure awareness and dispassionate observation. The fundamental technique of essential mindfulness is meditative breathing, the awareness of in-and-out breathing, and nothing else. The meditator fully concentrates on each inhalation and on each exhalation, and in that way, after a while, penetrates into the nature of things.

JOURNAL EXERCISES

1. In answer to Buddha's question about whether she had found any mustard seeds, Gotami said: "Done is the business of the mustard seed." What is the "business of the mustard seed"? What is the nature of Gotami's realization? Can you imagine a realization powerful enough to assuage your sorrow if you lost your only child?
2. Create a dialogue with the Buddha in which you ask him, among other questions, to elaborate upon his attitude toward death. Perhaps you might ask Buddha what happened to him after he died?
3. What does Nirvana mean to Buddha? Explain it in his words first, and then attempt to explain it in your words. Try to frame your remarks in a contemporary vocabulary (e.g., computerize).
4. Compare the Hindu conviction of rebirth with Buddha's teaching of rebirth or redeath. How do you describe the differences between them, or in your opinion is there really no difference at all? Explain your position.
5. Select any one of the points of view from which to meditate upon death in Buddhaghosa's *Path of Purity*. Why did you select that one? How does this point of view help you to come to understand death?
6. How might an intelligent, practicing Buddhist answer the following question: What does your tradition teach about how to die artfully? That is, what is the most sacred way to die?

Chapter 4 ZEN ATTITUDES
TOWARD DEATH

The Master said in answer:
Just by practicing dying.

Suzuki Shosan, *Collected Writings*

After Buddha's death, as a part of Buddhism's development, various schools formed to carry forth his *dharma* (teaching). In the next two chapters we will explore two cultural versions of, or two historical traditions within, Buddhism: Zen and Tibetan Buddhism. Our concern will not be to chart their respective differences and similarities, but rather, in keeping with our approach throughout the text, to highlight the unique contribution of each tradition's attitudes toward dying.

Zen uniquely begins with the absolute negation of everything, including itself. There are in fact four different faces of Zen: the sect within Buddhism, the heart of all Buddhism, the true center of all the world's spiritualities, and the Zen beyond Zen, the no-Zen Zen. Zen is one of the few major sacred traditions which, at the heart of its self-affirmation, denies itself. Ultimately there is nothing that can be called Zen, no myths, no creeds, no doctrines, no symbols, no initials. Zen is the sound of one hand clapping, the plop of a bull frog into a quiet pond, and the direct transmission of heart/mind to heart/mind. As a Zen monk might say: "I come from the No Organizational Temple, and I bow to every Buddha." In the following stories, we will touch upon this quiet essence of Zen.

D. T. Suzuki, who more than any other brought Zen Buddhism to America, writes: "The essence of Zen Buddhism consists in acquiring a new viewpoint on life and things generally."[1] He could have just as easily said: Zen consists in acquiring a new viewpoint on life and death. Zen Buddhist teachers have always maintained that a death to all false ideas about the self, and to god, is necessary before one can begin to understand the secrets of death and after-death. In response to the question: "What is death?" Zen Master Kobun Chino Sensei once said: "A room full of furniture!" The student continued. "But what happens at death?" "What happened to the events of yesterday!" Kobun answered: "At death, you wake up. You become aware that there is no death. And you can wake up at any moment!" In the following stories the impact of Zen is expressed in its essential nature.

Bodhidharma and Hui-Neng

Once, when Buddha's monks had assembled to hear him speak, Buddha simply lifted one flower and smiled. Zen traces its origins to that silence. From an exoteric point of view however, Zen originated when the 28th Indian Buddhist Patriarch, Bodhidharma, brought to China the following message:

> "A special transmission outside the scriptures;
> No dependence upon words and letters;
> Direct pointing at the soul of man;
> Seeing into one's nature and the attainment of Buddhahood."[2]

From these lines it is evident that whatever else Zen is, it is not conceptual, theoretical, speculative or understandable, but rather a direct, intuitive, spontaneous realization of Buddha-Mind.

Of all the stories about Bodhidharma, the following is especially appropriate to our presentation of Zen. When Bodhidharma was invited to have an audience with the Chinese Emperor Wu, the Emperor asked Bodhidharma to evaluate his achievements. "Of no merit whatsoever!" Bodhidharma replied. "Then what do you teach?" Wu retorted. "Vast Emptiness!" was the reply. Feeling one-upped, Wu shot back, "Then who now stands before me?" And Bodhidharma made the characteristic Zen reply: "I do not know, sire!"[3] Zen originates in this not-knowing who the knower is.

Hui Neng (638–713), whom some call the founder of Chinese Zen Buddhism, further illumines this not-knowing. One day after his father had died, he overheard a monk chanting from the *Diamond Sutra*. Enthralled and inspired, he left his job for the monastery of the fifth patriarch at Yellow Plum in Chin-Chou. As a novice, he was employed to pounder rice for the brothers. One day, after being there for eight months, he heard about a monastery-wide contest with the fifth patriarch's mantle as the prize. Whoever could express true realization in a *gatha* (short poem or chant) would become the sixth patriarch. Shen Hsiu, the oldest of the order, was the only one who dared to post a stanza outside the meditation hall. It read:

> Our body is the Bodhi-tree,
> And our mind a mirror bright.
> Carefully we wipe them hour by hour,
> And let no dust alight.[4]

Unlike the rest of the monks, Hui Neng was not impressed with this verse. Instead, he had his own posted alongside it:

> There is no Bodhi-tree,
> Nor stand of a mirror bright.
> Since all is void,
> Where can the dust alight?[5]

That is, since there is no permanent, fixed form, since everything is permanently changing, even as I write, there can be no reality attributed to either the Bodhi-tree, or to the mirror stand. Therefore, since all forms are empty from the beginning, there is no place where *karmic* dust can land or to which it can attach. Like Bodhidharma, Hui Neng too, though indirectly, answered the identity question with an "I do not know!" Common to each of these stories is an underlying "emptiness," an underlying "nothingness" out of which everything manifests. In the *Heart Sutra,* which we will discuss momentarily, emptiness is said to be form, and "form is emptiness." In other words, common to each of these stories is the equation: $0 =$ infinity.

In China and Japan, in recognition of this profoundly self-contradictory equation, a series of pictures was developed to illustrate the enlightenment process. Called the "Ox-Herding" pictures, each picture is framed in an asymmetrical, spontaneously brushed, free form circle (*enso* in Japanese). In the first six circles, the young man who is first pictured looking backward (that is, being dominated by his *karma*), searches for, discovers footprints of, perceives, catches, tames and rides an ox (that is, his Buddha Nature). In the seventh *enso,* the young man sits quietly and the ox too rests. The ox has been forgotten, or empathetically internalized.

The eighth picture is simply the *enso* alone, an empty circle, the formless form. Both ox and self are forgotten. A complete surrender to death in life has been actualized, a conscious death to the self-limiting, infantile self of one's ego-construction. A verse beneath the *enso* reads:

> Whip, rope, person, and bull all merge in
>   No-Thing.
> This heaven is so vast no message can stain it.
> How may a snowflake exist in a raging fire?
> Here are the footprints of the patriarchs.[6]

In this penultimate *enso,* the seeker enters *shunyata* (emptiness), he returns to the source and is content to dwell in his true abode, unconcerned about

Enso

Both forgotten all is none

awakening exper.

within versus without. Here both true self and the seeker are forgotten. Each has entered into the un-selfconscious awareness of true self identity.

But this Great Death experience is also a rebirth. The seeker cannot remain in *shunyata* but must return to the realm of forms. In the final *enso*, he enters into the market place, barefooted, bare-breasted, dusty and blissful. The last picture in the series depicts the herdsman awake, and returning to the world with false desires extinguished. His spiritual death results in a movement from controllable passions to a spontaneous compassion. Adapting to the needs of any situation, he is free from past personality. Having accomplished the sacred art of dying, he is changed, yet nothing is different. Over his shoulder he carries a fishing pole at the end of which hangs a fish, and he meets a Buddha-figure who carrying in one hand a bag bulging with anything one could want, and in the other an empty basket. The herdsman, also himself the Buddha, meets Buddha and everyone they look upon is enlightened in their viewpoint. There is only the Void, only the Great Death from which all creation arises.

Enso plus Buddha and Boy

The Great Death

We come now to the very heart of Zen, which is, it might be said, to commit spiritual suicide. Bunan wrote:

While living
Be a dead man,
Be thoroughly dead—
And behave as you like,
And all's well. [7]

Zen is one of the few traditions whose major practice is to live as though thoroughly dead. In fact, there is a term for this experience, namely the Great Death. In Zen the Great Death means dying to ordinary, dualistically conditioned consciousness in which: I am I, I am not you and I am not not-I. Dying to all ideas of self, to all dualistic clingings, to all dependency on the patriarchs, in Zen's awakening: I am I, I am you and simultemporally I am not-I. If one meets the Buddha, even the Buddha must be killed.

To achieve this, Zen has evolved two modes of what might be called a spiritual death-training, *zazen* and *koan*. In fact, these are not methods at all, for there is nothing to attain. Rather they are methodless methods.

Zazen (or seated Zen) is a cultivation of the cessation of ordinary consciousness such that, having denied everything, having nothing left to deny, one reaches absolute stillness. Wide awake, though fully dead, one awakens to *nirvana*. In this practice one sits, usually with others and with a teacher present, facing a wall, eyes opened, fully awake, just breathing. When asked what happens when he sits, Kobun Chino said: "When I sit, the world sits!" That is, to sit one needs to give up (die to) the actions of the world, and notions of self. Dying to self-reflective identity, one sits as if there is no one left sitting and yet is both fully dead and fully alive. The whole point of sitting is to cease sitting even while one sits, to cease identifying the self with any dualistically separated object, even the awakening itself.

The other spiritual death practice is the *koan* (a totally illogical challenge to ordinary dualistic consciousness). For example: "Without speaking and without not speaking—speak!" A *koan* is given to a student with the intention of driving the dualistically calculating mind out of existence. *Koans* force the human proclivity toward intellectualization to exhaust itself, once and for all. This Great Death, or *shunyata* (absolute void, emptiness), is also called the Great Birth, or *satori* (sudden enlightenment).

A monk once asked Joshu: "Has a dog Buddha-nature, or not?" Said Joshu, "Mu!" (no nothing) D. T. Suzuki was given this *mu* by his master as a *koan,* and he was instructed to think of it regardless of what else he was doing or where he was. Suzuki reports that when he finally ceased being conscious of *mu,* "I was one with *Mu,* identified with *Mu,* so that there was no longer the separateness implied by being conscious of *Mu.*"[8]

When the Great Death-Great Birth is achieved, the dualistic self has been annihilated. One becomes one's own not-self. Now, in Zen's illogical logic: I am I, and I am you, and I am not-I. In this mode of awareness, there is no struggle between life and death, for one is both fully alive (I am I, and I am you) and fully dead (I am not-I) at the same time. The Great Death uncovers what Zen calls the "Original Face," that is the nature of self before God said: "Let there be Light!"

To look at this more graphically we could say that the emptiness of the

Great Death, illustrated by an empty circle (*enso*), is the Great Birth, is the enlightenment depicted by the last Ox-Herding picture. Each picture, both empty and full, occurs spontaneously and simultaneously. Although there is a *difference* between the two, there is *no* real *distinction*. Both express awakening to the region of deathlessness.

Death Ritual

Reflect for a moment upon the following story:

An ancient Zen master took his disciple with him when went to console a family that was grieving over the recent death of one of its members. When they arrived at the house the disciple knocked on the coffin and asked, "Master, is he alive or is he dead?"

The disciple persisted, "Why won't you tell me one way or the other?"

"I won't say. I won't say," repeated the master.

On the way back to the temple the disciple, still deeply troubled by this question of life and death, suddenly turned to the master and demanded, "I must know! If you don't tell me, I won't be responsible for what I do to you."

"Do whatever you like," the master retorted, "but you won't get an answer from me." So the disciple struck him.

Years later, after the master had passed on, the disciple visited another master who had once been a disciple of the first master, and told him about the incident. Then the disciple asked, "Was he alive or was he dead?"

The master answered, "I won't say he was alive, I won't say he was dead."

Disciple: "Why won't you tell me?"

Master: "I won't say. I won't say."

The disciple suddenly had an awakening.[9]

The master's refusal to explain is like Bodhidharma's not knowing. By not saying, the master urges the questioner to discover that neither is right, and that both are right. At any rate, Zen is more interested in what one does as one reaches the threshold of dying.

From the Zen standpoint, all life is life after death if one dies artfully before dying. To prepare oneself for dying, therefore, the Zen practitioner, while fully alive, will read and meditatively reflect upon the inner meaning of the *sutras*. In that process, it could be said that one practices dying by entering into and identifying with the *sutra*. From the Zen standpoint, to truly understand the *sutras*, one must temporarily die to one's own predilections about self to become awakened into a new understanding of the text. At the same time, the text itself must die or, as it could be said, if you meet a *sutra*, burn it.

One Zen text often studied in relation to death is the "Heart of Perfect Wisdom" or the "Heart Sutra," which contains the core of Buddhist wisdom beyond birth and death. One who recites it, over and over, according to some forms of Buddhism, is prepared in the best possible way for the journey through death.

Addressing Shariputra, the Bodhisattva (or Buddha-minded one) begins the 38-line scripture by reminding Shariputra, and the reader at the same time, that:

> Form is emptiness and the very emptiness is form; emptiness does not differ from form, form does not differ from emptiness; whatever is form, that is emptiness, whatever is emptiness, that is form, the same is true of feelings, perceptions, impulses and consciousness.[10]

Therefore, death, to the extent that it has a form, is empty, without content or meaning. And to the extent to which death is empty, it has a form, a content, a meaning. The Bodhisattva continues.

> Therefore, O Sariputra, in emptiness there is no form, nor feeling, nor perception, nor impulse, nor consciousness; No eye, ear, nose, tongue, body, mind; No forms, sounds, smells, tastes, touchables or objects of mind; No sight-organ element, and so forth, until we come to: No mind-consciousness element; There is no ignorance, no extinction of ignorance, and so forth, until we come to: there is no decay and death, no extinction of decay and death. There is no suffering, no origination, no stopping, no path. There is no cognition, no attainment and no non-attainment.[11]

The secret of Zen of course is to dwell in *nirvana* before one dies, so that there will be no death left to die.

> Therefore, O Sariputra, it is because of his non-attainmentness that a Bodhisattva, through having relied on the perfection of wisdom, dwells without thought-coverings. In the absence of thought-coverings he has not been made to tremble, he has overcome what can upset, and in the end he attains to Nirvana.[12]

Facing death in *nirvanic* consciousness, there no longer exists anyone who dies. This is why the *sutra* exclaims that the person who reaches *nirvana* exists far apart from every perverted (ignorant) view of reality.

Therefore, the Bodhisattva concludes, one should practice chanting the great transcendent *mantra* (sacred saying or sound) which is contained in the last line of the *sutra*. By memorizing these lines one can repeat them over and over as the threshold of death is crossed: "*Gate, Gate* (Gone, Gone), *Paragate* (Completely Gone), *Parasamgate* (Totally Gone Through), *Bodhi! Svaha* (Hail transcendent Wisdom)!" This *mantra,* when uttered repeatedly, has the effect of transferring a transcendent spiritual principle from the realm of hearing and speaking to an inner appreciation. The dying person thus takes the *sutra* with him into the next realm and at the same time may realize that there is no *sutra,* and no next realm.

It is well known that in Japan samurai warriors often entered into Zen training to sustain and complement their profession because of Zen's attitude toward death. Part of the samurai's training involved what has been called the "practice of dying." By this practice, the samurai warrior continually worked for and prepared for the immediacy of his own death. Suzuki Shosan (1579–1655), who was trained as a samurai until he gave up his profession at forty-one to practice Zen, indicates how this practice of dying became part of his life:

> One day a certain monk said: How does one arouse and produce the power of Ni-oh?
> The Master said in answer: just by practicing dying. From the time I was a young man, by continually leaping into the midst of enemies of great strength, I was constantly practicing dying. Thus I could enter into [this death practice] soon. On one occasion I attacked these two or three men who had spears. I was pierced in my body and while experiencing death without [actually] dying, and throwing my body into this struggle, I struck off their heads, broke their spears and thus was not defeated. So while learning to die in various ways, I came to know this power of Ni-oh.[13]

Like Ramanamaharshi (cf. Chapter 14) Suzuki Shosan chose to face death head-on by a deliberate act of imagination. Thus Shosan passed from death-readiness training to Great Death training, the radical death-in-life which renders physical death as empty as the self is empty.[14]

When the Sixth Patriarch Hui neng was about to die, he admonished his gathered disciples not to mourn:

> Live as though I were still here. Do zazen together. When there is calm, neither activity nor passivity, without [notions of] birth or

death, coming or going, right or wrong, and without abiding or departing, then that is the great Way. When I am gone, just practice correctly according to the Teaching, just as you did during my days with you. Remember, even were I to remain in this world, if you disobeyed my teaching my presence among you would be pointless.[15]

Zen is a matter of life and death. When Dogo visited a sick fellow monk he asked where the monk could be seen if he died. The monk replied: "I will meet you where nothing is born and nothing dies." But Dogo replied: "You should have said that there is no place where nothing is born and nothing dies and that we need not see each other at all."[16]

NOTES

[1]William Barrett, editor, *Zen Buddhism* (New York: Doubleday Anchor Books, 1956), 83.

[2]*Ibid.*, 61.

[3]*Ibid.*, 64.

[4]Wong Mou-Lam, Translator, *The Sutra of Hui Neng* in the *Diamond Sutra* and the *Sutra of Hui Neng* (Boulder, Colorado: Shambala Press, 1969), 15.

[5]*Ibid.*, 18.

[6]Paul Reps, editor, *Zen Flesh, Zen Bones* (New York: Anchor-Doubleday, n.d.), 150.

[7]A paraphrase of Bunan's teaching found in Lucien Stryk, editor, *Zen: Poems, Prayers, Sermons, Anecdotes, Interviews* (New York: Doubleday, 1963), 15.

[8]D. T. Suzuki, *The Field of Zen* (New York: Harper & Row, 1969), 10. Whether one practices *zazen* or with a *koan* or both, the Great Death process is similar: to recognize the problem (dualistic consciousness); to be removed from distractions; to focus on the solution (non-dualistic consciousness); to reach an impasse or crises in which all attempts at a solution have been exhausted; to die thoroughly to all subject-object dichotomies; and to be reborn or renewed as the no-self Self.

[9]Philip Kapleau, *Zen Dawn in the West* (New York: Anchor-Doubleday, 1980), 73–74.

[10]Edward Conze, *Buddhist Wisdom Books* (New York: Harper & Row, 1958), 81.

[11]*Ibid.*, 89.

[12]*Ibid.*, 93.

[13]Quoted by Winston L. King in his "Practicing Dying: The Samurai-Zen Death Techniques of Suzuki Shosan" in *Religious Encounters with Death,* edited by F. Reynolds and E. Waugh (University Park, Pa.: The Pennsylvania State University Press, 1977), 145.

[14]Like those who practice *vipassana* (placing awareness in the breath), Shosan taught nembutsu (reciting "Namu Amida Butsu, Nama Amida Butsu" in synchronization with breath rhythms) as a spiritual device. In becoming one's own breath, no-mind awakens.

[15]Kapleau, 71–72.

[16]Gyomay M. Kubose, *Zen Koans* (Chicago: Henry Regnery Co., 1973), 18. According to Zen Buddhist philosopher Masao Abe in "Transformation in Buddhism," in *Buddhist-Christian Studies,* vol. 7, 1987, *nirvana* is at once: (1) the nonduality of life and death; (2) the beginningless endlessness of life and death; and (3) the total living-dying presence at this instant.

JOURNAL EXERCISES

1. What is the essence of Zen? Or to put it another way, what is no-Zen Zen? And how does this image of a Zenless Zen contribute to Zen's attitude toward death?
2. Reread the lines attributed to Bodhidharma and Hui Neng's four-lined *gata*. Are there any similarities which strike you? Does one or the other speak more directly to your life-situation? If so, which one and why?
3. What does it mean in Zen to live as if thoroughly dead? Try to create an ingenious dialogue between yourself, as you ordinarily are, and your thoroughly-dead-self.
4. What is the relationship, or potential relationship, between a dying person and the *mantra* at the end of the "Heart Sutra"? In what way(s) that you can imagine could the repetition of this *mantra* influence what happens at death?
5. In response to the age old identity question of "Who are You!" an ageless Zen philosopher responded: "Absolutely contradictory self-identity!" Ruminate upon this phrase for a while, and only then record your associations and responses to it.
6. How might an intelligent, practicing Zen Buddhist answer the following question: What does your tradition teach about how to die artfully? That is, what is the most sacred way of dying?

Chapter 5 TIBETAN ATTITUDES TOWARD DEATH

Buddhism
1) Vajrayana
2 of 3) mahayana
Bud 3) Hinayana

Tibet — death exper prac in life
Chinese — death in life
S.E. Asian — nirvana

O nobly-born listen.
Now you are experiencing The
Radiance of the Clear Light of
Pure Reality. Recognize it.

The Tibetan Book of the Dead

Tibetan Buddhism belongs to what is called the Vajrayana school of Buddhism, to distinguish it from Mahayana (Chinese and Japanese Buddhism), and Hinayana (or southeast Asian Buddhism). The Hinayana Vehicle or school develops the realization of *nirvana* and non-attachment to the world, which prepares one to personally enter into death undisturbedly and with deep assurance. The Mahayana Vehicle fosters great compassion for all its practitioners, and focuses on the experience of death in life. The Vajrayana Vehicle teaches its practitioners in great detail how to enter into the death experience prior to dying. In this chapter we will elaborate Tibetan insights and practices related to the sacred art of dying, especially ones found in the *Tibetan Book of the Dead*.

We will begin with a story told by Sogyal Rimpoche, a reincarnate lama, scholar and meditation master, which captures the essence of Tibetan convictions about death. In the early sixties in Sikkim, an old nun who had practiced Buddhism all her life became ill and knew she was about to die. She packed her belongings, gave things away and simplified her life. One morning Sogyal's aunt, herself a venerated teacher, saw the nun dying and called for an old family friend to come. Normally in the morning the old man, who was also a great teacher, would do the shopping for the family. When he arrived he said to the nun:

I think it is time for you to go. Now you have got to see whatever your teachers have taught you to see. This is the time to put your visualizations into practice. Whichever form of the Buddha you can best relate to, unite your mind with that Buddha, and don't think about us here behind. We'll be okay. I'm going shopping now. When I come back, perhaps I won't see you, so goodbye.[1]

70

During the entire time that the old man talked, he did so with a smile, and when he left the nun laughed. What a way to die. Imagine that you could die laughing.

The old man was not, as it might at first seem, cold-hearted. Rather, he and the nun were true to Buddhist practice. They had each read, studied and listened at the deathbed of others to the *Tibetan Book of the Dead*. They both knew exactly what she should do as she entered her last conscious moments.

From the Tibetan viewpoint it is crucial that a person die in a wholesome mind-state because of the pull of *karmic* operations. We have already seen that *karma* is the imprint which our actions make on the stream of our consciousness. If one dies in a wholesome mind-state, with concentrated awareness, that person's virtuous *karmic* imprint will ripen. If one dies in a negative mind-state, with strong attachments to this life, with incompleted emotions and needs, an unwholesome *karmic* imprint will develop in the next life-form. The old nun died with a clear consciousness—joyfully!

The Clear Light

The Tibetans teach that to understand what happens at death is to be aware of the nature of mind. Each person is a function of three levels of consciousness:

1. the gross level—empirical, sensuous, physical awareness (body);
2. the subtle level—cognition of mental constructs and objects (brain);
3. the subtlest level—innate, unconditional consciousness— which passes from life to life and becomes free from obstacles (Buddha-mind).

Just as life depends on the interaction of four basic elements—earth, water, fire and air, plus ether—the process of dying begins with the dissolution of these elements. The earth element of the body's functions is first absorbed by the water element in the body which is then dissolved and absorbed by the fire element. When at last, whether the process takes years or weeks, the fire element dissolves into air, heat escapes from the body. During this time, if one can meditatively be aware that nothing exists independently of mind, then one will become enlightened to Buddha-nature.

After the four elements dissolve, and the gross and subtle bodies have died, one awakens, in the subtlest body, to the Clear Light of the void. This is not to be confused with the so-called light at the end of a dark tunnel such as Ivan Ilych saw (cf. Chapter 1), for the Clear Light of Tibetan Buddhism is empty. It is a clear atmosphere of no color, like an autumn dawn when the sky is without clouds, and there is neither sunlight nor moonlight. As Buddha said, it is like the sky, luminously clear, yet empty. The Clear Light state is the awakening of the most subtle consciousness to the essential body of Buddha which is beyond form.

The lama prepares the dying person by reading from the *Book of the Dead* that "swifter than lightning, the luminous splendor of the colourless light of Emptiness . . . will surround you on all sides." Though terrified "try to submerge yourself in that light, giving up all belief in a separate self, all attachment to your illusory ego."[2] The Light happens in a brief instant which passes so quickly that few realize its true Reality. What prevents both the living and the dead from seeing the Clear Light of the Void is its reflection through karmic impressions. Imagine a film-projector showing images on the screen. Behind the projector is the Clear Light of pure consciousness. The film of one's life experience is an arrangement of karmic impressions which are recorded in the film stills and projected onto the screen of the mind.

When consciousness does not enter the Clear Light state it becomes a bardo body, a subtle or intermediate body between death and rebirth which goes wherever it thinks. If one is concentrated on *shunyata* (emptiness), then the Clear Light can be entered. But if a person has strong *karmic* attachments to earthly life, he or she will pass through the clear light stage quickly.

Most *bardo* bodies exist in a state of confusion and may not realize that they have experienced death. According to the *Book of the Dead,* upon awakening, the feeling is similar to awakening from sleep. Confusion becomes fear in the face of visions, phantasms, realities perceived as dreams, dreams as realities. Landslides, fires, hurricanes, shades and apparitions terrify the *bardo* body (or consciousness) as long as it is still attached to life.

Three and a half days after death, Buddhas and Bodhisattvas appear to the *bardo* body in radiantly peaceful manifestations. Once again, there is opportunity to merge into the heart of truth. Most, however, continue to desire to exist as individuals and are therefore destined to reenter the wheel of becoming. As desire for rebirth becomes more urgent, the deceased is brought to face King Yama, Judge of the dead. Yama holds up the shining mirror of Karma which reflects the deceased's past deeds. But as the *Book of the Dead* reveals:

> The mirror in which Yama seems to read your past is your own memory, and also his judgment is your own. It is you yourself who pronounce your own judgment, which in turns determines your next rebirth.[3]

The *bardo* state lasts no longer than forty-nine days, by which time a new body must be found. The to-be-born-again are encouraged to concentrate on the womb about to be entered, and to enter it in a state of supreme equilibrium. Then, the bardo body will be attracted to a couple making love and, at the moment of ejaculation, enter the woman's body.

Tibetan Book of the Dead

Tibetans are a deeply religious people, as evidenced by their prayer flags, prayer wheels, bells, masks, icons, prayer blocks, sacred dances and texts. One of the most interesting of these texts is the *Tibetan Book of the Dead.* Titled the *Bar-do-tho-dol,* or liberation by hearing the Bardo, it focuses on the gap between death and rebirth ("bar" means "in between" and "do" means "an island or mark"). Like the dream state, the bardo contains visions and images and presents the dying with opportunities for awakening or rebirth.

In the eighth century, Padmasambhava, called the second Buddha, essentialized the *Tantras* (esoteric or secret teachings of Buddha) into six cycles which are related to the six *bardos* or gaps. Three relate to life (birth to death, sleep to dream, self to *samadi,* nothingness) and three relate to death (the moment before death, the *dharmata,* or luminosity of things-as-they are, and the becoming). The *Book of the Dead* is a manual for the sixth cycle—becoming—and was written to help practitioners die consciously. Instructions in it are found on the nature of the mind, what happens in other *bardos,* how to assist the dying person and the self, what to do at the exact moment of death, how to deal with visions, how to enter the Buddha-realm, and how to choose rebirth.

As we have said, the *Book of the Dead* is a guidebook which deals with the period between death and rebirth. This *bardo* is divided into three stages: (1) when the soul is disincarnated, and glimpses the Clear Light, (2) when there is a recovery of objects in dream-like forms, and (3) when the soul is reincarnated into a womb of flesh and blood. The desire to be reincarnated comes from karmic illusions, and prevents a person from choosing to concentrate on the pure Buddha realm. In the process of reincarnation, the spiritual body (a *karmically* determined complex of energies) manifests in a physical form exactly the inverse of the process of dying. Thus it is seen that death is not extinction, for at death nothing is eliminated. There is only transition or change from one stage to another. The living read, study and memorize the *Book of the Dead,* and at the same time it was read to both the dying and to the corpse, for it was believed that the soul did not leave the body all at once. The book is read to the dying so that they can be liberated in the

Buddha and Consort

space of *Pure Awareness* (unborn, undying) and, to help those who choose to enter a womb again, to do it consciously, without projections or judgments.

On the cover of Chogyam Trungpa's translation of the *Book of the Dead*, one finds pictured the "Mandala of the Peaceful Deities." A *mandala* is a form of spiritual geometry in which the viewer's eye and awareness are drawn from the pattern's outer edges into the center of the cosmic design. Like a *mantra*, or words of power, a *mandala* is an image of spiritual power which symbolizes the true or real nature of Mind.

At the center of this *mandala* is a seated Buddha-like figure on whose lap, facing him, sits the female consort or *shakti* (the divine feminine). In esoteric forms of Tibetan Buddhism, sexuality and intimacy were practiced as a sacred science, a sexual yoga, in which the male and the female principles were balanced through harmonious interpenetration. When *yab* (the male) and *yum* (the female) are esoterically as well as physically at-one, each has died to separatistic self-identity and, as a result of this dying, is reborn in the wisdom of deathlessness. The point of this yoga which, needless to say cannot be practiced without discipline and guidance, is that through non-ejaculative penetration "male" and "female" enter into each other desirelessly. Not orgasm but non-dualistic union is the goal, and not erotic but meditative sexuality is the means.

Of the various suggestions provided for one's liberation in the *Book of the Dead*, constantly the reminder to beware of projections and unconscious tendencies emerges. Appearing in the forms of frightening and peaceful deities, these projections arise from the mental body. The Lords of Death too emerge from this mental body and therefore have no solid substance. When projections arise the *bardo* body is reminded to pray with deep devotion:

> When parted from beloved friends, wandering alone,
> my own projections' empty forms appear,
> may the buddhas send out the power of their compassion
> so that the bardo's terrors do not come. . . . [4]

The *Book of the Dead* concludes with instructions for: (1) transference into the pure Buddha-realm (to enter the Pure Realm of complete joy, one needs to concentrate intensely on it to be born into that realm), and (2) choosing an appropriate womb-entrance (to be reborn one needs to concentrate on being reborn in a body which can benefit all sentient beings).

> Transference to the Pure Realm of Space, of purified faculties, is directed like this: 'Ah, how sad it is that I still remain in this muddy swamp of samsara even now, after such a long time of countless

ages without beginning or end, and while so many others have already become buddhas I have not been liberated. From this moment on I feel sickened at this samsara, I dread it, I am worn out with it. Now it is time to get ready to escape, so I must bring about a spontaneous birth in a lotus flower at the feet of the buddha Amitabha in the western Blissful Realm.' With this thought concentrate intensely on the Blissful Realm in the west, it is vital to make this effort. Or else, if you direct intense concentration, one-pointedly and without distraction, toward whichever realm you wish, the Pure Realm, or Complete Joy, or the Densely Filled, or the Realm of Willow Leaves, or the Palm-tree Mountain, or the Palace of Lotus Light in Urgyan, you will immediately be born in that realm.[5]

If this cannot be done, instructions are given for being reborn:

Again, it is very important to concentrate like this: 'I will be born as a universal emperor for the good of all sentient beings, or as a brahmana like a great sala tree, or as the son of a siddha, or in a family of a pure lineage of dharma, or in a family where the father and mother have faith; and taking a body with merits which can benefit all sentient beings, I will do good.' Concentrating on this thought, the womb should be entered. At this time you should bless the womb you are entering as a palace of the gods, and supplicate the buddhas and bodhisattvas of the ten directions and the yidams, especially the Lord of Great Compassion, and enter the womb with the longing of a request for transmission.[6]

To avoid entering the wrong womb, everyone is instructed to first enter the pure state of equilibrium, and to be reborn in that state.

Death Ritual

The dying moment is filled with beauty and peace. It is the reverse of the process of birth. Everything in life is summed up in this moment. Thus the *Book of the Dead* stresses cultivating the proper last thoughts, for one's mental condition at death is likely to be retained after death. In this last moment the True Self can most directly be revealed.

At death, the *Book of the Dead* suggests a practice called the "Ejection of Consciousness" in which the dying person: (a) keeps a pure mind, clear of earth-bound distractions, (b) visualizes a seated Buddha over her or his head, surrounded by a rainbow arch, (c) feels the self in the presence of an enlightened being, (d) visualizes consciousness as a ball of fire in the abdomen which then rises up the spine until it leaves the top of the head, and (e) experiences self-consciousness mixing with the mind of the enlightened being like water mixing with water. By means of the ejection of consciousness, practitioners learn how to shoot awareness up the spine through the crown of the head into the Buddha and in this way they enter the Clear Light realm at death. Of course, it's not necessary to wait until death is near to begin such a practice. In fact, Tibetans bring death in an anticipatory way into life through this practice of transferring consciousness while yet alive. The more adept at this transference one becomes in life, the easier it becomes to accomplish just at the moment of death.

The *Book of the Dead* begins with instructions on how to liberate human beings. We end here with the most central one:

> First of all one should have studied the instructions, which should certainly liberate those of the highest capacities; but if they do not one should practice the ejection of consciousness, which liberates spontaneously as soon as it is thought of, in the bardo of the moment before death. This should certainly liberate yogins of average capacities, but if it does not one should strive in this "Great Liberation through Hearing" in the bardo of dharmata.[7]

Therefore, the dying person should first examine the sequence of the signs of death according to the "Spontaneous Liberation of the Signs of Death," and when they are definitely completed, she or he should effect the ejection of consciousness which, as soon as it is thought of, liberates spontaneously. If ejection is effected, there is no need to hear the *Book of the Dead,* but, if not, it should be read clearly and precisely, close to the dying or dead body. The reader is not to touch the dying person but reads as close to the ear as possible. The words are read correctly and clearly, even if the person is dead, even if there is no corpse present.

Just reading from the *Book of the Dead* in itself affects both the dying person, who becomes aware that a ritual is being performed, and the community involved in the dying process. As the deterioration of consciousness increases, the words from the *Bardo Thodol* provide a powerful confidence that the dying person is moving into luminosity.

The importance of these practices is twofold: to support the dead person through the bardo between death and rebirth, and to help the practitioners when they face death. Friends and family are advised to approach those who are dying or who have died, without weeping or making distracting noises. The corpse is not disturbed immediately so that the soul may concentrate on the becoming process. Furthermore, since in Tibetan culture death is not a problem, it is natural and important to tell dying persons that they are dying, especially so that they can begin their mental preparations.

The concluding words of the *Book of the Dead* encapsulate everything that has been spoken of before:

> One should read this continually and learn the word-meanings and terms by heart; then when death is certain and the signs of death have been recognized, if one's condition allows one should read it aloud oneself and contemplate it, and if one is not able to do that it should be given to a dharma-brother to read, for this reminder will certainly liberate, there is no doubt. This teaching does not need any practice, it is a profound instruction which liberates just by being seen and heard and read. This profound instruction leads great sinners on the secret path. If one does not forget its words and terms even when being chased by seven dogs, the instruction liberates in the bardo of the moment before death. Even if the buddhas of the past, present and future were to search, they would not find a better teaching than this.[8]

From the Tibetan viewpoint, it is during periods of change that the greatest possible growth occurs. That is why death and the proper manner of dying are so crucial to one's liberation. Death is the ultimate change in life, and if one allows himself or herself to die to self before dying, at death all confusion will cease in the peace of the last moment.

Perhaps now the opening story about the dying nun has a clearer meaning. Both the old man who did the family's shopping and the dying woman herself expressed the same understanding of death by their actions. He would not have left her to shop had it not been the "right time," the time for her to begin practicing her visualizations. "Unite your mind with Buddha," he said before leaving, "and don't think about us here behind. We'll be Okay."[9]

NOTES

[1]Sogyal Rimpoche, "The Gates of Death," in *The Laughing Man*, Vol. 2, No. 3, 22.

[2]Edward Conze, translator, *Buddhist Scriptures* (New York: Penguin Books, 1959), 227.

[3]*Ibid.*, 229.

[4]Chogyam Trungpa, translator, *The Tibetan Book of the Dead* (Boulder Colorado: Shambala Press, 1975), 69–70.

[5]*Ibid.*, 90.

[6]*Ibid.*, 90.

[7]*Ibid.*, 33. As specified by Glenn H. Mullin in *Death and Dying: The Tibetan Tradition* (Boston: Arkana, 1986), 142–145, self-liberation can be achieved simply by carefully observing the signs of death. After the elements dissolve and the breath totally stops, one awakens from unconsciousness into the Clear Light of luminosity. "When a yogi applies the correct meditations the mind here immediately transforms into the ultimate state of the unproduced, uncreated sphere of truth" (145). Richard W. Boerstler in *Letting Go* (So. Yarmouth, Mass., 1985) applies a Tibetan breathing approach to dying called "comeditation" in which a guide helps the patient breathe into death.

[8]*Ibid.*, 91.

[9]Rimpoche, *ibid.*

JOURNAL EXERCISES

1. In what ways does the old dying nun typify the Tibetan attitude toward death? Why did she laugh when the old man left her alone? Could you imagine yourself dying this way?
2. Imagine that you have died and that your essence has entered into the Clear Light stage of after-death travel. Describe it as best as you possibly can.
3. Reflect upon the image of the film-projector behind which shines the Clear Light. What does the viewer see projected onto the screen? What does the screen represent?
4. Do you know of any western version of the *Tibetan Book of the Dead*? If so, compare them; if not, do you see a need for such a practical guide to dying in the west?
5. Redescribe the process called the "ejection of consciousness." Can you imagine this practice transposed onto any other sacred tradition that you know? Describe this transposition.
6. How might an intelligent, practicing Tibetan answer the following question: What does your tradition teach about how to die artfully? That is, what is the most sacred way of dying?

Chapter 6 CHINESE ATTITUDES TOWARD DEATH

> In Life I follow and serve (Heaven and Earth).
> In death I will be at peace.
>
> Chang Tsai, *Hsi Ming*

One theme that emerges in this text is that answers to death-related questions are often found in a culture's creation stories. This is especially true of a rather atypical, exceptional Chinese creation account which vividly depicts the paradoxical nature of the beginning of all things:

> There is a beginning. There is a not yet beginning to be a beginning. There is not yet beginning to be a not yet beginning to be a beginning. There is being. There is non-being. There is a not yet beginning to be non-being. There is a not yet beginning to be a not yet beginning to be non-being. Suddenly there is being and non-being. But between this being and non-being, I don't really know which is being and which is non-being. Now I have just said something. But I don't know whether what I have said has really said something or whether it hasn't said something.[1]

In this Taoist story, Chuang Tzu captures the being-non-being aspect of the beginning, the birth-death aspect. In other words, contained within the beginning is the not-yet-beginning-to-be-a-beginning nature of creation, to say nothing of not-yet-beginning-to-be-non-being. In this sense, the true beginning is beginningless, and birth already contains its opposite, death.

Still another version of the mysterious nature of the beginning teaches that:

> There was something formless yet complete,
> That existed before heaven and earth;
> Without sound, without substance,
> Dependent on nothing, unchanging,
> All pervading, unfailing.
> One may think of it as the mother of all things under heaven.
> Its true name we do not know;
> 'Way' is the by-name that we give it.

81

Were I forced to say to what class of things it belongs
I should call it Great.[2]

This verse is attributed to Lao Tzu, or the venerable master, who alleg-
edly lived during the time of Confucius (551–479), and who, before he died,
was asked to record his teachings by virtue of his revered status. As a result,
he left two books which describe the *way* (Tao) and its *virtue* (Te). Here Lao
Tzu depicts the Tao as that which is both formless yet formed, silent and
void, and which can be called the mother of all. But while he names it the
Tao, it is, as he indicates in his opening verse, beyond name.

The way (Tao) that can be spoken of
Is not the constant way (Tao);
The name that can be named
Is not the constant name.
The nameless was the beginning of heaven and earth;
The named was the mother of the myriad creatures.
Hence always rid yourself of desires in order to observe its secrets;
But always allow yourself to have desires in order to observe its
    manifestations.
These two are the same
But diverge in name as they issue forth.
Being the same they are called mysteries,
Mystery upon mystery
The gateway of the manifold secrets.[3]

It should be noted that while the Tao is a name for that which cannot
be named, its secrets can be grasped by one who has rid the self of, or died
to, desires. Even though, as Lao Tzu writes, one must have desires to observe
the manifestations of the Tao, to truly observe its inner nature one must be
desireless. While we will return to this later when we discuss the process of
reversal, at this point we will focus on the connection between creation and
death.

Many images have been given to depict the Tao, the way, that which
generates itself, mother of the universe, the nature of nature. Over and over
again, it is referred to as the flowing of water which subtly, non-aggressively,
rhythmically, streams around all obstacles. Ultimately, the Tao is a mirror in
which one discovers one's own, original harmonious nature.

Lao Tzu further teaches that:

The Tao engenders one,
One engenders two,

Two engenders three,
And three engenders the myriad things.
The myriad things engender the yin vapors and embrace the yang,
And through the coalescing of these vapors,
They attain a state of harmony.[4]

Crucial in this verse is the generative relationship depicted between Yin and Yang. Creation occurs at the moment of the separation of being into Yang and Yin:

In the beginning there was the unity of Yang-Yin (light-darkness, heat-cold, dry-moist). When the subtle went upward, and the gross downward, when heavens formed from the subtle, and earth from the gross, then there was and is now Yang and Yin (active and receptive, male and female). From the harmonious interaction of Yang and Yin come the seasons and all of earth's products. Yang produced fire whose subtlest parts formed the sun; Yin produced water whose subtlest parts formed the moon. The sun's interaction with the moon produced the stars which fill heaven, just as rivers and dust fill earth. When Yang combines with Yin, all creatures are produced. In these two is the All (Tai Chi).[5]

YIN 陰

YANG 陽

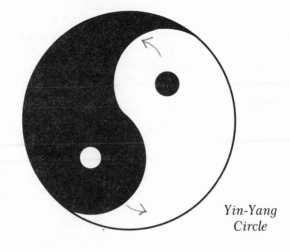

Yin-Yang
Circle

As the graphics illustrate, not only is there a common character in the Chinese script for both Yin and Yang, but also each "half" of the circle is penetrated by its "opposite" while each of the two "opposites" (the smaller circles) are again divided into "halves" with interpenetrating "opposites." Of course there is no end, either on a macro- or micro-cosmic level to this patterning. It is both natural and cosmic. The ancient sages viewed nature as a bi-polar reality in which each dimension contains its opposite, and in which each dimension is constantly transforming into its opposite. Thus there is no female without male, no day without night, no evil without good, no life without death, no Yin without Yang, and vice versa. As one can see in the accompanying drawing, the Yin/Yang symbol represents the complementary nature of opposites (or harmonious dualism) in which opposites always interpenetrate and replace each other. The following list enumerates the harmoniously balanced opposites:

YANG (Sun)
 1. Positive charge
 2. Heaven (aspiration)
 3. Day
 4. Male
 5. Active, aggressive
 6. Hard (the river bank)
 7. Hot (dry)
 8. Transcendence
 9. Discipline, order
10. Life

YIN (Moon)
 1. Negative charge
 2. Earth (matter, mother)
 3. Night
 4. Female
 5. Receptive, yielding
 6. Soft (the river)
 7. Cold (moist)
 8. Immediacy
 9. Spontaneity, flowing
10. Death

In the Chinese theory of natural evolution, Yin is always in the process of changing to Yang, and Yang to Yin, for the nature of nature is never fixed. Like Buddha's teaching of *annica* (the impermanence of all phenomena), the Chinese understood, integrated and applied the implications of natural changes. Yin was seen as mother earth, night, female, receptive, soft, flowing and spontaneous, whereas Yang was viewed as heaven, day, male, active, hard, ordered, and disciplined. While each seems to have a separate existence, at the same time each harmoniously interfuses the other.

For our purposes we can better understand the significance of the mutual interpenetration of Yin and Yang if we examine the Chinese art of dying. To the ancient sages, life was already in death, and death already in life. To separate one from the other would be to render each incomplete. Life (Yang) is seen as the foreground of death, and death (Yin) as the backdrop to life. The process of death then is the natural and necessary transition from a conscious state to an unconscious one, from a life-body to a death-body.

Perhaps one of the most affirmative attitudes toward death to be found in world literature is in the writing of Chuang Tzu (399–295 BCE). Believing that life and death are merely human distinctions for one reality, he writes:

> Life is the companion of death, death is the beginning of life. Who understands their workings? Man's life is a coming together of breath. If it comes together, there is life; if it scatters, there is death. And if life and death are companions to each other, then what is there for us to be anxious about?[6]

This predilection toward the non-distinction between life and death explains how Chuang Tzu was able to face his own death with such seeming nonchalance:

> When Chuang Tzu was about to die his disciples expressed a desire to give him a sumptuous burial. Chuang Tzu said, "I will have heaven and earth for my coffin and coffin shell, the sun and moon for my pair of jade discs, the stars and constellations for my pearls and beads, and the ten thousand things for my parting gifts. The furnishings for my funeral are already prepared—what is there to add?" "But we're afraid the crows and kites will eat you, Master," said his disciples. Chuang Tzu said, "Above ground I'll be eaten by crows and kites, below ground I'll be eaten by mole crickets and ants. Wouldn't it be rather bigoted to deprive one group in order to supply the other?"[7]

For Lao Tzu, legendary founder of the Taoist school, the perfect man, the man of Tao, does not waste energy being anxious about dying.

Thus when Lao Tzu says "Death arises from life itself," one needs to understand that for the Chinese sages, at death the power of death emerges to the foreground from the midst of life where it has always been. As Lao Tzu writes:

Human life commences in birth
And terminates in death.
The disciples of life are about one-third,
While the disciples of death are about one-third.
[Those who originally could have lived to an old age but who of their
    own accord] walk the path of death also number about one-third.
Why is this?
Because their desire for life is too excessive.
I have heard it said that one who is adept at nourishing life,
While travelling on land, will not meet with a wild rhinoceros or tiger.
And amidst the fray of battle
Will not meet with injury from the sword and buckler.
The wild rhinoceros has nothing into which to pierce its horn,
The tiger has nothing in which to sink its claws,
And the sword has nothing in which to lodge its blade.
Why is this?
Because of his not entering the sphere of death.[8]

A third of humanity is full of life, a third heads toward death, and a third, because they value life, move into the realm of death, or what is called the process of reversal. Taoist sages teach that by reversing the ordinary life direction, by returning to one's original simplicity, it is possible to become a true sage, and to discover not only the art of dying, but also the art of grieving. Although Lao Tzu does not speak with one voice, his main emphasis is linked with how to live a long life and have a natural death. Chuang Tzu, on the other hand, had accomplished the art of this reversal and had become like a child in spirit. He responded in an unusual way when his wife died:

When Hui Tzu went to convey his condolences, he found Chuang Tzu sitting with his legs sprawled out, pounding on a tub and singing. "You lived with her, she brought up your children and grew old," said Hui Tzu. "It should be enough simply not to weep at her death. But pounding on a tub and singing—this is going too far, isn't it?" Chuang Tzu said, "You're wrong. When she first died, do you think I didn't grieve like anyone else? But I looked back to her beginning and the time before she was born. Not only the time before she was born, but the time before she had a body. Not only the time before she had a body, but the time before she had a spirit. In the midst of the jumble of wonder and mystery a change took place and she had a spirit. Another change and she had a body. Another change and she was born. Now there's been another change and she's dead. It's just like the progression of the four seasons, spring, summer, fall, winter.

"Now she's going to lie down peacefully in a vast room. If I were to follow after her bawling and sobbing, it would show that I don't understand anything about fate. So I stopped."[9]

Beyond all human change, nature continues to express itself within never-ending cycles of transformation. Waves swell and fall from the horizon flowing to the lap of the beach, finally to crash and dissipate into white froth, only to return to the sea beneath the next wave. So, too, human life terminates with a reversal of direction, from oncoming to outgoing, from Yang to Yin.

As Tibetans do, the Chinese Taoists also practice a dying before dying through meditative practices, the fine arts and the martial arts. More specifically, the Chinese are known for their spiritual practices of "T'ai Chi" and the more ancient Ch'i Kung ("chee" "gung"). In each, the practitioner cultivates the spontaneous art of activating and circulating *ch'i* (life-force), which flows from the base of the abdomen. Called "embryonic breathing," in the Taoist system of esoteric physiology the circulation and recirculation of *ch'i* activated an inner balance of Yin and Yang energies. Taoists also believed that gradually, through such exercises, a new "embryo body" (a subtle body within the physical body) developed. It was through this body that one achieved immortality.

Through repeated practice of such meditation forms, and through tracing patterns of light with one's hands in slow motion, the one who moves experiences, at the same time, being moved by *ch'i*. One way to characterize these movements would be to refer to the Taoist notion of spontaneous reversal, of *wu wei* (actionless action); another way would be to refer to the Confucian notion of cultivated ritual, of *li* (prescribed action). Each way provides a way of dying before dying, so that the practitioner never again fears death.

Veneration of Ancestors

If Lao Tzu and Chuang Tzu can be characterized as spontaneously Yin-like, the sage Confucius (551–479) can be called Yang-like because of his reliance on ritual, manners and the cultivation of social and family virtues. Confucius attempted to restore China's ancient values, including through what has been called the worship of ancestors, but which more accurately should be termed veneration of ancestors. It was thought that the dead benefit the living with next-worldly wisdom, whereas the living benefit the dead through prayers, sacrifices, and commemorations. Just as there is a synchronistic relationship between humans and natural processes, there is there a synchronistic connection between the living and the dead. To revere the aged as wise, and the dead as most wise, is to participate in the sacredness of all life through funeral rites, mourning observances and continual sacrifices. Such rituals were confined to one's blood-family, for only the emperor could worship imperial ancestor and *Shang Ti,* by law.

The dominant Confucian attitude toward death can be summed up in the tone of the following dialogue with one of his disciples, Tzu Lu:

> Chi lu (Tzu lu) asked about serving the spiritual beings. Confucius said, "If we are not yet able to serve man, how can we serve spiritual beings?" "I venture to ask about death." Confucius said, "If we do not yet know about life, how can we know about death?"[10]

Just as Confucius refused to talk about god or heaven, so too he refused to speak about death or after-death. When he was asked to pray at his own death, he responded that he had already been praying for a long time. Instead, Confucius focused his teaching on propitious behavior, on the most mannered action in each situation. He taught a ritually correct way to do everything: to rise, to wash, to dress, to eat, to speak, not to speak, to work, to socialize, to study, to sleep and to die. Each gesture, each request, each birth, each marriage, each funeral is given meaning by personal presence fused with ceremonial actions. For example, Chinese traditionalists greet their teachers with a probing reserve, with a respectful deference which is spontaneously, acknowledged without words.

To better understand what later tradition attributed to Confucius about the sacred art of dying, consider the following passage from the *Scripture on Filiality,* in which the correct procedures for mourning are outlined:

> When mourning, a filial son weeps without wailing; he performs funeral rites without attention to personal adornment; he speaks without rhetorical flourish; he feels uncomfortable in fine clothing; he feels no joy on hearing music; he does not relish good food—all this is in the nature of grief. After three days he breaks his fast to show men that the dead should not hurt the living and that disfigurement should not lead to the destruction of life—this is the rule of the sages. The period of mourning is not allowed to exceed three years, thus showing the people that all things come to an end. The

body, shrouded, is lowered into the encased coffin. The sacrificial vessels are set out with grief and sorrow. Beating the breast and jumping up and down, the mourners bid a last sad farewell. The body is laid to rest in the burial place selected by divination. Offerings are made to the spirits in the ancestral temple. Spring and autumn sacrificial rites are performed in order to be mindful of the dead at stated times. When parents are alive, to serve them with love and reverence; when deceased, to cherish their memory with deep grief—this is the sum total of man's fundamental duty, the fulfillment of the mutual relations between the living and the dead, the accomplishment of the filial son's service of his parents.[11]

The psychological and moral tone implicit in Confucius' teachings is made more explicit by Hsün Tzu (298–238 BCE). In his *locus classicus,* "Discussion of Rites (*Li Chi*)," part of a larger well-ordered philosophic system, he begins by discussing the origin of ritual as the fulfillment of human desires for sacred action. "All rites begin in simplicity, are brought to fulfillment in elegant form, and end in joy." Hsün Tzu writes, "When rites are performed in the highest manner, then both the emotions and the forms embodying them are fully realized." The meaning of ritual for Hsün Tzu is deep indeed, like a plumb line, and always operates in a timely fashion:

When conducting a sacrifice, one divines to determine the appropriate day, fasts and purifies oneself, sets out the tables and mats with the offerings, and speaks to the invocator as though the spirit of the dead were really going to partake of the sacrifice. One takes up each of the offerings and presents them as though the spirit were really going to taste them.[12]

There are a multiplicity of rules governing everything from dress, to food offerings, to types of coffin decorations; in this way life and death are regarded equally.

Death Ritual

After death, the dying person's name was no longer used because it was thought that naming the dead person would call forth his or her presence. According to the ritual prescriptions, the son assumed a major responsibility. He wore special clothing and fasted from certain types of food and behavior. His grief was to be demonstrated only in an appropriate manner (i.e., "jumping up and down" as opposed to "beating the breast" for women).

Later Confucian philosophers developed the idea that as each person contains the masculine principle and the feminine principle, so too in each person there is a "higher" or Yang soul, and a "lower" or Yin soul. The Yin-like soul is more dense and clings to the body. It stays near the grave site and is acknowledged at least once a year in the spring when families "sweep the grave" of their dead relatives. The Yang-like soul, which is less dense, less malevolent, remains around the house. Daily, incense is brought to a home altar, and twice a month, and at the new year, food is prepared for the Yang soul and placed on the altar. While anthropological studies have raised questions about the universal acceptance of such a two-soul theory, its practice indicates that the ancestor's soul was approached quite differently at the home altar than at the grave site.

It is the family altar at which relatives of the dead ritualistically honor and venerate their ancestors. As we have already indicated, there is a mutuality and reciprocity between the living and the dead, as there is between heaven, earth and being human, or between the Yang-soul and the Yin-soul. Prayers, remembrances and sacrificial offerings made to the dead, it is believed, benefit not only these dead, but also the sacrificer. The Chinese indicate, by their actions at the home altar, that they are both offering their oblations to the departed and, at the same time, receiving benefits from the family's spiritual resources.

The altar itself, which occupied the most honored place in the home, is where the ancestral cult is focused. The altar may be a "hand-carved heirloom displayed in the upper floor of the central structure on a vast estate or simply a board fixed high upon one wall of a single-room dwelling."[13] Aside from incense pots and perhaps some foods and wine on the altar, there is a tall, thin wooden ancestral tablet with the names, titles and dates of death of family members inscribed therein. It was on this altar that food and chopsticks are placed so that the ancestors can eat with the living on special occasions, like the New Year celebration.

The Yin-soul on the other hand remains close to the gravesite and is approached with a bit more caution than with domestic joy. Graves are places where disembodied spirits, ghosts and/or spirit-bodies dwell, and where beleaguered souls cause trouble for other souls. Nevertheless, during the grave-sweeping festival in mid-spring (April 5, one hundred and five days after the winter solstice), the entire family visits the gravesite. Each mourner renews his or her relationship with the dead, renews pledges, seeks favors, asks advice and fondly remembers the relatives. Then the ancestor's graves are swept and after all obligations are met a family celebration begins.

Of the many rites and customs performed by the ordinary Chinese family when one of its members died, there was always a chief mourner whose ultimate purpose was to promote safe passage for the deceased soul into the next world. The fullest responsibility for the performance of appropriate customs normally rested with the filial son(s). This is not always the case today however, as Ida Pruitt tells us in *A Daughter of Han: The Autobiography of a Chinese Working Woman*. She writes of being chosen, instead of her husband, to be the chief mourner for her aunt, and the one to carry the Heredity Jar:

> This is a small earthen jar into which all the members of the family, of the next generation, put food—rice, chiaotze, bread. They stuff the jar full that there may be many descendants and that there may be food for the person about to go on the long journey, also that there may be luck for those who put in the food. The child who stuffs in the most food will have the greatest fortune. The youngest son puts the round loaf of bread on the top of the jar and sticks a pair of chopsticks into it. I had to be all the children and stuff the jar, and also the youngest son and stick in the chopsticks, and the oldest son and carry the jar. Carrying the jar is the sign of the chief mourner. It is placed in the grave at the coffin head.[14]

Ida was by her aunt's bedside when she died. From the Chinese viewpoint, it is extremely important that some of the family are present at death of a loved one, because it is believed that those who die alone will have no descendants after their transmigration. As soon as her aunt died, she stuffed a little red bag containing a piece of silver, a pinch of tea, a piece of candy and a bit of salt vegetable into her mouth, so that she would have food and currency for her journey. Then she bound her aunt's feet together so that the body would not get up again. Shortly thereafter, she went to the Tu Ti Miao (the Temple of the Earth God), the next day to Cheng Huang Miao (the Temple of the City God), and on the third day to the Temple of Tien Chun Lao Yeh (the Temple of the Hosts of Heaven).

On the fifth day, the body was buried. The night before, the family and chief mourner knelt near the coffin in unbleached, unhemmed white garments, and quietly wept as music softly played in the background. This was done to help the deceased's soul begin its difficult journey away from the body. Wearing sackcloth, Ida walked in front of the coffin carrying the Heredity Jar in her arms. At the gravesite, the coffin was lowered into the ground against a backdrop of chanting priests, mourning relatives and funeral music. Here we might say the funeral service ended and the veneration of her ancestor began.

NOTES

[1]Burton Watson, translator, *Chuang Tzu* (New York: Columbia U. Press, 1964), 38.

[2]Arthur Waley, translator, *The Way and Its Power* (New York: Grove Press, 1958), XXV.

[3]D. C. Lau, translator, *Lao Tzu: Tao Te Ching* (New York: Penguin, 1963), I.

[4]Ch'en Ku-ying, translator, *Lao Tzu: Texts, Notes, and Comments* (Chinese Materials Center, 1961), XLII.

[5]Composed from varying sources. This view of creation is not as old as early "picture writing" in China; it is in spirit. In this actual form, it is no earlier than Han dynasty commentaries on the *I-Ching*.

[6]Burton Watson, trans., *The Complete Works of Chuang Tzu* (New York: Columbia University Press, 1968), 235.

[7]*Ibid.,* 361.

[8]Ch'en Ku-ying, L.

[9]Watson, *Chuang Tzu,* 113. In popular Taoism, the quest for longevity and immortality appears in myths, yoga and alchemical practices. Chuang Tzu resisted this. "What makes my life good makes death good," he said.

[10]*Analects* 11:11, in Wing Tsit Chan, *A Sourcebook in Chinese Philosophy* (Princeton: Princeton University Press, 1963), 36.

[11]Mary Leila Makra, translator, *The Hsiao Ching* (Asian Institute translations, No. 2), XVIII. It may be necessary here to know that the real source of this brilliant symbolic analysis of funeral and mourning activity is Hsün Tzu (third century BCE). The "Discussion of Rites (Li)" chapter in Hsün Tzu is its locus classicus (ref. pp. 98–100 in Watson's translation).

[12]Burton Watson, translator, *Hsün Tzu, Basic Writings* (New York: Columbia University Press, 1963), 110.

[13]Christian Jochim, *Chinese Religions* (New Jersey: Prentice-Hall, 1986), 171.

[14]Ida Pruitt, *A Daughter of Han: The Autobiography of a Chinese Working Woman* (Palo Alto: Stanford University Press, 1967), 315.

JOURNAL EXERCISES

1. Discuss the opening paradox of the chapter—that there is a not-yet beginning to be beginning. What is the significance of the speaker's last lines: "But I don't know whether what I have said has really said something or whether it hasn't said something"?
2. Draw a picture of the Yin/Yang symbol in complete detail. Ruminate upon its parts, its unity, its movement. In what ways, if any, does this symbol influence your view of death?
3. Redescribe the Taoist process of reversal. In what way does this spiritual path relate to the Taoist attitude toward death?
4. Reread what Confucius and his followers taught about the filial son's responsibility to the deceased. Can this be compared to any western practices? What is the role of the daughter?
5. What is the difference between, and the relationship of the Yin-soul and the Yang-soul? Are they two souls?
6. How might an intelligent, practicing Confucianist or Taoist answer the following question: What does your tradition teach about how to die artfully? That is, what is the most sacred way of dying?

Chapter 7 MESOPOTAMIAN AND EGYPTIAN ATTITUDES TOWARD DEATH

What is this sleep which holds you now?
You are lost in the dark and cannot hear me.

The Epic of Gilgamesh

According to archaeological research, the earliest skeletal remains of *homo sapiens* date back to approximately 30,000 BCE. These early Paleolithic peoples were concerned with three fundamental realities: birth, food and death. Their approach to these concerns was both practical and supernatural and is evidenced by their burial customs. Paleolithic peoples buried their dead ritualistically as follows:

1. Often the corpse was covered with a red pigment (associated with blood or vitality) which suggests a hope that vitality would be restored, and a belief in an afterlife.
2. Food, tools and weapons were found in the graves which indicates a belief that they would be needed in some way in the next world.
3. The dead were usually buried on their side, legs tightly flexed, hands covering their face, in the fetal position, as if to prepare them for a rebirth from the grave/womb of Mother Earth.
4. Stone or bone ornaments and figurines were placed in the grave; their accentuated sexual features and blank faces suggest that these figurines represent not individual women but the Mother Goddess.

When we examine the earliest written texts of ancient western cultures we find two dominant attitudes. In the first, represented here by the Sumerian story the "Epic of Gilgamesh," the search for immortality discloses its non-existence, whereas in the second, represented by Egyptian and Greek stories and practices, the soul is immortal. In the rest of this chapter, we will contrast the Mesopotamian (Sumerian) view with that of the Egyptians, because in some sense the bifurcation between the two still exists today, though in different forms.

94

Enkidu and Gilgamesh

[handwritten: search for immortality — a dis closes its non exist]

The "Epic of Gilgamesh" is not only the earliest surviving epic poem, but it is the earliest surviving attempt to reflect on the problem of fate. In its most complete form, the epic is contained on twelve clay tablets written in Semitic Akkadian which were recovered from King Ashurbanipal's palace library at Nineveh. While the versions quoted here date from the seventh century BCE, scholars date other remaining fragments of the story to ancient Babylon, about 2000 BCE.

Told as if in stages or scenes, the epic begins with Gilgamesh ("He who discovered the source" or "He who saw all").

> I will proclaim to the world the deeds of Gilgamesh. This was the man to whom all things were known; this was the king who knew the countries of the world. He was wise, he saw mysteries and knew secret things, he brought us a tale of the days before the flood. He went on a long journey, was weary, worn-out with labour, returning he rested, he engraved on a stone the whole story.[1]

It is important to notice the point of view of the story. The first words—"I will proclaim to the world"—introduce Gilgamesh, and his noble, powerful and tragic quest for immortal life. The readers are reminded that they are "reading" an oral presentation told by an epic story-teller of what Gilgamesh himself wrote, for Gilgamesh returned from his journey only to engrave the whole story on stone. What we are hearing is Gilgamesh's story, told by a contemporary poet to both eulogize and venerate the memory of Gilgamesh, and to reanimate the power of his quest in the hearer's psyche.

First, the listener is told that the gods created Gilgamesh two-thirds god and one-third mortal. He was made King of Uruk, which is situated near the Persian Gulf in the Arabian peninsula, not far from Ur, Abraham's home city. In Uruk, he built great walls and temples for Anu and the goddess Ishtar, the artistry of which no later king could equal.

The listener is invited to climb Uruk's walls, to walk its stones along with the narrator and to look out over Gilgamesh's city:

> Walk along it, I say;
> Regard the foundation terrace and examine the masonry:
> Is it not burnt brick and good?
> The seven sages laid the foundations.[2]

These crucial lines will reappear at the end of the story when Gilgamesh returns from his quest for immortality, and provide a clue to the only meaning that immortality can hold for him.

As the first scene begins, we are told of Gilgamesh's dynamic tyranny. No woman, be she wife or daughter, was safe from his insatiable advances. To protect the people of Uruk, and in response to their pleadings, the goddess Aruru (who had created Gilgamesh) mixed water and clay and let it fall in the wilderness. Thus, Enkidu was created—a hairy, wild man who ate grass and drank from animal's waterholes.

To civilize Enkidu, Ishtar, the (goddess of love and fertility and Queen of Heaven), sends a courtesan to seduce Enkidu, and they lie together for six days and seven nights. Thereafter, the wild beasts no longer recognize him and run away, for he can no longer keep pace with them. Having accomplished her purpose the courtesan takes him to Uruk to meet Gilgamesh. Enkidu robustly announces his plans to challenge him boldly and cry out aloud:

> I am the strongest here,
> I have come to change the old order,
> I am he who was born in the hills,
> I am he who is strongest of all![3]

Entering Uruk, he meets Gilgamesh and a titanic struggle ensues. When Gilgamesh finally conquers Enkidu, the two embrace, and their friendship is sealed.

In the next scene, the new friends set out to rid the forest of an evil demon, Humbaba, and to establish the name of Gilgamesh where it has never before been heard. Each is accomplished. However, on their victorious return, they refuse the advances of Ishtar since, as Gilgamesh says, she has had too many lovers. Furiously, she sends the Bull of Heaven to kill Gilgamesh, but instead Gilgamesh and Enkidu cut out the bull's heart and offer it to Shamash (god of the sun). For this, the gods decide that Enkidu must be put to death, and they reveal this to him. He dreams that he is carried off to "the House of Darkness," from which there is no return for those who enter.

Enkidu falls sick and bitterly laments the day he was lured to the city by the courtesan. When he dies, Gilgamesh deeply mourns. Four thousand years later, his lament still strikes a deep response in the reader:

> Hear me, great ones of Uruk,
> I weep for Enkidu, my friend.
> Bitterly moaning like a woman mourning
> I weep for my brother.
> O Enkidu, my brother,

You were the axe at my side,
My hand's strength, the sword in my belt,
The shield before me,
A glorious robe, my fairest ornament;
An evil Fate has robbed me . . .
What is this sleep which holds you now?
You are lost in the dark and cannot hear me.[5]

Refusing to bury Enkidu's body, Gilgamesh laments seven days and seven nights until worms began to fasten on the dead body. Only then is Enkidu buried. Gilgamesh summons the finest artisans and commissions them to fashion a statue of Enkidu. When it is finished, the breast of lapis lazuli and the body of gold, they set it on a hardwood table. A bowl of cornelian, filled with honey, and one of lapis, filled with butter, are set beside the statue. When Gilgamesh offers the shrine to the sun, he departs, weeping.

With the chilling fact of his own mortality facing him—"When I die, shall I not be like Enkidu?"—Gilgamesh then announces his intention to search for everlasting life. He wonders: If this is what life comes to, what is its point? Why did I bother to build Uruk if I am not going to continue to live within them? For the first time in his life Gilgamesh faces his own death, and is plunged into turmoil and doubt. Gilgamesh decides to seek the meaning of death, and he departs on a journey to find Utnapishtim—the only mortal ever to achieve eternal life—who now lives beyond the edge of the world.

Far from an easy journey, he travels over steppes and grassland, through mountain passes and over ranges. Along the way he meets three people, each of whom attempts to dissuade him from the journey. To the Scorpion-Man (guardian of the entrance to the underworld), Gilgamesh says that he wished his weeping would bring Enkidu back, but when it did not, he decided to seek out Utnapishtim (the far away one). "No man born of women has ever achieved what you wish to achieve," he is told. "What you seek is impossible."

After Gilgamesh has left and has traveled through total darkness, he comes to Shamash (judge, law-giver, god of the sun) who speaks in the same way. But Gilgamesh will not be diverted. He then meets Siduri, the alewife, the divine winemaker (perhaps a form of Ishtar), who dwells by the deep sea (perhaps the Mediterranean). When she learns of his quest, she replies:

The life thou pursuest thou shalt not find.
When the gods created mankind,
Death for mankind they set aside,
Life in their own hands retaining.

Thou, Gilgamesh, let full be thy belly,
Make thou merry by day and by night.
Of each day make thou a feast of rejoicing,
Day and night dance thou and play![6]

These words most accurately capture the Mesopotamian attitude toward death. Their speaker, Siduri, counsels Gilgamesh to live his life to the fullest while he still can. But when this suggestion fails to dissuade his single-minded resolve she gives him an invaluable gift—she reveals to Gilgamesh where to find Urshanabi, Utnapishtim's ferryman. Meeting Urshanabi Gilgamesh reveals that he is afraid of death because his brother's fate lies heavy upon him.

How can I be silent,
How can I rest?
He is dust and I too shall die
And be laid in the earth forever.[7]

Moved by Gilgamesh's lament, Urshanabi agrees to take him to Utnapishtim, but warns him not to let his hands touch the waters in the Sea of Death over which they must cross.

The journey does not take long, nor does it, after meeting Utnapishtim, for all of his hopes to evaporate. Gilgamesh asks, "How shall I find the life for which I am searching?" Sounding like Buddha, Utnapishtim replies that there is no permanence:

Do we build houses forever?
Do we seal (contracts) forever?
Do brothers divide shares for ever?
Does hatred persist forever in the land?
Does the river forever rise (and) bring on floods?
The dragon-fly leave (its) shell
That its face might (but) glance on the face of the sun?
Since the days of yore there has been no performance;
The resting and the dead, how alike they are![8]

He reveals that while the gods alot both life *and* death, the day of death they do not disclose. But Gilgamesh will not yet be quieted, for now he asks Utnapishtim: "Tell me, how come you entered into the company of the gods and came to possess immortality?" And Utnapishtim replies: "I will reveal a hidden matter to you. I will now tell you a secret of the gods."

In the next scene, that secret is revealed, and the story of the Great Flood which destroyed all of humankind is told. That the author of the epic decided to include the flood story—a myth within the epic—affords a fascinating parallel to the later flood story in Genesis. But unlike Noah's story, Utnapishtim and his wife alone escaped in a great ship which they built. As a consequence of their courage and skill, the gods decreed that they should never die: "In times past," Enlil (god of earth, wind, spirit) said, "you were mortal; henceforth you and your wife shall live forever far away at the mouth of rivers."

What follows may at first seem anti-climactic but, in fact, it forms an integral component of the drama.

Utnapishtim's wife, takes pity on Gilgamesh. She persuades her husband to reveal the secret location of a miraculous plant called, "The Old Man Becomes Young Again," or the plant of rejuvenation. Utnapishtim then tells Gilgamesh:

> Thou hast come hither, toiling and straining.
> What shall I give thee that thou mayest return to thy land?
> I will disclose, O Gilgamesh, a hidden thing,
> And . . . about a plant I will tell thee:
> This plant, like the buckthorn is its . . .
> Its thorns will prick thy hands just as does the rose.
> If thy hands obtain the plant, thou wilt attain life.[9]

Immediately Gilgamesh dives for it and brings it back to his boat. Somewhat relieved, he and his boatman set out to return to Uruk but while bathing at a waterhole, a serpent sniffs the fragrance of the plant and carries it off. When Gilgamesh sees that the plant has been stolen, he takes Urshanabi's hand and weeps: "Is this what I have suffered for? I have gained nothing. I found a sign, and now it is lost!"

With empty hands and a disconsolate heart, Gilgamesh finally returns home. Without moving, he instructs Urshanabi to climb the walls of Uruk:

> Inspect the base terrace, examine its brickwork,
> If its brickwork is not of burnt brick,
> And if the Seven Wise Ones laid not its
> foundation.[10]

By reaffirming the excellent construction of his city, and thereby implying its ethical virtues as well, Gilgamesh indicates that this was the only immortality he could attain. He then engraved the whole story, and the story within the story, on stone tablets.

When he was about to die, his servants gathered around him in the palace and intoned:

The king has laid himself down and will not rise again,
The Lord of Kullab will not rise again;
He overcame evil, he will not come again;
Though he was strong of arm he will not rise again;
He had wisdom and a comely face, he will not come again;
He is gone into the mountain, he will not come again;
On the bed of fate he lies, he will not rise again,
From the couch of many colours he will not come again. [11]

The people of the city lamented and ritualistically weighed out their offerings both to the departed Gilgamesh, and to all the gods of the dead. They had no further hopes. Like his friend Enkidu before him, Gilgamesh was dead, never to rise again. [12]

From the "Epic of Gilgamesh" the reader can glean at least five responses toward the reality of death, none of which holds any real promise:

Everyone
1. That to find answers to questions raised by death one has to search life with a single-minded passion.

Not enough to know you are going to die.
2. That the only valid answers to death's mystery come from one's own experience, not from someone else's attempt to provide answers.

3. That there is no personal immortality for humans, only for the gods, that human fate is in the hands of the gods and that only the gods know when a person will die.

4. That even though the key to rejuvenation is possible to grasp momentarily, it cannot be kept. *maintain youth*

5. That society (the polis) outlasts the individual and is the only immortality humans can achieve, that is, to live on in the memory of the living, indeed in the memory of this story itself.

Isis and Osiris

To move from the pessimistic Mesopotamian view in which there is no personal immortality, to that of her sister civilization, the Egyptian, is to move to a civilization with an intensely positive preoccupation with death. Pyramids, tombs, mummies, mortuary tools, funerary writings, and the *Egyptian Book of the Dead* all testify to a fundamental optimism in the face of death. From about 2300 BCE on, an elaborate cult of the dead arose in Egypt in which techniques were developed for the preservation of corpses, some of which have been preserved for more than three thousand years. From the building of pyramids as monumental tombs for the dead to the sacred art of mummification, Egyptian culture developed ritual and accompanying mythologies which give this cult a significant place at the beginnings of recorded western culture.

Egyptian mythology as a whole reflects the fact that different gods and goddesses were worshiped in different city states. While each god or goddess belonged to its own family, there developed a more universally accepted mythology which superseded, in importance, the local one. It is fairly certain that by the very beginning of the First Dynasty (ca. 2850 BCE), the Egyptian king was believed to be the God Horus, symbolized by a seated or standing falcon. The king was also equated with the sun, and later in Egyptian mythology Horus would fuse with the great sun god Re (himself identified with the god Atum).

This cult of the worship of Atum-Re, of the divine king, was taken over by the famous Pharaoh Akhenaton (1364–1347 BCE), who attempted to introduce the sole worship of Aten, a word taken from his name Akhenaton ("Glory to Aten"). He made no use of the ancient myths of creation of the ancient rituals to the gods; yet he claimed to be the Son of Re.

In reaction to this the Amon-Re priests emphasized the mystery of the Amon (The invisible one) in their hymns:

> One is Amon, hiding himself from them,
> concealing himself from the (other gods) . . .
> He is far from heaven, he is (absent from) the Underworld,
> (So that) no gods know his true form.[13]

Although Amon is invisible, formless, and beyond all names, poets attempted to describe the god through speaking negatively. In the following, all three adjectives are used in the negative:

> All gods are three: Amon, Re, and Ptah,
> And there is no second to them.
> Hidden is his name as Amon, he is Re in face, and his body is Ptah.[14]

Insofar as Amon is formless, he/she is wind; insofar as Amon has a face, he/she is sun; and insofar as Amon has a body, he/she is earth.

Given the complex nature of Egyptian mythology and the numerous examples we could discuss, we will explore here only the myth of Isis and Osiris, since it is so central to our purpose, since the myth formed the functional rationale of the cult of the dead, and since the slain King Osiris' resurrection assures his followers a new life.

And the story begins, when Osiris ruled, and there was no death in the land. A just and wise king, Osiris, while certainly associated with vegetation and fertility myths, was always depicted as a real person who suffered a violent death. Egyptian icons depict Osiris with his body swathed, mummy-like, but with his head free of wrappings. Osiris became the prototype of every soul who hoped to conquer death. In the *Egyptian Book of the Dead* Osiris says of himself:

> I am he who cometh forth advancing, whose name is unknown. I am Yesterday. "Seer of Millions of Years" is my name. I pass along, I pass along the paths of the divine celestial judges. I am the Lord of Eternity. . . . [15]

Now it is told that Osiris and his sister Isis loved each other as husband and wife, and that together they ruled the land. Isis, sister and wife, stood loyally at his side and protected Osiris by her skillful tongue. Nevertheless, his enemies plotted against him, especially Seth, Osiris' jealous brother. One

Osiris-Isis

evening, Seth gave a banquet. As part of a game, he proposed to give away a chest he had skillfully made of fragrant diversified woods to the person who most perfectly fit inside it. When none present fit, Osiris took off his crown and fit into the chest perfectly. Immediately Seth and his attendants nailed it shut, soldered the edges and flung it into the river. Osiris became the first man to die.

Undaunted, Isis followed the casket to the sea on which it disappeared. But Isis did not rest until one day she found the coffin under the bark of a tree that stood as a column in the palace of the King of Byblos. When she returned with the casket to Egypt, she and her sister Nephthys embraced and wept for their brother Osiris. The faithful Isis then moved close to her husband, opened the chest and breathed into Osiris' mouth. With this breath, and with the motion of wings which she grew, she brought Osiris back to life. There they lived happily together.

Soon thereafter however, when Seth learned of Osiris' resurrection, he fell upon his brother again, this time cutting him into fourteen pieces, which he scattered over the land. Again, Isis searched the world and gathered each of the pieces of her dead husband, and formed them again into his complete body. According to the Pyramid Texts, Horus and Thoth lift Osiris from his side, and before them he is vindicated. His kingdom is restored. All the gods dwelling in the sky and on the earth are satisfied—and sky and earth are given to him. But the twice reborn Osiris no longer belongs to sky and earth. His dominion is in the Nether World beneath the earth:

> He entered the secret gates in the (splendid) precincts of the lords
> of eternity, at the goings of him who rises in the horizon, upon the
> ways of Re in the Great Seat.[16]

A voice then comes to Isis to tell her that Osiris lives again, but now as judge of the dead in the underworld.

What is unique about Osiris, when compared to all of the other Egyptian gods, is that instead of being associated with splendorous power, he is primarily associated with death and resurrection. This became a meaningful symbol of immortality to the followers of his cult.

Weighing the Soul

The two main sources of Egyptian mythology are the Pyramid Texts, inscribed on the interior walls of pyramids (2400–2000 BCE), and the Coffin Texts, inscribed on coffins during the succeeding centuries (2000–1580 BCE). Written in hieroglyphic, the Pyramid Texts consisted mainly of rituals, magical charms, prayers, and hymns referring to the funeral of the Pharaoh, while the Coffin Texts were elaborations of traditional myths designed for the commoners. From about 1600 BCE, these were replaced by the *Book of the Dead* which was similar to the Coffin Texts but was written on papyrus rolls and were placed in the tombs of the dead.

The title, *Book of the Dead,* given to a large body of religious literature drawn up for the use of dead kings, priests and other royalty, is depicted composed in hieroglyphs on the walls of pyramid tombs. It represents a system of theology in which the supremacy of Osiris, among the gods, is upheld. The book deals with the welfare of the deceased, and provides clues about their new life after death. The *Book of the Dead* tells the story of an afterworld trial and judgment in terms of a court trial carefully conducted by a divine council and headed by Osiris. At the center of the trial ritual, the heart of a deceased person was weighed on a double scale and balanced against the weight of an ostrich feather, the symbol of Maat (the divine creative power or "substance"). Finally, the deceased was made to testify, and a verdict was presented to the court. Since the only recorded verdicts are positive—e.g., He shall be given food yielded to Osiris and granted a permanent share in the field of satisfaction—the *Book of the Dead* was undoubtedly aimed at helping the deceased to obtain a favorable verdict.

By far the most prominent feature of the *Book of the Dead* is the process of judgment whereby forty-two judges, in the presence of Osiris, determined a person's fate. First the dead uttered a confession to the judges which included a list of personal wrongdoings. The deceased scribe Ani, for instance, accompanied by his wife, is depicted entering the Hall of Double Right and Truth to address the forty-two gods. Ani makes his negative confession in which he says that he has not "done iniquity," or "robbed with violence," or "stolen," or "murdered," or "defrauded offerings," or "minished oblations," or "plundered the god," or "spoken lies," or "snatched away food," or "caused pain."[17]

After his confession, there is a climactic weighing of the deceased's soul. If his heart balances evenly against a feather, the soul is granted the pleasures of paradise. Ani then addresses a prayer to his heart that he will hear a verdict like that given to Osiris:

> Thoth, the righteous judge of the great company of the gods who are in the presence of the god Osiris, saith: "Hear ye this judgment. The heart of Osiris hath in very truth been weighed, and his soul hath stood as a witness for him; it hath been found true by trial in the Great Balance. There hath not been found any wickedness in him; he hath not wasted the offerings in the temples; he hath not done harm by his deeds; and he uttered no evil reports while he was upon earth."[18]

Weighing Soul

This scene vividly attests to the Egyptian belief that the heart, or seat of consciousness, would be the final witness for or against the judged person. The judgment scene also indicates that for the Egyptians, individuals had to answer in the next world for their earthly conduct.

Death Ritual

As we have seen, the Egyptians placed great importance on the survival of the body. At death, it was believed that the *ka* (spiritual personality or a double of one's earthly body) and the *ba* (true soul which was shown as a bird with a human head) depart. Later the body would be needed by the *ka;* therefore a special room was built in the tomb, with scenes from the dead person's life pictured in it, so that the *ka* could return to enjoy afterlife as if still among the living.

Of all the preparations made for eternal life, the sacred art of mummification was one of the most remarkable. The Egyptians sought to preserve the body so that the spirits of the dead could reinhabit them. They believed that a corpse, though dead to earth, could be reinvigorated for eternal life. To accomplish this, embalming took place in the "House of Vigour" (or "vitality"), and the process itself was called *senefer* (the restoration of vitality to the dead body).

For seventy days the body was prepared by priests and skilled workers who were supervised by the "Reader," a priest who recited appropriate formulas as the work took place. All the internal organs and anything that would putrefy were removed and the brain was withdrawn through the nostrils and thrown away. The abdomen was filled with various aromatics. The vital organs were immediately prepared for storage in four stone jars and the empty body, entirely shaven, was placed for forty days in dry natron which absorbed all its remaining humidity.

The last state of embalming was the bandaging. Hundreds of yards of fine linen were used to wrap the body in several protective layers. During the wrapping, prayers were recited and sacred formulas were pronounced. Depending on how wealthy and how powerful the person was, a network of jewels and amulets might be inserted into different layers of the bandages. The necklace of amulets was to protect the neck of the mummy and it formed a magical net uniting the deceased with the eternal world. Around the waist a belt was fastened from which were hung archaic ritual objects and a ceremonial dagger.

During the wrapping, prayers were given and unguents and oils were poured on the bandages to help preserve the body, and to favorably scent the mummy. Finally, the body was wrapped in a large linen sheet. A solid gold mask was placed over the face if the body was that of royalty. Reciting chapters from the *Book of the Dead,* a priest placed a small headrest under the nape of the neck in the form of an amulet which, it was believed, would generate a miraculous heat that would enable a person to raise his or her head.

The mummy was then taken by those who had prepared the body along with essential pieces of burial furniture to be placed in the tomb (e.g., bed, vases, wine jars and ritual garments) which were brought by the women. If royalty, the body was taken to the Nile and boarded on a boat which floated to the burial temple. When they reached the necropolis, the mourners wept loudly and dancers, dressed like ancient spirits in short loinclothes, performed ritual dances at the head of the procession.

When all the furniture was in place in the tomb, the mummy was set standing at the entrance to the tomb. A libation of blessed water was poured over the mask as formulas from the *Book of the Dead* were recited. When the king's mummy was to be placed in the tomb, his wife raised her voice:

> I am thy wife, O great one—do not leave me!
> Is it thy good pleasure, O my brother, that I should go far from thee?
> How can it be that I go away alone?
> I say: "I accompany thee, O thou who didst like to converse with me,"
> But thou remainest silent and speakest not![19]

Outside torches would be lit and music and dance would be performed. The mourning period was now completed.

Clearly, what is most significant about the Egyptian attitude toward death is its emphasis on judgment. Unlike the Mesopotamian view that nothing survives death except one's reputation in the memory of society and the family of the deceased, the Egyptians believed that one not only lives on after death, but also undergoes a moral judgment. As Lord of the great judgment, Osiris (the god who died and was restored to life) became the symbol of immortality, so much so that it was by identification with Osiris that believers were able to share in the afterlife. In that land of eternity, where all the ancestors from the beginning of time rest, is the land of the Beautiful West where millions yet to be born will come. For no one can linger long in the land of Egypt.

NOTES

[1]N. K. Sandars, translator, *The Epic of Gilgamesh* (New York: Penguin, 1960), 61.

[2]*Ibid.*

[3]*Ibid.*, 65.

[4]Old Babylonian version translated by E. A. Speiser in *Ancient Near East: An Anthology of Text and Pictures,* ed. by James B. Pritchard (Princeton, New Jersey: Princeton University Press, 1958), 40–75.

[5]Sandars, 94–95.

[6]Mircea Eliade, *From Primitives to Zen* (New York: Harper & Row, 1967), 329.

[7]Sandars, 103–104.

[8]Eliade, 330.

[9]*Ibid.*, 333.

[10]*Ibid.*, 334.

[11]Sandars, 118–119.

[12]An Assyrian version of the *Epic of Gilgamesh* contains a twelfth tablet, undoubtedly added later, depicting Gilgamesh meeting the shade of Enkidu who tells him about the underworld including a grim description of decomposing bodies.

[13]Cornelius Loew, *Myth, Sacred History and Philosophy* (New York: Harcourt, Brace & World, 1967), 85.

[14]*Ibid.*, 86.

[15]E. A. Wallis Budge, translator, *The Book of the Dead* (Secaucus, New Jersey: University Books, Inc., 1960), 609.

[16]Quoted in J. H. Breasted's *Development of Religion and Thought in Ancient Egypt* (New York: Harper Torchbooks, 1912), 36.

[17]E. A. Wallis Budge, translator, *The Egyptian Book of the Dead* (New York: Dover Publications, 1967), 347–49.

[18]*Ibid.*, 258.

[19]Christiane Desrockes-Noblecourt, *Tutankhamen* (New York: George Rainbird Limited, 1963), 241.

JOURNAL EXERCISES

1. Gilgamesh's lament for his friend Enkidu is deeply poignant. Aside from the fact that he is weeping for Enkidu, in what ways is Gilgamesh also weeping for himself?

2. Imagine that you are Gilgamesh and that for some reason (which you can supply if it is crucial to your letter) you cannot return home. You have learned the "secret" of immortality—that it is reserved for the gods, and that humans are mortal. Select someone you would want to write a letter to, and tell him or her of your discoveries. Tell that person what it is about Uruk (home) which you now can appreciate the most.

3. Discuss the story of Isis and Osiris. In what ways is the resurrection of Osiris similar to, and different from, the resurrection of Jesus the Christ?

4. What is the connection between the Egyptian *Book of the Dead* and the *Tibetan Book of the Dead*? List as many ideas as occur to you and then examine one in depth.

5. Discuss the process of mummification. What do you think the real intention of the practice was? Are there any modern-day practices like it and, if so, do they have similar intentions?

6. Compare and contrast the Mesopotamian and Egyptian attitudes toward death and the afterlife. Can you think of present-day examples of each?

Chapter 8   GREEK ATTITUDES TOWARD DEATH

> Then it is a fact, O Simmias,
> that true philosophers make death
> and dying their profession. . . .
>
> Socrates, *Phaedo*

When we come to consider the Greek approaches to death and dying, it would be appropriate to examine two complementary aspects of its intellectual heritage—the mythic and the philosophic—since each plays an important role in Greek culture. In the first, or more feminine approach, we will review the myth of Psyche and Eros, and examine the presence of *thanatos* (the death urge) in her life. In the second, or more masculine approach, we will review the story of the death of Socrates and then consider his teaching of the immortality of the soul.

Psyche and Eros

The myth of Psyche and Eros depicts several aspects of death, some of which do not and one of which does lead to rebirth. The story begins when Psyche, the youngest, most beautiful, goddess-like third daughter of an ancient king and queen arouses Aphrodite's jealousy because of her beauty. Aphrodite has the oracle announce that Psyche is to be chained to a rock, and to be ravished by Death, the ugliest creature imaginable. Her wedding is to be her funeral. Eros, Aphrodite's son, is sent by his mother to accomplish this bidding, but he accidentally pricks his finger on one of his own arrows and falls in love with Psyche. Eros takes Psyche as his wife on the condition that she will never look at him or inquire into his ways.

While she really has no other choice, her new life is paradisiacal for her and soon she becomes pregnant. Eros tells Psyche that her child will be a god but warns her that if she breaks her vow, the child will be mortal and he will depart. Meanwhile Psyche's sisters visit her and question her about her husband. What does he look like? What does he do? Why won't he let her see him? What if when the baby is born he plans to devour the child?

To avert this, the sisters propose a plan. They tell her to prepare a lamp and a knife and, when Eros is asleep, to murder him. Influenced by their jealousy she takes a knife and a lamp to Eros' bed to kill him but she pricks

Psyche-Eros

herself on his arrow and falls in love with him. Awakened by a drop of hot oil from her lamp, Eros tells her that she has broken her covenant and he flies away.

Devastated that her husband, whom she now knows to be divine, has flown away, she immediately wants to drown herself in the face of the seeming death of her relationship. But Pan, the god of nature, dissuades her and tells her that she must pray to the god of love. Psyche's prayers are only partially effective, for Eros is the god of love and he is still beholden to his mother's wishes.

After rejecting the temptation to suicide, she begs Aphrodite to reunite her with Eros. In response, she is given four tasks to accomplish and is warned that if she fails, she will surely die. To win Eros back she must:

1. sort a mound of seeds;
2. return with a golden fleece;
3. fill a crystal goblet with water from the river Styx;
4. return from the underworld with a cask of Persephone's beauty ointment.

When with help she completes the last task and returns from the underworld, she is tempted to open the casket and to look for herself. But instead of beauty, a deadly sleep emerges and pours over her. She falls, as if dead. When Eros discovers this, he flies to her rescue, wipes the sleep from her lids, puts it in the casket, and takes Psyche with him back to Olympus. With Zeus' blessing, Psyche is made a goddess. Eros and Psyche are married, and they name their daughter Pleasure.

In and through this myth, at least four dimensions of *thanatos*, the death instinct, are expressed, each of which is intimately related to Eros. First, Psyche was to be married to Death, which at a deeper level signified that her wedding was to be her funeral. In fact, as it has been suggested, traditionally the bride's loss was more than just a name change, but included freedom, her individuality and her virginity.[1]

Second, Psyche was instinctively tempted to commit suicide when her grief at losing Eros became unbearable. In that moment, the loss of her lover became overwhelming, and she was ready to sacrifice herself until shown another way by Pan.

Third, knowing that if she failed to complete any of the tasks she would die, Psyche agreed to undertake the heroine's quest and to accept Aphrodite's four challenges. Her instinct for love was great enough to overcome her fear of death. At the same time, she was willing to die for her love, so strongly was she motivated to see Eros again.

Fourth, and most significantly, Psyche brought the sleep of death upon herself when she opened the cask of beauty ointment. Like Persephone, when Psyche became preoccupied with beauty, she instead clothed herself with symbolic death. But in this case, *thanatos* was fulfilled by *eros*, for Eros brought her back to life. Like Isis, who brought Osiris back to life after he had been dead, the power of Eros' divine love saved Psyche from the power of death. Like Osiris, she was raised back to life by love.

It could be said that three manifestations of *thanatos* in this myth parallel the three faces of death discussed in the first chapter. First, Psyche must experience the psychological death of being taken in "marriage" by a man she is not permitted to see. Not only does she surrender her innocence, she also becomes pregnant by Eros, thereby surrendering her psychological independence. Second, when Psyche discovers what she has done and whom she has lost in the process, she contemplates her own physical death. And third, when she opens the casket which she has brought from the underworld for Aphrodite, she does it so that she too will become more beautiful, so that Eros will love her more deeply. Instead, it contained a death-like sleep which became a death to her old self. For Eros' sake she almost died, and by the power of love she was brought back to life.

Socrates

Any discussion of Greek attitudes toward death inevitably leads to the philosopher Socrates. Born in Athens in 469 BCE, Socrates lived a hundred years after the Buddha. While he wrote nothing himself, his brilliant pupil Plato (427–347 BCE) recorded his words more or less systematically. It was Plato who provided us in the *Phaedo* with an account of Socrates' last hours, and his last conversations which we will discuss later in this chapter.

A stonemason and carver by trade, Socrates lived at a time of intellectual ferment. He exchanged ideas with the Athenians everywhere in the marketplace, in the open air parliament, under colonnades, for he believed that it was his mission to question the validity of everything he heard. By testing all so-called truths, Socrates developed a method of teaching through dialogue. At the same time, by relentlessly searching for the truth behind statements, he made himself unpopular with many of the established citizens of Athens.

In 399 BCE, when he was nearly seventy, Socrates was accused by Citizen Meletos and others of impiety, of rebelliousness toward the state, and of corrupting minors. The court had no judge or jury, but rather was based on a majority vote among 501 men. Socrates argued in his own behalf, but was pronounced guilty by a vote of 281 to 220. Since his chief accuser Meletos sought the death penalty, by law Socrates was required to propose his own penalty as an alternative. Somewhat whimsically, Socrates said that because he sought only to benefit the people of Athens he should receive free board and lodging in the town hall. In a more serious vein, since he was too old to be banished, and since he had wronged no one, he proposed that his friends Crito, Critobulos and Apollodoros pay a fine of thirty minas of silver. As one would suspect, the court would not be persuaded and, after going into session again, voted to condemn him to death.

Undisturbed, and without bearing any grudges against his persecutors, Socrates told them that the most difficult task was not to escape from death, but to escape from wickedness. A master teacher to the end, as he left the court he said: "And now it is time to go, I to die and you to live, but who gets the better part?"

Once in prison, Socrates' friends arranged for his escape, which he refused. Responding to his shocked followers' disbelief, Socrates reasoned:

1. If Athenians will not accept me, who will?
2. Is there any reason to live if I cannot discuss virtue?
3. Do they not want my body to live and my beliefs to die?
4. In choosing to die (bodily), am I not chosing to live (spiritually)?

To escape, Socrates reasoned, would be to renounce his beliefs. And in response to another disciple's question—"How do you know you are doing the right thing"—he answered, "By doubting the truth as others have found it, I have had to discover it myself." In this sense Socrates did not teach any doctrine, but rather a method. He taught his followers to search for truth (their own) and to distrust the truths of others, especially when seeking the meaning of life after death. By the principle of searching dialogically for the truth, Socrates felt confidently that dying was the right action to take.

To save the women the trouble of washing his body after he was dead, Socrates retired to bathe. When he returned, he rejected a fine garment that was offered to him, indicating that the garment he lived in would be good enough to die in. And then he added: "Bury me the normal way."

When the prison ward appeared with the hemlock, Socrates congratulated him: "See what a fine fellow he is. See how generously he is shedding his tears for me. Let us do as he says." "But," said Crito, "the sun has not gone down yet. There is still plenty of time."

> "It is natural that these people whom you speak of should act in that way, Crito," said Socrates, "because they think that they gain by it. And it is also natural that I should not; because I believe that I should gain nothing by drinking the poison a little later—I should only make myself ridiculous in my own eyes if I clung to life and hugged it when it has no more to offer. Come, do as I say and don't make difficulties."[2]

At this, he made a sign to a servant who was nearby to hand him the poison. Socrates then asked if there was enough to also offer a libation to the gods, but was told that there was just the right amount for him.

> "I see," said Socrates. "But I suppose I am allowed, or rather bound, to pray the gods that my removal from this world to the other may be prosperous. This is my prayer, then; and I hope that it may be

granted." With these words, quite calmly and with no sign of distaste, he drained the cup in one breath.[3]

Up until this time, Plato records, most of his disciples and friends had held back their tears, but when they saw Socrates actually drink the poison, they wept. "I wept broken-heartedly," Phaedo declares, "not for him but for my own suffering at losing such a friend." But Socrates responded:

> "Really, my friends, what a way to behave! Why, that was my main reason for sending away the women, to prevent this sort of disturbance, because I am told that one should make one's end in a tranquil frame of mind. Calm yourselves and try to be brave."[4]

After walking about, the feeling of heaviness came into his legs. He laid down on his back on the bed and was covered with a blanket. A coldness spread in his body. The sun had almost set. Socrates whispered: "Crito, we owe a cock to Asclepius; pay it without fail." With this he died.

The Immortal Soul

Socrates was a philosopher's philosopher. For him, life's most sacred concern was to uncover the purpose of philosophy. In other words, that a philosopher examine his or her own life in the process of being a philosopher was axiomatic for Socrates. Furthermore, he taught that since the purpose of philosophy was to discover the meaning of life in the face of death, and to understand the nature of the soul, a true philosopher was one who practiced the art of dying all the time. As Socrates says to Simmias:

> "Is not what we call death a freeing and separation of soul from body?"
> "Certainly," he said.
> "And the desire to free the soul is found chiefly, or rather only, in the true philosopher; in fact the philosopher's occupation consists precisely in the freeing and separation of soul from body. Isn't that so?"
> "Apparently."
> "Well then, as I said at the beginning, if a man has trained himself throughout his life to live in a state as close as possible to death, would it not be ridiculous for him to be distressed when death comes to him?"
> "It would, of course."

"Then it is a fact, Simmias, that true philosophers make dying their profession, and that to them of all men death is least alarming."[5]

The art of dying, Socrates contended, was nothing more than accepting death as the separation of the soul (which continued to exist) from the body (which ceased to exist). In outline form, one might say that Socrates believed that:

- The eternal soul is the only substantial reality that is incorruptible.
- The body is an outer garment for the soul and they are dualistically opposed to each other.
- The soul is eternal essence and is therefore not subject to death.
- The soul is confined within the body.
- Death liberates the soul back to its eternal home.
- The soul, after death, migrates through several lives.
- The soul, when purified and free of blemish, is free to associate with the gods.

The key to understanding this list is to understand what Socrates means by the soul (*psyche*). In a conversation with Cebes Socrates speaks in this vein:

"Now, Cebes," he said, "see whether this is our conclusion from all that we have said. The soul is most like that which is divine, immortal, intelligible, uniform, indissoluble, and ever self-consistent and invariable, whereas body is most like that which is human, mortal, multiform, unintelligible, dissoluble, and never self-consistent."[6]

As it was for Parmenides and Heraclitus before him, the soul for Socrates is the vital core of selfhood whose life is sustained by a constant dialogue with itself and with others. Due to its nature, the soul therefore is not subject to the inevitability of death as the body is.

Returning to this same line of reasoning, Socrates expresses his belief in the immortality of the soul when in a conversation with Cebes, he asks:

"Then tell me, what must be present in a body to make it alive?"
"Soul."
"Is this always so?"
"Of course."
"So whenever soul takes possession of a body, it always brings life with it?"

"Yes, it does."

"Is there an opposite to life, or not?"

"Yes, there is."

"What?"

"Death."

"Does it follow, then, from our earlier agreement, that soul will never admit the opposite of that which accompanies it?"

"Most definitely," said Cebes.

"Well, now, what name did we apply just now to that which does not admit the Form of even?"

"Uneven."

"And what do we call that which does not admit justice, or culture?"

"Uncultured; and the other unjust."

"Very good. And what do we call that which does not admit death?"

"Immortal."

"And soul does not admit death?"

"No."

"So soul is immortal."

"Yes, it is immortal."

"Well," said Socrates, "can we say that that has been proved? What do you think?"

"Most completely, Socrates."[7]

What happens to the soul when a person dies is vividly described. The body dissolves, but the soul, if free from worldly stains, can forever associate with the gods. If the soul is polluted and impure, contaminated with incompleted desires, it was likely to wander among tombs and graves until it could enter a body and continue to fulfill the desires of the past life. This later statement, of course, sounds interestingly close to the Upanishadic teaching of reincarnation. In the following quotation, Socrates encapsulates this to Cebes:

"Of course you know that when a person dies, although it is natural for the visible and physical part of him, which lies here in the visible world and which we call his corpse, to decay and fall to pieces and be dissipated, none of this happens to it immediately; it remains as it was for quite a long time, even if death takes place when the body is well nourished and in the warm season. Indeed, when the body is dried and embalmed, as in Egypt, it remains almost intact for an incredible time; and even if the rest of the body decays, some parts of it—the bones and sinews and anything else like them—are practically everlasting. That is so, is it not?"

"Yes."

"But the soul, the invisible part, which goes away to a place that is, like itself, glorious, pure, and invisible—the true Hades or unseen world—into the presence of the good and wise God (where, if God so wills, my soul must shortly go)—will it, if its very nature is such as I have described, be dispersed and destroyed at the moment of its release from the body, as is the popular view? Far from it, my dear Simmias and Cebes. The truth is much more like this: If at its release the soul is pure and carries with it no contamination of the body, because it has never willingly associated with it in life, but has shunned it and kept itself separate as its regular practice—in other words, if it has pursued philosophy in the right way and really practised how to face death easily: this is what 'practicing death' means, isn't it?"

"Most decidedly."[8]

As in other cultures, Socrates too presents his own conceptions of what actually happens to the soul after death. When a person dies a guardian spirit comes to lead the soul to a place where it must face a trial and then pass on to the house of Hades. This guidance is absolutely necessary since there are many "breaks and branches" along the way. As Socrates says:

"This is how the story goes. When any man dies, his own guardian spirit, which was given charge over him in his life, tries to bring him to a certain place where all must assemble, and from which, after submitting their several cases to judgment, they must set out for the next world, under the guidance of one who has the office of escorting souls from this world to the other. When they have there undergone the necessary experiences and remained as long as is required, another guide brings them back again after many vast periods of time."[9]

Beyond this, Socrates does not speak. For Socrates, the fear of death was based on the assumption that one knows exactly what will happen in death. But since no one knows beyond a doubt what in fact takes place at death, this fear is groundless. For Socrates therefore, there is nothing tragic about death, and one should die within an attitude of reverence, thankfulness and peace, with patience and acceptance.

Death Ritual

As in the Chinese practice, the family remains close to the dying person in Greek culture. When the last breath is taken, a family member closes the eyes, and the hands, feet and jaw of the deceased are bound. In popular practice, it was believed that at the moment of death, the soul is released by the heart in a breath of air through one's mouth. The corpse was cleaned, covered with expensive garments and left exposed for family and friends to pay their last respects. This was all done quickly so that the body could be buried quickly. It was believed that the soul could not fully depart from the body until the body was buried, and the soul could not reach the other world until the body had completely disappeared, leaving only the white of the bones.

Death rituals in Greek culture were aimed both at appeasing the gods and at assisting the soul's smooth transition from this world to the next. As in many other cultures, burial was preceded by a procession with family and friends carrying the coffin. This was done before daybreak. Torches were carried to light the path and, symbolically, to light the way for the deceased's soul.

When the procession reached the gravesite, the hands, feet and jaw were untied and the coffin, while still open, was lowered into the earth. A priest poured wine on the body after which family and friends threw handfuls of earth on the coffin. A shroud was then pulled over the deceased's face and the coffin was covered and the grave filled with earth. Before leaving, family and relatives washed their hands to purify themselves.

Three days after death, in the evening, women relatives gathered for the first time at the grave to lament. No one was allowed to visit the grave before that. However thereafter, during every anniversary of the deceased's birth, the family visited the tomb and performed a ceremonial reminder for the loved one. At least five years after the burial, when all the flesh had disappeared, the family of the deceased exhumed the remains of the body from the grave. The sight of the bones served as a reminder that the beloved's soul had entered paradise.

NOTES

[1]Robert Johnson, *She: Understanding Feminine Psychology* (New York: Harper & Row, 1977), 12.

[2]Hugh Tredennick, translator, *Plato: The Last Days of Socrates* (New York: Penguin, 1954), 181.

[3]*Ibid.*, 182.

[4]*Ibid.*

[5]*Ibid.*, 112–13.

[6]*Ibid.*, 132.

[7]*Ibid.*, 167.

[8]*Ibid.*, 132–33.

[9]*Ibid.*, 170.

JOURNAL EXERCISES

1. Retell the story of Psyche and Eros in your own words, perhaps in a modern idiom or context. In what ways does your version differ from the original story?
2. Imagine that you could engage Socrates in a conversation. What would you question him about with regard to his views on dying?
3. What did Socrates say to those who wept at his impending death? From Socrates' viewpoint, what should be the relationship between one's state of mind and the dying process?
4. How does Socrates prove that the soul is immortal? Do you agree with his logic? If not, why? If so, elaborate.
5. From Socrates' standpoint, what is the best way to prepare one's mind for death? In other words, how does the philosopher die?
6. How might an intelligent, practicing Socratic philosopher answer the following question: What does your tradition teach about how to die artfully? That is, what is the most sacred way of dying?

Chapter 9 HEBRAIC ATTITUDES TOWARD DEATH

You should repent one day
before you die. . . .
Thus . . . repent every day.

Rabbi Eliezer

We come now to the three great Semitic religions—Judaism, Christianity and Islam—which form the monotheistic bedrock of western culture. Though young compared to Egyptian society (i.e., by 3000 BCE Egypt had already built the pyramids), the Hebrew people for the first time in history developed a thoroughgoing monotheism coupled with ethical righteousness. As a result of this unique blend of theology and *praxis*, and in the general trajectory of Egyptian and Greek views, the Jewish attitude toward death, as toward life, is that each is from God and each is good. As the following chart illustrates, the Hebrew response to death, at least in the biblical period, was much less certain about an afterlife than were the Egyptians and the Greeks.

WESTERN VIEWS OF DEATH

After Death	Egyptian	Greek	Hebrew
1. Soul/Body	1. Separate	1. Separate	1. Separate
2. Soul	2. Migrates	2. Migrates	2. Migrates
3. Body	3. Mummified	3. Ritually Buried	3. Ritually Buried
4. Reuniting of Body and Soul	4. Yes	4. No	4. Maybe
5. Final Judgment	5. Yes	5. Yes	5. Maybe

In Jewish tradition there is no death since both body and soul continue on, that is, return to their source. In the Midrash it is written that just as creation in God's sight was good, so God looked at death (*Maweth*) and said "Behold death is good." Death thus is neither a decree nor a punishment but is a part of creation.

As we shall see, the Jewish tradition is not of one accord theologically. In fact, Judaism contains a range of beliefs, from no view of an afterlife to a belief in the resurrection of the body and the immortality of the soul. Yet deeper than these seeming differences is a continued search for meaning despite life's absurdities. Indeed what could be more absurd than the Nazi concentration camps during the Second World War and the mass extermination of six million Jews? The question this nightmare raised was, and is: How could a just and loving God allow such an inhumane atrocity to occur? On a different scale, this was also Job's question to God: Why am I, a righteous man, caused to suffer? And the answer given by God—"Where were you when I created the world?"—does not fully satisfy the question which is asked anew by each generation. But for the Jew, what is important is not so much the answer, but the search for meaning in life, one which offers no easy or completely satisfying answers.

Dr. Viktor Frankl, a Viennese author and psychiatrist, could be called a modern Job, for in the midst of suffering through three grotesque years at Auschwitz, he discovered meaning which sustained him.[1] During his imprisonment, he later discovered, his father, his mother, his brother and his wife had died in the camps. Like other prisoners, Frankl was deprived of his possessions, malnourished, reduced to a number, and incessantly dehumanized by the camp guards. Everywhere, death surrounded him, and he had no certainty of ever leaving the camp alive. Yet, in the midst of this profound suffering, he came to experience an equally profound freedom.

In *Man's Search for Meaning*, Frankl tells his story in three phases: the period following admission, the camp routine, and the period following release.

As soon as he was admitted to the camp, he was stripped of all his possessions, clothing, identification, his entire body was shaved, and he was given ragged clothes and shoes that did not fit. Frankl soon discovered the truth of Dostoevski's statement that it is possible for a person to get used to anything. Yet there would be inmates who could not adjust, and who took their own lives by running into electrically charged barbed wire fences.

If the first phase of camp life was characterized by shock at the reality of mass death and human deprivation, the second phase was characterized by apathy or emotional death. Prisoners sought to deaden the tortures of their longings for home and their disgust with the immediate surroundings. As Frankl writes: "The sufferers, the dying and the dead, became such commonplace sights . . . that they could not move (us) any more."[2] As with the others, he experienced what we have called a psychological death which, in this situation, was a necessary condition for personal survival.

Despite the horror of his surroundings, Frankl experienced brief moments of transcendence. He recounts that he grasped the "greatest secret of human life, that one's salvation is through love and in love."[3] By contemplating his wife, and through his mental conversations with her, he discovered that "love is as strong as death."[4] This intensification of his inner life provided him with a refuge from the cruelty and suffering which was an everyday reality in the camps.

Within his story, Frankl tells two suggestive vignettes which illustrate contrasting ways of facing death. In the first story, a wealthy Persian was walking in his garden with one of his servants who told him that he had just encountered Death. He begged his Master for his fastest horse so that he could flee to Teheran. When the master consented, the servant galloped off. On returning to his house, the master himself met Death, and asked him: "Why did you terrify my servant in that way?" And Death replied: "I did not threaten him; I only showed surprise in still finding him here when I planned to meet him tonight in Teheran."[5] The moral of course is that there is *no* escape from Death.

In the second story, Frankl tells of a young woman who knew that she would die within a few days. When he talked to her, she was cheerful and said: "I am grateful that fate has hit me so hard. In my former life, I was spoiled and did not take spiritual accomplishments seriously." Pointing through the window of her prison hut, she said, "This tree here is the only friend I have in my loneliness." Through that window one could see just one branch of a chestnut tree, on which were two blossoms. "I often talk to this tree," she told him. This surprised Frankl. When he asked her if the tree replied she answered, "It said to me, 'I am here—I am here—I am life, eternal life.' "[6]

As a result of his camp experiences, Frankl concludes that if there is any meaning in life, there must be, as well, a meaning in suffering. He discovered "that everything can be taken from a man but one thing: the last of the human freedoms—to choose one's attitude in any given set of circumstances, to choose one's own way."[7] He discovered that the way a person accepts and responds to suffering reveals meaning in life. Therefore Nietzsche's words—"He who has a *why* to live for can bear with almost any *how*"—become Frankl's experience. Frankl discovered that suffering deepens a person's life, provides an opportunity for self-transcendence, and is necessary for growth and maturity, and that through suffering each person is uniquely, fully free.

A few days after he was liberated, he tells of walking through a country meadow for miles and miles with no distractions, no people, no buildings, nothing but wide open space. After such a long confinement, one can imagine the overwhelming, almost disbelieving, sense of joy he felt in being free to walk anywhere he wished. Hearing a lark sing jubilation, he experienced a profoundly intimate moment:

> I stopped, looked around, and up to the sky—and then I went down on my knees. At that moment there was very little I knew of myself or of the world—I had but one sentence in mind—always the same: "I called to the Lord from my narrow prison and He answered me in the freedom of space." How long I knelt there and repeated this sentence memory can no longer recall. But I know that on that day, in that hour, my new life started. Step by step I progressed, until I again became a human being.[8]

Biblical Perspectives

In the Hebrew Bible, the word death is used in at least three ways: as biological cessation, as a power which opposes God's creation, and as a metaphor for anything which leads a person away from God. The emphasis, however, was upon the first.

Biologically speaking, death occurs when the vital force (*ruah*), or breath, withdraws through the throat. Earlier Jewish attitudes toward death did not hint at a return to God and what remained was a "shadow" or "shade," an impermanent residue in *sheol* (probably meaning "underworld" or "nonland" or "unland"). In a later understanding, the human soul (*ruah*) was believed to have memory and personality. In this belief, humans are born with a pure soul and a sacred body which are inter-dependent. The soul precedes and outlives the body since the soul was with God before the body was created. Humans are created as animated bodies, that is, body-forms animated by the life-force (*ruah*). There are two loci of this vital force; the breath and the blood. The Hebrew idea of personality as an "animated body" is to be contrasted with the Greek notion of a "incarnated soul" (a soul which occupies a body).

Death was therefore not an enemy. The writer of 2 Samuel 14:14 says: "We must all die; we are like water spilt on the ground, which cannot be gathered up again." Nor is death viewed as an irrational intrusion upon life. The writer of Ecclesiastes 3:1 says: "To everything there is a season and a time to every purpose under heaven." Life and death are not separate, but are bound together by God's will. "The Lord gives, and the Lord has taken away; blessed be the name of the Lord" (Job 1:21).

In one of the most remarkable passages on death and dying formed in Hebrew Scriptures, the psalmist cries out to Yahweh, for his soul is troubled:

My life is on the brink of Sheol;
I am numbered among those who go down to the Pit,
A man bereft of strength:
A man alone, down among the dead,
Among the slaughtered in their graves,
Among those you have forgotten,
Those deprived of your protecting hand.[9]

He feels God's wrath weighing heavily, upon his heart, and his friends have forgotten him. Then from the depths of his lament he cries out:

Yahweh, I invoke you all day,
I stretch out my hands to you:
Are your marvels meant for the dead,
Can ghosts rise up to praise you?
Who talks of your love in the grave,
Of your faithfulness in the place of perdition?
Do they hear about your marvels in the dark,
About your righteousness in the land of Oblivion?[10]

"May there not be room in *Sheol* for God's wonders?" the psalmist wonders aloud. May it not be that God hears prayers uttered from the Pit?
    In a brutally honest self-evaluation, the psalmist concludes:

Wretched, slowly dying since my youth,
I bore your terrors—now I am exhausted;
your anger overwhelmed me,
you destroyed me with your terrors
which, like a flood, were around me, all day long,
all together closing in on me.
You have turned my friends and neighbors against me,
now darkness is my one companion left.[11]

The two possible interpretations of this psalm again point to the two ends of the Jewish attitude toward death and dying. The one interpretation indicates that like Job, the psalmist prays to the end, protestingly. Why, he asks, has he been rejected by God and by his friends? This interpretation offers little hope beyond the immediate darkness. The other interpretation indicates that Yahweh will hear his prayer, and that the psalmist will discover it answered when he awakens from death. His hope is in the eternal light which in scriptures always overcomes the darkness. Consistent with this interpretation is a later psalm in which the psalmist crys out:

Alleluia!
I love! For Yahweh listens to my entreaty;
he bends down to listen to me when I call.
Death's cords were tightening around me, the nooses of Sheol;
distress and anguish gripped me.
I invoked the name of Yahweh:
"Yahweh, rescue me!"[12]

And because Yahweh is merciful and tenderhearted, he saves the singer from the Pit.

Creation and Death

To understand how death entered the world, we must consider the Hebrew story of creation. No matter how it is translated, Genesis 1:1 ("In the beginning God created . . . ") has often been interpreted as a description of creation *ex nihilo,* that is, creation out of nothing. The word for create, *bara,* which is used exclusively of God's actions, does not in itself express the idea of making something out of nothing. But if the "beginning" means the absolute beginning of created things, then before God made the world, nothing existed out of which the world could have been created. This understanding is stated explicitly in a later apocryphal book (2 Maccabees) when a mother says to her child:

I implore you, my child,
observe heaven and earth,
consider all that is in them,
and acknowledge that God made them
out of what did not exist,
and that mankind comes into being
in the same way.[13]

After the spirit (*ruah*)—or wind or breath of God—initiated creation, God said: "Let us make man in our image" (*imago Dei*) which in Hebrew means the reflection of God's wisdom or grace. It is to be noted that humans, composed of body and soul, are made in the likeness of God, and that in some mysterious way God, too, is body and soul, male and female together.

In the second chapter of Genesis, first a man was formed of clay from the earth, and when God breathed into his nostrils, he became a living person. We remember here how significant the breath was to Hindu, Buddhist and Chinese practitioners of meditation. God caused a deep sleep to fall on man (*ish*), and while he slept, God took one of his ribs which he made into a woman (*isha*). Just as in Chinese culture Yin comes from Yang and Yang from Yin, so too does woman come from man, and vice versa.

The woman, Eve, and the man, Adam, were placed in the garden of Eden along with the tree of immortal life and the tree of the knowledge of good and evil, and they were told that of all the trees in the garden they could eat of any one except from the tree of the knowledge of good and evil. To eat of that tree would be to die. "Not true," says the serpent (the power of evil) to Eve. "You will not die; in fact your eyes will be opened for the first time."[14] The entrance of the serpent into the story may remind the reader of the serpent, in the *Epic of Gilgamesh,* who stole the Plant of Rejuvenation.

Believing the serpent's half-truths, Adam and Eve choose to eat the fruit of the forbidden tree and their eyes are opened to the knowledge of good and evil. When God comes into the garden, they hide, ashamed. And God says to Adam and Eve:

> With sweat on your brow
> shall you eat your bread,
> until you return to the soil,
> as you were taken from it.
> For dust you are
> and to dust you shall return.[15]

Then God banned Adam and Eve from ever returning to the garden of Eden, and God posted angels with revolving swords of fire to guard the way to the tree of immortal life, lest they eat from it while yet in a sinful state.

Traditionally, this passage has been interpreted to indicate that due to human sin, or what could be called existential mistrust, death entered the world. At the same time, some scholars suggest that death (the body's return to the ground) was not caused by disobedience, but was rather one's natural end, and that it was *anxiety* (in the face of death), not death itself, that God used and continues to use to punish his created children.

Either way, the question is asked: Why did God create humans in such a way if God knew that they would sin? Of course the question assumes wrongly that God "knew" they would sin, as if God operated according to the conditions of time and history. But according to the story human beings were created with free choice, with freedom not to sin. But then another question can be asked: Why didn't God explain more fully the consequences of eating the fruit? And the later rabbis and sages answer because such a narrative would have restricted free choice since the man and the woman would have obeyed God more from fear than from respect. In the story as it is, Adam and Eve are asked to obey on the basis of what could be called existential trust in the Creator. It is this human inability to trust God that leads to sin, and subsequently to death. The mystery in the story is how God's will and human will operate freely and fully.

As the story of salvation history unfolds, God finds it necessary to punish men and women for their corruption, and when they refuse to repent, a flood is unleashed. Like Utnapishtim in the *Epic of Gilgamesh,* Noah built an ark so that he, his family and all living creatures could be saved from the corruption which surrounded them. This flood (perhaps the rising of the Tigris and Euphrates rivers which would have flooded the area) lasted forty days. As a result of the flood, God entered into a covenant with Noah to establish the election of the people of Israel, a covenant strengthened and extended through the father of the Jewish people Abraham, who migrated from Mesopotamia and its polytheistic practices, and took up a nomadic life in Canaan.

Aside from Moses, there is no more significant figure in Hebrew scriptures than the patriarch Abraham. And among the events in his life, what became the most significant to Jews was the attempted sacrifice of his "only" son Isaac. Because of its narrative and religious power it is quoted in full here.

> Some time afterward, God put Abraham to the test. He said to him, "Abraham," and he answered, "Here I am." And He said, "Take your son, your favored one, Isaac, whom you love, and go to the land of Moriah, and offer him there as a burnt offering on one of the heights which I will point out to you." So early next morning, Abraham saddled his ass and took with him two of his servants and his son Isaac. He split the wood for the burnt offering, and he set out for the place of which God had told him. On the third day Abraham looked up and saw the place from afar. Then Abraham said to his servants, "You stay here with the ass. The boy and I will go up there; we will worship and we will return to you."
>
> Abraham took the wood for the burnt offering and put it on his son Isaac. He himself took the firestone and the knife; and the two walked off together. Then Isaac said to his father Abraham, "Father!" And he answered, "Yes, my son." And he said, "Here is the firestone and the wood; but where is the sheep for the burnt offering?" And Abraham said, "God will see to the sheep for His burnt offering, my son." And the two of them walked on together.
>
> They arrived at the place of which God had told him. Abraham built an altar there; he laid out the wood; he bound his son Isaac;

he laid him on the altar, on top of the wood. And Abraham picked up the knife to slay his son. Then an angel of the Lord called to him from heaven: "Abraham! Abraham!" And he answered, "Here I am." And he said, "Do not raise your hand against the boy, or do anything to him. For now I know that you fear God, since you have not withheld your son, your favored one, from Me." When Abraham looked up, his eye fell upon a ram, caught in the thicket by its horns. So Abraham went and took the ram and offered it up as a burnt offering in place of his son. And Abraham named that site Adonai-yireh, whence the present saying, "On the mount of the Lord there is vision."[16]

To understand the impact on Abraham of God's request, that he would be required to offer his son Isaac as a burnt offering, the reader must be aware that human sacrifice was practiced in Abraham's time, and that Isaac was Abraham's only son. Ishmael, his other son by Hagar, the maid servant, was banished into the desert at Sarah's request. To sacrifice Isaac, therefore, would have meant that Abraham would never father a great nation. But Abraham's faith was stronger than his fear of death. Just as the sacrifice was about to take place, on what today is called the Temple Mount in Jerusalem, God intervened. Not only Abraham's but also Isaac's faith had been proven. A ram was substituted for Isaac, who was "reborn" to become the father of Jacob, and thereby with Abraham, a father of the Jewish people. Both Abraham and Isaac, in their willingness to follow God, experienced a spiritual death which became a spiritual rebirth.

In Jewish history, this story was given a deeper interpretation by the Talmudic sages who pointed out that the would-be sacrifice of Isaac takes on the dimension of atonement for the sins of Israel. It is suggested that Isaac knew he was about to be sacrificed, and yet he was willing to die for the sins of others. It is suggested further that not only Isaac makes a self-sacrifice, being willing to die for others, but that Abraham and Sarah as well sacrificed themselves in and through their son's sacrifice. It is further suggested in the homiletical literature that when Abraham took the knife to Isaac, Isaac's soul departed from his body and he was dead. But when the angel of God spared him, his soul returned to his body, and he was as-if "resurrected" back to life. As was noted earlier, Isaac's sacrifice is a biblical image of spiritual death and rebirth, for it is in his willingness to die to himself that he is reborn not only to himself, but also to God.

Shortly thereafter, Abraham's wife, Sarah, who miraculously conceived Isaac at ninety, died at Hebron in Canaan at the age of one hundred and twenty-seven. According to tradition she died when she saw Abraham returning from Mount Moriah without Isaac whom she feared to be dead. After

Abraham-Isaac

mourning for her according to custom, Abraham purchased a piece of land from the Hittites so that he could bury his wife in a hidden cave. There is no mention here, or at the burial of Moses, or of Joshua, or of David, of any possibility of a life after death. But, by the time of the prophets, the notion that the dead would be raised from the grave was beginning to surface.

Messianic Hopes

After the destruction of the first temple and the exile of the Jewish people, the post-exilic prophet Ezekiel was taken by the spirit of God to a valley full of the bones of the dead. And God said to Ezekiel:

> "Prophesy over these bones. Say, 'Dry bones, hear the word of Yahweh. The Lord Yahweh says this to these bones: I am now going to make the breath enter you, and you will live. I shall put sinews on you, I shall make flesh grow on you, I shall cover you with skin and give you breath, and you will live; and you will learn that I am Yahweh.' "[17]

God told Ezekiel that the bones were the house of Israel, and that he would raise them up and put God's spirit in them so that they might return to their native land. But when was this to take place?

The answer to this question is found in the prophet Isaiah who refers to the messianic age which, when it comes, will destroy death.

> On this mountain,
> Yahweh Sabaoth will prepare for all peoples
> a banquet of rich food, a banquet of fine wines.
> On this mountain he will remove
> the mourning veil covering all peoples,
> and the shroud enwrapping all nations,
> he will destroy Death for ever.
> The Lord Yahweh will wipe away
> the tears from every cheek;
> he will take away his people's shame
> everywhere on earth
> for Yahweh has said so.[18]

The writer of Isaiah makes a clear distinction between the wicked, who will not rise after death (they shall be annihilated from memory), and the corpses of the righteous of whom he says, "Rise, awake, exult, all you who lie in the dust, for your dew is a radiant dew and the land of ghosts will give birth" (Is 26:19).

According to later rabbinic literature, the messianic age (*Yemot Ha-mashiah*) will take place on earth after a period of calamity, and in its place peace (*shalom*) will spread throughout the world. Jerusalem will be rebuilt, and the dead will be resurrected and rejoined with their souls. From Isaiah on, the biblical tradition speaks of a Messiah who, like King David, will come to establish a perfect society. Lion and lamb will now dwell together, and a branch from Jesse's trunk will now rule righteously.

Who is this Messiah who will redeem humankind, who will instigate the kingdom of God on earth? Except for Orthodox Jews who believe in a personal Messiah, many Jews perceive the Messiah not as an individual savior, but as a collective redemption. Messiah is interpreted to mean a messianic age, the age of true peace between humans and their world, an age when humanity has reached a level of enlightenment and justice. That will be the day of the Messiah, and in that day there will be no more death as we now understand it. The Messiah, one could say, will bring eternal life for all living creatures great and small.

Hebraic conceptions of afterlife also developed in this bifocal way—both individually and collectively. As we have already noted, the shade—the weakest aspect of the person—survives in *sheol*. In later Judaism, *sheol* became the place of disembodied souls and was divided into paradise for the good and *gehenna* for the wicked.

Early Hebraic thought also developed the notion of a corporate person and of a communal immortality. In contrast to individual survival in *sheol,* it is the on-going community that is immortal, Much like Gilgamesh's discovery, identity after death continues among people. It was for this reason that Abraham, when his death grew near, expressed concern that Isaac's wife must not be a Canaanite but an Israelite so that the lineage of Abraham's descendants would be guaranteed.

Apocalyptic Visions

Despite these views, we can observe a shift from an earlier scriptural silence or negativity toward life after death to the later biblical descriptions of the resurrection of the body, especially when we reach the inter-testamental period. In the Book of Daniel, written about 165/164 BCE, we find the oldest and only clear reference in Hebrew scriptures to the resurrection of the dead:

At that time Michael will stand up, the great prince who mounts guard over your people. There is going to be a time of great distress, unparalleled since nations first came into existence. When that time comes, your own people will be spared, all those whose names are found written in the Book. Of those who lie sleeping in the dust of the earth many will awake, some to everlasting life, some to shame and everlasting disgrace.[19]

This reflects biblical anthropology in which body and soul (life-force) have no existence apart from each other. Unlike the Hindu and the Greek view, which maintain that the soul exists independently of the body, for the Jew *psyche* and *soma* (body) are unified. Here the connection between the Messiah and awakening to everlasting life is made through the image of the book which is opened in God's presence in the heavenly court. Daniel says:

I gazed into the visions of the night.
And I saw, coming on the clouds of heaven,
one like a *son of man*.
He came to the one of great age
and was led into his presence.
On him was conferred sovereignty,
glory and kingship,
and men of all peoples, nations and languages
became his servants.
His sovereignty is an eternal sovereignty
which shall never pass away,
nor will his empire ever be destroyed.[20]

This then is the apocalyptic answer to questions of justice and reward raised by the Jewish martyrs in the face of their deaths under the Seleucids' rule. This time of suffering will be followed by an apocalyptic time when Israel will be saved; her dead will rise, not as disembodied souls, but as animated body-souls, and will be with God eternally.[21] Though nothing is stated here about the nature of the resurrection, in the Talmud and later homiletical writings, the dead are said to rise apparelled in their own clothes (bodies), the completely miraculous act of God. During the Talmudic period the Jewish tradition became more specific about resurrection, heaven, hell and judgment.

Death Ritual

One day the disciples of Rabbi Eliezer came to him as he was about to die and asked him for a last teaching. Rabbi Eliezer replied: "You should repent one day before you die!" His disciples were confused. "How can we know just when that day comes?" They asked. "Thus you should repent every day," was his answer.[22] In Jewish cultures, a person who is about to die must be attended to constantly. At death, the dying person makes a confession for which no rabbi need be present. Prayers are then offered including the *Shema*—"Hear, O Israel, the Lord is our God, the Lord is one" (Dt 6:4)—which in Hebrew sounds like "*Shema* yis-ro-ayl, A-do-noy el-lo-hay-nu, A-do-noy e-hod." The *Shema* may very well be one's last words.

Throughout the entire period between death and the funeral, the body is never left unattended. A son, or the nearest relative, closes the eyes and mouth and extends the arms and hands to the side of the body. Prior to burial, the body is lovingly washed and dressed in a white linen or a shroud, a custom that goes back into Jewish tradition when people were buried in shrouds as a sign of humility, and to protest the lavish Roman garb. Since embalming and cremation are not practiced among orthodox Jews, the deceased is buried as quickly as possible after death in a pine box.

At the end of the service and at the graveside, the relatives recite a mourner's prayer (*kaddish*) which is a prayer to life praising God: "The Lord gives and the Lord takes away; blessed be the name of the Lord." And then the rabbi says: "To the departed whom we now remember, may peace and bliss be granted in life eternal. May they find grace and mercy before the Lord of heaven and earth. May their souls rejoice in that ineffable good which God has laid up for those who fear Him, and may their memory be a blessing unto those who treasure it." Famous for its rhythmic cadence, the *kaddish* prayer is an essential part of the mourning experience. It is important and expected that the next-of-kin will recite the *kaddish* prayer regularly during the year of mourning. After the casket is lowered into the ground, the mourners then throw handfuls of dirt on it to mark the final farewell.

For the next seven days, the family observes an intense period of mourning (*shiv'ah*) in a place, usually the home, designated as a "House of Mourning." Except for the sabbath, which is always a day of joy, the mourners sit low to the floor, thinking, praying and reading from the Mishnah and Zohar. During this period all other normal activities are ceased. There is no entertainment, no shaving, no sex, no working, no looking in mirrors, and no wearing of shoes. Each day a member of the family says the mourner's prayer, a practice which continues for a full year.

Beyond these rituals however it should be noted that the principal qualification for entrance into heaven (*gan eden*) is to have lived one's life in accordance with God's law. Conversely, by willfully disobeying God's commandments, one is doomed to hell (*gehinnom*). When a person dies, one's good and righteous acts are weighed against one's evil acts. Whereas in *The Egyptian Book of the Dead* the entire soul is weighed against a feather, in the Jewish belief one's soul is weighed against itself. If righteousness outweighs evil, one is assured a heavenly eternity. For that reason, the Jew today concentrates more energy on right living, on doing righteous acts (*mitzvah*), than upon developing an elaborate afterlife theology.

But how, we might ask, is the experience of dying brought into life in such a way so to prepare the believer for death?

Ritually speaking, the answer is obvious, for the most important Jewish holiday is Yom Kippur, the Day of Atonement. This is the one day in the year that one fasts, visits the synagogue to personally reflect upon past sins or shortcomings, and is diligent in prayer. Certain prayers and readings remind the congregation that sin also has a corporal nature. It follows, in fact, that as a symbolic or spiritual death occurs, that is, as the ego-bound individual dies, the community emerges and the people of Israel are renewed.

For the religious Jew then, perhaps it can be said that there need be no fear of death. Death is a sacred and natural part of God's creation. It was, and is, the result of sinful nature; yet, the dead will be raised again with the coming of the Messiah. There is no need to weep too much for a dying person. When Rabbi Bunam's wife wept bitterly over her husband who was about to die, with words that were nearing his last, he said: "Why are you weeping? All my life has been given simply so that I might learn how to die!" And, at the hour of his death, the Baal Shem Tov said: "Now I know the purpose for which I was created!"

NOTES

[1]Genesis Rabbah 9:5. Death for Jewish culture is not a result of sin but is intertwined in the theory of reward and punishment. The death of a righteous person for instance can be looked at as a reward since it marks an end to life's struggle. In one of the Talmudic passages the sages say that each person has three partners, the father, the mother and God. When death comes, the earth takes back its part (the body) and God takes back God's part (the soul). For further reference see Nidda 31a; Eccl. Rab. 5:10; Gen. Rab. 4:10; and Lev. Rab. 4:5.

[2]Viktor Frankl, *Man's Search for Meaning* (New York: Pocket Books, 1959), 33. Viktor Frankl, Professor of Neurology and Psychiatry at the University of Vienna Medical School and Distinguished Professor of Logotherapy at the U.S. International University, is the founder of what has come to be called the Third Viennese School of Psychotherapy—the school of logoth-

erapy. During World War II, he was interred for three years at Auschwitz, Dachau and other concentration camps.

[3] *Ibid.*, 59.

[4] *Ibid.*, 61.

[5] *Ibid.*, 89.

[6] *Ibid.*, 109–110.

[7] *Ibid.*, 104.

[8] *Ibid.*, 142.

[9] Ps 88:4–6. The following scriptural quotations unless otherwise indicated are taken from *The Jerusalem Bible* (New York: Doubleday, 1966). The pit (*sheol*) was not a reward or a punishment, but rather a place cut off from God in which one led a zombie-like existence.

[10] Ps 88:10–13.

[11] Ps 88:14–17.

[12] Ps 116:1–4.

[13] 2 Macabees 7:28.

[14] Gen 3:4–5.

[15] Gen 3:19.

[16] Gen 22:1–14. The Torah (The Jewish Publication Society of America, 1962).

[17] Ez 37:4–7.

[18] Is 25:6–8. By the tenth century a notion of two Messiahs had developed within Jewish thought, the Messiah ben Joseph who was/is to be political leader and who would gather the exiles back to Jerusalem before being killed in battle, and the Messiah ben David who will be a spiritual leader and who will bring peace and restore the law (cf. Gen 49:1–27 and Ez 37:15–28).

[19] Dan 12:1–2.

[20] Dan 7:13–14.

[21] The word apocalypse (Greek, to uncover) when applied to Jewish and Christian writings (from 200 BCE to 150 CE) refers to visions of an imminent cosmic cataclysm in which God triumphs over evil, and at which time the messianic kingdom will arise.

[22] Rabbi Eliezer, *Tractate Shabbat*, 153a.

JOURNAL EXERCISES

1. Which of the two stories that Viktor Frankl tells about death makes more of an impact on you, and why? Do you know of any other versions of either story? Perhaps you would like to create your own version in a contemporary metaphor.
2. What did Frankl discover in the death camp which allowed him to survive the experience? Is there any area of contemporary life to which his insight might well apply?
3. Did Adam and Eve really have the free choice not to eat of the Tree of the Knowledge of Good and Evil when, prior to eating from it, they had no way of knowing the difference (between good and evil), or of the consequences of that difference?
4. What images does Ezekiel use to describe the resurrection of the dead? In what ways does it relate to the creation account?
5. Reflect on the story of Abraham and Isaac once again. In what way(s) is self-sacrifice the major motif, and is such self-sacrifice possible today?
6. How might an intelligent, practicing Jew answer the following question: What does your tradition teach about how to die artfully? That is, what is the most sacred way of dying?

Chapter 10 CHRISTIAN ATTITUDES TOWARD DEATH

> Anyone who wants to save his life
> will lose it; but anyone
> who loses his life for my sake
> will save it.
>
> *Jesus*

Christianity, in its many forms, has developed elaborately rich traditions about life everlasting. Few beliefs in fact have a more personal and universal importance for the practicing Christian than a belief in eternal life. In the Catholic and Orthodox traditions, for example, eternal life or heavenly joyfulness is described as flowing from two sources: one, the perfect knowledge and love of God; the other, the loving knowledge of all persons in God's family. The apostle John describes heavenly life as consisting of an immediate or beatific vision of God in which "we shall be like him because we shall see him as he really is" (1 Jn 3:2). Heaven then for the Christian is the possibility of one's eternal participation in the eternal purpose of God. But first, we must return from the raptures of heaven's gardens back into history, to Jerusalem, to the time of Jesus, for it is upon his life and passion that all Christian views of death are based.

As a prophet, teacher and healer, Jesus appeared in the context of Judaism as one who taught both the coming of God's kingdom and an ethics of mercy and justice, that is, of loving neighbor and enemy alike (though not necessarily in the same way). In the process, as the Gospels report, he healed the sick, gave sight to the blind, exorcised the possessed, forgave sinners, reinterpreted the Torah, and spoke "with authority," prophetically challenging everyone to repent and believe in the imminent presence of his Father's kingdom. Understandably, he was perceived as a threat by the conservative members of the Sanhedrin (i.e., aristocratic administrators of ritual practices) and by the legalistic Pharisees (e.g., those whose practices subordinated the spirit of God to the correct performances of ritual, and who felt "justified" through scrupulous obedience to the letter of the elaborated law). Jesus' seeming transgressions against the Torah convinced some that he had to be eliminated for the sake of the nation's well-being.

The Trial

There are four distinct, historical pictures of Jesus in the New Testament: Mark's, Matthew's, Luke's and John's. Each has a slightly different style, point of view and audience. For our purposes we will read the Gospel accounts side by side to arrive at the story of Jesus' arrest, trial and execution.

Jesus was arrested in Jerusalem near the time of Passover, which placed the Jewish council and its officiating high priests and scribes under extreme pressure. After witnesses testified against him, Caiaphas, the high priest, asked Jesus the one question that would force a verdict: "Are you the Christ, the Son of the Most High?" In response, Jesus answered directly and definitively—"I am!" Immediately Caiaphas did what the law prescribed for blasphemy—he tore his robes and pronounced the death sentence (cf. Dt 13:2–12). At that moment, the Sanhedrin declared that Jesus should die and the Roman soldiers took him to Pilate's judgment hall.

"We have found this man subverting our nation," the crowd cried, "opposing the payment of taxes to Caesar, and calling himself Messiah, a king." Thus began Jesus' second trial, this time under the Roman procurator Pilate who was sojourning in Jerusalem due to the Passover feast. Pilate, looking at Jesus, asked: "Are you the King of the Jews?" Jesus answered: "Are you saying this on your own or have others been telling you?" Finding no case against him, Pilate announced that he would release Jesus once he had taught him a lesson. Thereupon, he had Jesus scourged with a leather strap to which sharp pieces of metal or bone were attached. But the crowd continued to cry out: "Crucify him, crucify him." Jesus was then clothed in purple, struck with reeds, spat upon and given a crown of thorns to wear. He was mockingly called "King of the Jews."

Meanwhile, Pilate tried once more to reason with the crowd. According to a Passover custom, the governor at that time could release one prisoner at the people's request. Pilate asked if they would have him release the King of the Jews. But instead the crowd shouted in unison to release Barabbas, a convicted murderer. Pilate then ordered Jesus to be brought before the mob and he said: "Take him yourself and crucify him, for I find no crime in him." To that the priests said: "He has made himself the Son of God; he must die."

Turning to Jesus, Pilate asked: "Where are you from?" Jesus gave no answer. "Don't you know I have the power to release you or to crucify you?" Pilate asked. "You would have no power over me unless it had been given to you from above," Jesus said. All the while the crowds cried out: "If you release this man, you are no friend of Caesar's."

Charges of "blasphemy" were viewed by the Romans as a religious transgression, and no Roman judge would sentence a man to death for such an infraction. Knowing this, the crowds pressed a different charge, that Jesus passed himself off as the Christ-King which implied that he was a political agitator and revolutionary. Finally, attempting to wash his hands of the whole affair, Pilate agreed. All that remained was the crucifixion itself.

Jesus was led to a hill just outside Jerusalem called Golgotha because the hill had the appearance of a skull. There Jesus was nailed to a cross through his wrists and feet and suffered an excruciating death. The inscription over his head read, "Jesus of Nazareth: the King of the Jews."

Last Words

One way to begin to understand his experience at this hour would be to reflect upon his last words, words which reflect both his humanity and his divinity, words such as: "Eloi, Eloi, lama sabachthani—My God, My God, why hast thou forsaken me?" (Mt 27:46; Mk 15:34), and "Father, forgive them; they do not know what they are doing" (Lk 23:34). The first words (quoted from the beginning of Psalm 22 which ends with praise of Yahweh) sound confused and abandoned, sound totally human, while the second express almost unbelievable compassion from one who felt forsaken yet forgiving. These two "words" from the cross embrace both a human, aching heart and a more-than-human compassion, together in the same person.

In John's account of the crucifixion we are told that Jesus' mother Mary and the unnamed, beloved disciple were standing at the foot of the cross.

Looking down, Jesus tenderly addressed them as a part of his eschatological family, the family of God which is beyond blood-ties. He said to his mother, "Woman, behold your son," and to the disciple "Behold, your mother" (Jn 19:26). It is implied that they were to care for one another as Christ cared for each of them, and that they were thus to be bearers of Christ's compassionate identity in and to the new community of believers. Eastern Orthodox theologians point to this moment—just as Jesus is dying—as the very first beginnings of the Church (which was to blossom at Pentecost).

To understand Jesus' suffering at this moment, we must remember how he was killed. Not only was he nailed to a cross, but likely a platform was built under his feet to prevent him from suffocating within minutes. The platform allowed the victim to push up, enough to gasp for air, before slumping down again. He constantly struggled between suffocation and gasping for air. Toward the end, Jesus again quoted from the Hebrew Psalms: "Into your hands I commend my spirit." Like a child who runs to mother or father sure to find safety in the parent's arms, Jesus spoke these words in trusting surrender to his Father. His mission on earth was completed. He sacrificed himself and in that final act transformed the cross from a death-giving post and crossbeam to the tree of eternal life.

The Resurrection

Through the narrow passageway of death, theologians say, the way to resurrection is opened, a resurrection which reverses human expectations. The force of the Christian attitude toward death and dying, and the impact of its claims, stand or fall on the reality of Christ's resurrection. As Paul states, if Christ has not risen, then one's faith is in vain. In fact, the Gospels were all written through eyes of faith in Christ's resurrection, seen in the early Church as both the center of history, from which and to which everything flows, and the end of history, the fulfillment of God's promises.

Indeed, before he died Jesus talked about the resurrection with one of his favorite followers, Martha, whom Jesus loved. The discussion occurred in response to Martha's displeasure at his not arriving in time to save her brother Lazarus from death. "If you had been here," Martha chides, "my brother would not have died." But Jesus said: "Your brother will rise again." Taken aback by his response, and being a good Pharisaic Jew, Martha said: "I know he will rise again at the resurrection on the last day." But Jesus countered:

I am the resurrection.
If anyone believes in me,
even though he dies he will live,

and whoever lives and believes in me
will never die,
Do you believe this?[1]

Martha replied, "Yes, Lord, I have come to believe that you are the Messiah, the Son of God" (Jn 11:27). Here, in John's Gospel, Martha is the one, not Peter as in the Synoptics, who identifies Jesus definitively as the "Messiah." Her sister Mary, on the other hand, fell at Jesus' feet and wept. Jesus too wept. Troubled in spirit he approached the tomb and prayed in thanksgiving for being heard by his Father. Then Jesus called loudly:

> "Lazarus, come out!" The dead man came out, bound hand and foot with linen strips, his face wrapped in a cloth. "Untie him," Jesus told them, "and let him go free."[2]

By saying "I am the resurrection" Jesus identifies himself both as one who has the power to revive Lazarus and as the power of resurrection itself. At the same time, he identifies himself as "the life," or as the power of eternal life. To see Jesus in this way is to recognize that Jesus' resurrection reconciles death with life, darkness with light, and completes the life cycle by overcoming death. In the person of Jesus the resurrection, which was yet to come, had already occurred in its initial phase.[2]

Since for the Christian resurrection is *the* key to the mystery of death, we must now ask a crucial question: What does the resurrection of Jesus' body really mean?

Of the countless attempts to describe the resurrection, they generally fall into three perspectives. First there are those who claim that just as Christ brought Lazarus back from the dead, it was Christ's actual physical body that was resuscitated. As John Updike writes:

> Make no mistake: if He rose at all it was as His body;
> If the cells' dissolution did not reverse,
> The molecules Reknit, the amino acids Rekindle,
> The Church will fall.[3]

The difficulty with this literal interpretation lies in the Gospel indication that the resurrected Christ was able to walk through doors and to suddenly appear and disappear.

Some theologians and psychologists have maintained that the resurrection occurred in the imagination or faith or hopes of those close to him. The difficulty with this theory of psychic reconstitution lies within the New Testament accounts of an empty tomb, and of his appearances in which he ate fish with the disciples and was touched by Thomas.

A third perspective suggests that the resurrection of Jesus is a spiritual mystery far greater than the human mind can grasp, and that in some unfathomable way Jesus appeared in several different modes or manifestations on different occasions. This interpretation depicts a resurrection in which the risen or spiritual body is transformed and is no longer bound by finite space and time.

This last view is based on the earliest testimony to the resurrection, one not found in the Gospels (which emphasize both the empty tomb and Christ's appearances) but in the Pauline letters which repeatedly stress Christ's appearances or revelations. For Paul, the bodily resurrection was to be viewed not in physiological terms but as *soma* or personality. The resurrected body is the consummation of one's entire personal reality and earthly history. Paul points to this transformation when he writes:

> It is the same with the resurrection of the dead: the thing that is sown is perishable but what is raised is imperishable; the thing that is sown is contemptible but what is raised is glorious; the thing that is sown is weak but what is raised is powerful; when it is sown it embodies the soul, when it is raised it embodies the spirit.[4]

Here Paul pictures a transformation of the earthly body (*psychikos*) into a spiritual body (*pneumatikos*), such that what was once merely physical now appears in an exalted, glorified, eschatological body far too mysterious to grasp.

In other words, unlike the Buddhist notion of reincarnation in which one's personal history is negated, unlike the Hindu notion that the awakened at death enter into Brahman as a river enters into the sea, and unlike the Greek eternal disembodiment of the soul, the Christian resurrected body is fully, eternally human. The fundamental difference between Jesus and for instance Krishna, the incarnation of Vishnu, is that Jesus must be understood through the eyes of historical consciousness. The life of Jesus cannot be reduced to a mythological expression like Lord Krishna, nor to a psychological type like Jung's "Self." Christianity has always maintained that Jesus is an historic person who actually lived, died, resurrected and ascended. But in what sense one might ask is Christ's resurrection *historical*?

According to the German theologian Wolfhart Pannenberg, since we can only know God in and through the Jesus of history, it follows that the resurrection is an utterly historical event, not simply a matter of faith. For Karl Rahner, the most influential Catholic theologian of this century, a careful distinction must be drawn between what Christians mean by "salvation history" and how that is different from ordinary history. Salvation history includes those events in ordinary history (and beyond it) which became transparent to the God of Abraham, Isaac, Jacob and Jesus. From the standpoint of ordinary history which is in part determined by the requirements of the sciences, the resurrection is a physical impossibility and a scientifically nonverifiable event. It could not have been photographed for example. The Shroud of Turin notwithstanding, from the perspective of ordinary history, the resurrection was either a subjectivistic reality in the minds or imagination of the faithful, or it was an objectivistic and literal description of an actual physical resuscitation.[5]

But from the standpoint of salvation history, the resurrection is viewed differently, radically differently. As Rahner writes:

> Jesus' resurrection, finally, takes on a unique salvation-history character because through faith we recognize it as being the eschatologically irreversible, historical appearance of God's promise of himself to the world.[6]

The resurrection then is finally both an event in ordinary history and an eschatological event in salvation history, both in but not of history. If this were not so, as Saint Thomas notes, Christians would not speak of a resurrected body, but of the assumption of a new body. And if this were not so, Rahner concludes, the statement "he is alive" would not have been able to activate the early Church development as it in fact did.

New Testament Teachings

In the previous chapter we discussed the character of Jewish apocalyptic writing in the Book of Daniel, an emphasis which is also developed in the New Testament. The Hebrew belief that with the coming of the Messiah death will be overcome once and for all becomes an accomplished fact revealed by the life and death of Jesus. Moreover, in the New Testament teachings about death at least four key aspects arise: death is a consequence of sin, death is a temporary separation of body and soul, death to sin is birth into eternal life, and the dead will be raised and judged at the second coming of Christ.

First, for Jews and Christians alike sin and death are closely related. In Paul's letters, sin is the cause of death, just as death is the consequence of Adam's sin. "Sin entered the world through one man, and through sin death, and thus death has spread through the whole human race because everyone has sinned" (Rom 5:12).

After the exile from paradise, Adam's son Abel was slain. Carrying his

son back to Eve, Adam laid his limp body in her arms. Cain, their jealous
son, had murdered his brother Abel. Feeling deeply sorrowful they remembered what God had said: "On the day that you eat the fruit of that tree, you
shall most surely die" (Gen 2:17).

If Adam had not sinned, he would have fulfilled his days here on earth,
and then passed from this world without dying. He would have experienced
what theologian Karl Rahner has called "a death without dying." In other
words, Adam would not have died the type of bodily death we now die. For
Paul, sinning meant the opposite of holiness, the opposite of righteousness.
To sin means to miss the mark, to disobey God, to turn away from the divine
gift of love. As a result, at death body and soul are separated temporarily, the
corrupted body dissolves and the soul begins its after-death journey. The
body then "sleeps" or "rests" in the earth of all bodies when body and soul
are reunited.

The second aspect—the separation of body and soul—is found pointedly
in the Coptic Egyptian Church where this separation is personified by the
word *Mu*. In an extracanonical, apocryphal work known as the *History of
Joseph the Carpenter* (a fourth century translation of a Greek original) Jesus
is shown telling his disciples that he saw Death enter his house to take his
father Joseph away. When Death sees Jesus, he hides behind the door. Jesus
is obliged to call Death in to fulfill his role of separating his dying father's
soul from his body. As we have said, at death the body goes the way of all the
earth, while the soul begins its after-death journey. While the body "sleeps,"
the soul travels either to paradise (or Abraham's bosom) or to Hades.
Whereas paradise and Hades are temporary, pre-final-judgment existences,
heaven and hell are final domains for the re-embodied soul. In Christian theology heaven and hell are not restricted in Christian theology to spatio-tem-
poral places where one goes after death, but are described as trans-temporal
possibilities which are also experienced in our present life.[7]

In the midst of a series of parables in the Gospel of Luke, which present
Jesus' teaching on the coming of the kingdom of God, we find the parable of
Lazarus which is a parable of afterlife. In life, a rich man who dressed in fine
linen and who had feasted sumptuously every day virtually ignored the beggar Lazarus, who lay at his gate covered with sores and longing for scraps
from the rich man's table. When each died, Lazarus was carried away by
angels to Abraham's bosom, while the rich man went to Hades.

> In his torment in Hades he looked up and saw Abraham a long way
> off with Lazarus in his bosom. So he cried out, "Father Abraham,
> pity me and send Lazarus to dip the tip of his finger in water and
> cool my tongue, for I am in agony in these flames." "My son," Abra-

ham replied, "remember that during your life good things came your way, just as bad things came the way of Lazarus. Now he is being comforted here while you are in agony. But that is not all: between us and you a great gulf has been fixed, to stop anyone, if he wanted to, crossing from our side to yours, and to stop any crossing from your side to ours."[8]

In the next world the situation was irrevocably reversed: the beggar became rich and the rich man poor. There was no means for bridging the gulf between the two dimensions prior to the final judgment.

> The rich man replied, "Father, I beg you then to send Lazarus to my father's house, since I have five brothers to give them warning so that they do not come to this place of torment too." "They have Moses and the prophets," said Abraham; "let them listen to them." "Ah no, father Abraham," said the rich man, "but if someone comes to them from the dead, they will repent." Then Abraham said to him, "If they will not listen either to Moses or to the prophets, they will not be convinced even if someone should rise from the dead."[9]

There are two "judgments" implied by this story—first, the *particular* judgment of each individual person to decide whether his or her soul is to be sent immediately to heaven, hell or purgatory, and, second, a *final* judgment on the last day when the bodies of the dead arise from their sleep in the earth to become re-ensouled.[10] The suggestion of two judgments points to the dual nature of human testing, in both its individual and its social nature. These two judgments mutually and harmoniously confirm each other.

But what is purgatory? Rather than a place, purgatory in Catholic faith is a process of purgation in which one's soul becomes purified from venial sins prior to Christ's second coming. While it is implied in 2 Maccabees 12:39–45, it is based more on Church tradition than on scripture. Of course it should be remembered that neither eternal life, nor hell for that matter, occupies a supernatural location. Heaven is rather the trans-temporal, invisible domain of God's presence which is forever beyond human understanding.

The third aspect of the New Testament teaching has to do with what could be called a mystical or the immediate experience of death, a dying beyond dying, the art of self-emptying that can take place while one is yet alive. To be thoroughly prepared for death from the New Testament viewpoint, one must die to all that is false and enter into the beginnings of eternal life while yet alive. Foretelling his own death and subsequent glorification, Jesus tells Andrew and Philip:

> I tell you, most solemnly,
> unless a wheat grain falls on the ground and dies,
> it remains only a single grain;
> but if it dies,
> it yields a rich harvest.
> Anyone who loves his life loses it;
> anyone who hates his life in this world
> will keep it for eternal life.[11]

The one who was "crucified" as Saul and reborn as Paul writes: "I have been crucified with Christ; it is no longer I who live, but Christ who lives in me" (Gal 2:20), and "For to me to live is Christ, and to die is gain" (Phil 1:21). Just as Jesus emptied himself of his divinity to become human, even to accepting death, so disciples should empty themselves of self and take on Christ. Speaking to those who have died into Christ and who have been raised with him, Paul writes: "After all, you have died! Your life is hidden now with Christ in God" (Col 3:2–3). The old self has been put to death, replaced by the new self formed anew in the image of the Creator.[12]

Nowhere in the New Testament is this doorway evidenced more dramatically than in the lives of martyrs and saints. Aside from Stephen (who in the hour of his martyrdom looked toward heaven and saw the skies open up and saw Jesus standing at the right hand of God's glory), Peter and Paul, the most famous early Church martyr was Polycarp who lived in the middle of the second century CE. The bishop of Smyrna sealed his fate when he refused to take an oath to revile Christ. When the Romans threatened to throw him to wild beasts he replied: "Call for them; for a change from better to worse is impossible for us; but it is laudable to change from evil to good."[13] As he spoke these words, courage and joy filled his heart and his face was bathed in grace. Deciding to burn him alive, the Roman proconsul bound him like a ram ready for sacrifice.

Before the pyre was lit Polycarp looked up to heaven and thanked God for the opportunity to enter "unto the resurrection of eternal life both of soul and body in the incorruption of the Holy Spirit."[14] But when the fire was lit his body was encircled by a wall of wind so that the executioner had to plunge a dagger into him. Polycarp died the way he lived, always willing to die for the sake of Christ's will, and always praying to die into the resurrected life of Christ. That the life of the Christian can be, in fact should be, a spiritual martyrdom is witnessed by a Christian's willingness to suffer and to surrender all aspects of the un-Christ-like self to God.

The last aspect of the New Testament attitude toward death, while difficult to understand, stimulates the most curiosity, namely the end of time or the last judgment. Paul writes:

> For we know that when the tent that we live in on earth is folded up, there is a house built by God for us, an everlasting home not made by human hands, in the heavens. In this present state, it is true, we groan even as we yearn to have our heavenly habitation envelop us. This it will, provided we are found clothed and not naked. While we live in our present tent we groan; we are weighed down because we do not wish to be stripped naked but rather to have the heavenly dwelling envelop us, so that what is mortal may be absorbed by life. God has fashioned us for this very thing and has given us the Spirit as a pledge of it.[15]

At death, the soul becomes naked until rejoined to its transformed or resurrected body which will occur when "the Son of Man comes in clouds with great power and glory" (Mk 13:26).

Paul takes this further in 1 Thessalonians where he proclaims that when Christ returns in glory (at the sound of God's trumpet) the dead will rise first, and then "we who are alive, who are left, shall be caught up together with them in the clouds to meet the Lord in the air" (1 Thes 4:17). At that time, Paul teaches, "in the twinkling of an eye":

> The trumpet will sound and the dead will be raised incorruptible, and we shall be changed. This corruptible body must be clothed with incorruptibility, this mortal body with immortality. When the corruptible frame takes on incorruptibility and the mortal immortality, then will the saying of Scripture be fulfilled: "Death is swallowed up in victory." "O death, where is your victory? O death, where is your sting?" The sting of death is sin, and sin gets its power from the law.[16]

When the Son of Man takes his seat on the throne of glory to face every reunited soul, some will be sent away to eternal punishment. Eternal life will be awarded to those who served Jesus by serving their neighbors:

> For I was hungry and you gave me food, I was thirsty and you gave me drink. I was a stranger and you welcomed me, naked and you clothed me. I was ill and you comforted me, in prison and you came to visit me.[17]

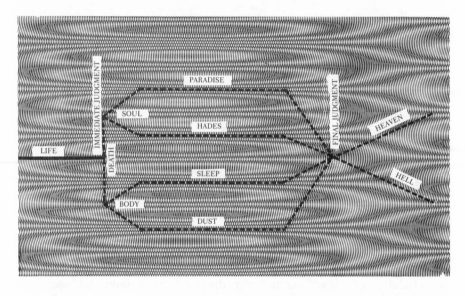

In the Book of Revelation (the last book in the New Testament), we are presented not with pictures but with descriptions of eternal life breaking into the author's own history. In John's Apocalypse one could say that eternity and time emerge from and return each other. The book opens with John's vision of a figure like the "Son of Man" in a long robe with white hair and flaming eyes: When I saw him, John reports, I fell in a dead faint at his feet, but he touched me with his right hand and said:

> There is nothing to fear. I am the First and the Last and the One who lives. Once I was dead but now I live—forever and ever. I hold the keys of death and the nether world.[18]

After Satan and his armies are consumed by a heavenly fire, John envisions "a new heaven and a new earth" which comes down as the new Jerusalem "as beautiful as a bride all dressed for her husband."

> Then I saw new heavens and a new earth. The former heavens and the former earth had passed away, and the sea was no longer. I also saw the new Jerusalem, the holy city, coming down out of heaven from God, as beautiful as a bride all dressed for her husband. Then I heard a loud voice call from the throne, "You see this city? Here God lives among men. He will make his home among them; they shall be his people, and he will be their God; his name is God-with-them. He will wipe away all tears from their eyes; there will be no

more death, and no more mourning or sadness. The world of the past has gone."[19]

The holy city is pictured as a crystal-clear jewel with twelve gates, streets of gold, and containing no temple. "Happy are those who washed their robes clean," says Christ, for "they will have the right to enter into the city and to feed on the tree of eternal life" (Rev 2:13–14).

In the lives of the saints, there are numerous descriptions of souls entering heaven where they are joined by a company of inhabitants and where, whatever else they experience, they experience Christ face-to-face. St. Andrew (ninth century) writes of a vision he experienced while lying in a city street in Constantinople nearly frozen to death. Suddenly he felt an inner warmth and was taken to paradise. He writes:

> After this a kind of fear fell upon me, and it seemed to me that I was standing at the peak of the firmament of heaven. . . . And behold, a flaming hand opened the curtain, and like the prophet Isaiah I beheld my Lord, sitting upon a throne, high and lifted up, and above it stood the seraphim. He was clothed in a purple garment; His face was most bright, and His eyes looked on me with love. Seeing this, I fell down before Him, bowing down to the most bright and fearful throne of His glory. The joy that overcame me on beholding His face cannot be expressed in words.[20]

Death Ritual

There are many various funerary practices among Christian denominations, some more and some less fully elaborate. One of the more highly developed forms is the Catholic Mass of the dead, now called the "Mass of the Resurrection" which includes Eucharist, rosary, prayers, music, flowers and procession to the cemetery. The rosary and other prayers are offered to assist the soul on its pilgrimage through purgatory. Here instead of discussing the Mass I will conclude by mentioning two practices which are likely to attend dying: dying sacramentally and dying prayerfully.

The early Church realized the significance of the manner and context in which a person died. Early in its history the Church developed what has been called "last rites" or "extreme unction," and which today is called "anointing of the sick." "Extreme unction" is usually accompanied by two other sacraments, confession (now called the "rite of reconciliation") and the Holy Eucharist. At the heart of each sacrament lies the believer's remembrance and participation in the real presence of Christ.

Each of the Christian sacraments (outward signs and symbols of inward spiritual graces) offers a ritualized participation in the death and resurrection of Christ. Viewing death sacramentally gives the Christian courage to leap into the unknown of death, assured that he or she will be supported by Christ and transformed thereby.

In the sacrament of "anointing of the sick" (cf. Jas 5:14–16), the sick person is prayed over, and traditionally six parts of the body (eyes, ears, nostrils, lips, hands and feet) are anointed with holy oils which have been blessed by the bishop for this purpose. As the priest anoints the person he says, "May the Lord who frees you from sin save you and raise you up." Upon hearing the dying person's confession so that on behalf of the Church he may absolve the person of any guilt, the priest then gives the Holy Eucharist (Communion) which brings Christ into the center of the dying person's experience. The rite concludes with a prayer that the dying will be refreshed by the presence of the body and blood of Jesus and will be led into God's kingdom. This sacrament is primarily intended to fortify the soul, to give spiritual aid and comfort, and to enable the person to meet death tranquilly, even victoriously.

In the end one dies alone, and from the Christian standpoint, therefore, prayerfully. Because Christ freely accepted suffering and death in order to liberate all humans from the fear of death, the Christian's attitude toward death includes an anticipated encounter with God. And because Christ prayed both in Gethsemane and from the cross just before he died, Christians too pray their way into death. Therefore, the believer cultivates a prayerful attitude of heart and mind in order to keep Christ's presence alive throughout the dying process.

Aside from one's personal concerns and planetary hopes, aside from any unfinished spiritual business, it becomes increasingly more important as death approaches to pray again and again a prayer that embodies and reanimates the source of a believer's faith. As a religious Hindu might at death mediate on Lord Krishna, as a Buddhist might chant "Gate, Gate, Paragate, Parasamgate! Bodhi Svaha!" and as a religious Jew might pray the "*Shema*," at death a Catholic or Orthodox Christian's last prayer might be: "Lord Jesus Christ, have mercy on us sinners," or "Holy Mary, Mother of God, pray for us sinners now, and at the hour of our death!"

NOTES

[1]Jn 11:25–26. All scriptural selections are taken from the *Jerusalem Bible* (New York: Doubleday, 1966). More concretely, in the Synoptic Gospels

(Matthew, Mark and Luke), soon after Peter's confession that Jesus is the Christ, his closest apostles see Jesus transfigured with Moses (the law) and Elijah (the prophets) to each side. At least three of his disciples—Peter, James and John—experienced a pre-figuring of the resurrection at Jesus' transfiguration. They saw Jesus with his clothes dazzlingly white, his appearance changed and his body brilliant as lightning.

[2]Jn 11:43–44.

[3]John Updike, "Seven Stanzas at Easter," in *Seventy Poems* (New York: Penguin, 1962), 28.

[4]1 Cor 15:42–44.

[5]Recently there has been increased scholarly interest in the image of a man on a burial shroud kept in Turin, Italy for centuries and now the property of the Vatican. The Shroud of Turin is kept in a silver casket high above the main altar of the Capella della Santa Sindone in Turin's Duomo San Giovanni. Since the first photograph of the man's face turned out to be in 1898 a negative, with light and shade reversed, theologians and scientists have been investigating the image. A forensic examination of the photograph reveals the image of a 5′10″, 175 pound male who could have been between the ages of thirty and thirty-five, with wounds on the back, skull, wrist and feet consistent with scourging and crucifixion. Pollen samples taken from the cloth indicate that its fibers came from plants that grow in the Palestinian region. U.S. Air Force Academy scientists Dr. John Jackson and Dr. Eric Jumper, after putting the shroud image under a VP-8 image analyzer usually used to enhance photographs taken of the planets, cautiously advanced the following thesis: the image on the shroud was caused by an intense burst of radiant energy in a millisecond of time, enough to imprint, but not destroy, the cloth.

[6]Karl Rahner, *Theological Investigations*, Vol. XVII (New York: Crossroad, 1981), 22.

[7]Lk 16:23–26. Abraham's bosom is elsewhere called paradise (Lk 23:43; Rev 2:7), a Persian word for a pleasure garden which, along with Hades or Sheol, describes the immediate and intermediate after-physical-death existence of one's soul. Heaven and hell become the final judgment's consummation.

[8]Lk 16:27–31.

[9]According to Catholic theologians, Mary, Joseph, the angels and the saints are already in heaven. By solemn declaration the Church proclaims: "The Immaculate Mother of God, Mary ever Virgin, after her life on earth, was assumed, body and soul, to the glory of heaven" (*Munificentissimus Deus*, of Pope Pius XII, November 1, 1950). Traditionally, venial sin is defined as a sin capable of impairing the health but not destroying the supernatural life of the soul. It is an impairment of the soul rather than the death of the soul, as mortal sin is. A mortal sin is defined as a serious offense against

God in which the soul loses sanctifying grace. To be guilty of mortal sin, three things must be present: the act must be morally serious, the person must have full knowledge of the action's sinfulness, and the act must be deliberately done.

[10]The Church has consistently proclaimed its belief in these two judgments.

[11]Jn 12:24–25.

[12]To facilitate this mystical death, this dying before dying, early Christian monks sought to incorporate death daily into life. St. Benedict advised his monks to keep the thought of death before them every day. Their vocation was, if possible, to die in God and to live eternally in God's presence. As an early Egyptian monk remarked in response to questions about eternal salvation: Become a dead man, and take no account of earthly praises. In monastic prayer therefore, the one who prays dies to an egocentric level of being, and becomes prayed-through. It is not the I who prays, but the Spirit who prays through the I. Practicing the sacred art of dying in this way, one realizes that death is the doorway to transcendence.

[13]Jack Sparks, editor, *The Apostolic Fathers* (New York: Thomas Nelson Inc., 1978), 143.

[14]*Ibid.*, 146. In our time, of many stories of such a faith, the Polish priest Father Maximilian Kolbe who was at Auschwitz in the Second World War stands out. At one point during his captivity, ten inmates were selected at random by a German commandant to be executed by starvation (a slow, painful death). When one man cried out that he did not want to die because his wife was pregnant, Kolbe voluntarily substituted himself. He encouraged the others with constant prayers, hymns praising God and venerating his spiritual mother Mary. On August 14, 1941, when the SS troups needed the cell for other victims, Kolbe was injected with carbolic acid, and on August 15, the Feast of the Assumption of Mary, his body was cremated. Forty-one years later, he was canonized a saint. Of course he is just one of the many martyrs of the Church whose blood became the "seed of the Church," and whose lives and deaths testify to a resurrected attitude toward death.

[15]2 Cor 5:1–5.

[16]1 Cor 15:52–56.

[17]Mt 25:35.

[18]Rev 1:17–19.

[19]Rev 21:1–4.

[20]An in-depth depiction of these experiences is found in Hieromonk Seraphim Rose's book *The Soul After Death* (Platina, Cal.: St. Herman of Alaska Brotherhood, 1980), 145–146 and especially Chapter 10. In the history of Greek and Russian Orthodox Christianity, a highly imagistic view of heaven and life after death has developed. Drawing upon scripture, the Church Fa-

thers and the lives of saints, Orthodox theologians speak first of angels who have the appearance of lightning and who appear after death to escort the soul into the next life. Unbound by time and space, these angels are spirits or aerial bodies which guard the soul in its battles with what Paul calls "the spirits of wickedness under the heavens" (Eph 6:12). Besides angels, Orthodox theologians speak of "aerial toll houses" through which the pilgrim soul wanders. Each toll house tests a special sin (e.g., lying, pride and murder) committed from childhood till that moment in the person's history. The length of one's journey is of course determined by the residue of sin which needs to be purified.

[21]Lk 22:42.

JOURNAL EXERCISES

1. Imagine that you can have a dialogue with the historic Jesus, and that you ask Jesus about death. What would he say? And then imagine being able to talk with the resurrected Jesus. What would he say?
2. Of the last words of Jesus from the cross, which are/is the most significant to you, and which reveals the deepest insights about the death process?
3. In Paul's perspective, in what ways does the resurrection of Jesus liberate other humans who believe in him from death? What is your point of view on what Paul says?
4. What is mystical death? What does Jesus say about it? How does Paul talk about it? Is it possible? For example . . .
5. What is meant by dying sacramentally? Is this the same as, or different from, death rituals in other sacred traditions? Compare, for example, "extreme unction" with Tibetan ritual practices.
6. How might an intelligent, practicing Christian answer the following question: What does your tradition teach about how to die artfully? That is, what is the most sacred way of dying?

Chapter 11 ISLAMIC ATTITUDES TOWARD DEATH

The happiness of the drop
is to die in the river.
Ghazal of Ghalib

"There is no other God but Allah, and Muhammad is his prophet." Such is the first statement of every Muslim's faith (*iman*): to surrender (*Islam*) totally to the oneness of Allah, and to honor and practice the teachings of the prophet Muhammad (570-632). To be a member of the Islamic holy community (*ummah*), one must acknowledge and worship Allah as the creator of all life and as its final judge, and one must honor, not worship, the prophet Muhammad, because it was through him that Allah revealed his divine word in the Holy Qur'an.

The Arabic (MUHAMMAD)　　　　　*The Arabic (ALLĀH)*

In order to understand the Islamic attitude toward death and dying it is necessary to begin with the Qur'an's portrayal of creation, and to note the parallels to the Judaeo-Christian creation story. One of several versions begins:

Then We made the sperm
Into a clot of cogealed blood;
Then of that clot We made
A (foetus) lump; then We

157

Made out of that lump
Bones and clothed the bones
With flesh; then We developed
Out of it another creature.
So blessed be God,
The Best to create!
After that, at length
Ye will die.
Again, on the Day
Of judgment, will ye be
Raised up.[1]

Recalling the Genesis account of creation, we notice some significant differences. To the biblical account of creation the Qur'an adds not only the announcement of death's inevitability, but also the Day of Resurrection. Creation, death and resurrection are therefore each sacred, and inexorably linked from the beginning.

Another version of the creation account elaborates this:

O mankind! if ye have
A doubt about the Resurrection,
(Consider) that We created you
Out of dust, then out of
Sperm, then out of a leech-like
Clot, then out of morsel
Of flesh, partly formed
And partly unformed, in order
That We may manifest
(Our power) to you;
And We cause whom We will
To rest in the wombs
For an appointed term,
Then do We bring you out
As babes, then (foster you)
That ye may reach your age
Of full strength; and some
Of you are called to die,
And some are sent back
To the feeblest old age,
So that they know nothing
After having known (much).[2]

Addressed to those who may have doubts about the resurrection, these lines indicate that Allah's creation is too wonderful to end with death. Furthermore, these stages have no meaning until one completes the full cycle—through them the soul itself develops. Life then is a preparation for the soul to pass through the stage of death, and to be fit to progress in the life after-death.

The Qur'an's story of the creation, temptation and fall of Adam is similar to its biblical counterpart, as it too functions; to explain the origins of death. The story begins with God speaking to the angels about the creation of humanity. Though holy and pure, the angels ask God an earth-bound question: "Will they make mischief and shed blood while we praise thee?" And God replied, "I know what ye know not" (*Sura* 2:30).

After Adam was created, God taught him the inner nature or quality of things. In Arabic, the passage reads literally: "And He taught Adam the names of things." This offers a variant of the Genesis account in which God gives Adam the power to name God's creations. In the Qur'anic account, God bade the angels to bow down to Adam, to the one who "tells them their natures (names)." And Adam and Eve were told that they could eat of all things within the garden except from the one tree which would produce harm and transgression.³ But as in the Genesis account, in the Qur'an Satan tempts them, makes them "slip from the garden," and "dislocates their felicitous state."⁴

It is written that both Adam and Eve eat from the tree at the same time, and are thus cast out of the garden and bound to live a mortal life on earth. Fortunately, however, God inspires spiritual knowledge in Adam and tells him:

> We said: "Get ye down all from here;
> And if, as is sure, there comes to you
> Guidance from Me, whosoever
> Follows My guidance, on them
> Shall be no fear, nor shall they grieve.
> "But those who reject Faith
> And belie Our Signs,
> They shall be Companions of the Fire;
> They shall abide therein."⁵

One's soul either grows nearer to the mercy of God, or abides in a spiritual fire. The choice is between a second birth or a "new creation" for those who follow the will of Allah, and a second death, an eternal death for those who remain unbelievers. Except for first physical death, which believers and unbelievers alike must suffer, believers never again taste death.

Therefore, God creates humans not to bring about their death, but, to free them from their sinful mistakes:

It is He Who gave you life,
Will cause you to die,
And will again give you
Life: truly man is
A most ungrateful creature![6]

Day of Judgment

From the Muslim standpoint, death is a transition from this world to Eternity. The purpose of life, as attested in the Qur'an, is to prepare for eternal life. For "every soul shall taste death" (*Sura* 21:34), but only after the tests and trials of life: "Blessed be the one who created death and life, so He may test which of you is finest in action" (*Sura* 67:2). This testing, the context of the Qur'anic concern for death, is the Day of Judgment, to which we now turn our attention.

But first the question can be asked: What happens to the deceased between death and the resurrection of the body? The Qur'an tells us of a barrier (*barzakh*) which separates the land of the living from those who have died (*Sura* 23:100). The deceased have thus no way to return to earth, no way to be reincarnated. The soul now begins a period of waiting for the day of resurrection and judgment. According to traditional accounts, once separated from the body the soul begins a journey heavenward. Modeled on the mystical journey taken by the Prophet Muhammad from Mecca to Jerusalem to heaven, the soul is escorted by the angel Gabriel through seven layers of heaven.

A favorite episode in Muhammad's life tells of the Prophet being taken from Mecca during the night to Jerusalem, and from there up into the presence of Allah. As Abraham and Moses spoke directly with God, as Jesus had a Son's relationship with his Father, Muhammad too had an intimate acquaintance with his Lord. Once in paradise, all the prophets assembled to meet Muhammad and together to offer praise to God. Allah instructed His prophet to institute the *salat* (prayer five times a day) as a way of surrendering to the God of creation.

The goal of the journey is for each person to reach a vision of God. One such vision is described in vividly imaginative terms by the medieval mystic Al-Ghazali: eighty thousand moons shine upon God and eighty thousand believers glorify Him. Afterward the soul returns to the grave to wait the judgment day.

According to Islamic teaching and belief, at the Day of Judgment the dead will rise from their graves amidst cataclysmic events which will disrupt the natural order. They will be judged according to the number of good and bad entries that have been recorded into a set of heavenly books by secretary angels whose duty it is to record all human deeds. In depicting the results of the Day of Judgment, the Qur'an describes a difficult life for unbelievers, who will be cast, chained together, into a roaring blaze:

> Hast thou not turned
> Thy vision to those who
> Have changed the favour of God.
> Into blasphemy and caused
> Their people to descend
> To the House of Perdition?—
> Into Hell? They will burn
> Therein,—an evil place
> To stay in!
> And they set up (idols)
> As equal to God, to mislead
> (Men) from the Path! Say:
> "Enjoy (your brief power)!
> But verily ye are making
> Straightway for Hell!"[7]

On the other hand, those who do good work will inherit paradise (*al-janat*), wherein they will live forever. The Qur'an assures the believer that at death:

> Gardens of Eternity . . . they
> Will enter: beneath them
> Flow (pleasant) rivers: they
> Will have therein all
> That they wish: thus doth
> God reward the righteous.[8]

There are two passages in the Qur'an where Muhammad especially speaks of the Day of Judgment. In the first, when the inevitable event comes to pass, when the earth shakes and mountains crumble into atoms, the resurrected shall be sorted out into three classes:

> Then (there will be)
> The Companions of

The Right Hand;—
What will be
The Companions of
The Right Hand?
And the Companions of
The Left Hand,—
What will be
The Companions of
The Left Hand?
And those Foremost
(In Faith) will be
Foremost (in the Hereafter).[9]

Righteous

agony

nearest to God

The companions of the Right Hand are the righteous people and the companions of the Left Hand are those who suffer in agony because of their sin. The foremost in Faith are the spiritually advanced persons who are "nearest to God." Prophets and teachers, from old, will recline on gold crusted thrones. No frivolities will be heard there, only the sound of "Peace! Peace!" And those on the right dwell among flowers and trees in shade by flowing waters, virgin-pure equal in age, while those of the left dwell in a blast of fire and in boiling water, with nothing there to refresh its inhabitants. And God commands: If anyone questions the resurrection of the body, tell them:

And they used to say,
"What! when we die
And become dust and bones,
Shall we then indeed
Be raised up again?—
(We) and our fathers of old?"
Say: "Yea, those of old
And those of later times,
All will certainly be
Gathered together for the meeting
Appointed for a Day
Well-known."[10]

The second account also depicts the Last Judgment, but in more graphic and poetic images. Earth and mountains are crushed to powder in one motion. And on that day will be brought forth a record book:

That Day shall ye be
Brought to Judgment:

Not an act of yours
That ye hide will be hidden.[11]

Based therefore on one's earthly deeds, the assignment is made either to a life of Bliss or Blazing Fire. This message is sent down from God through his Prophet Muhammad.

Preparing To Die

How then does a Muslim prepare for the certainty of the Final Judgment? And how does one prepare for the dying process itself?

In Islam, at least in Sufism, preparing for one's death is a spiritual necessity. The Sufis (from *suf*, a white wool garment) were ascetics and mystics so devoted to the love of Allah that they often experienced a spiritual dying into Allah's presence. Sufi poet Dhu'l-Nun writes:

I die, and yet not dies in me
The ardour of my love for Thee,
Nor hath Thy Love, my only goal,
Assuaged the fever of my soul.[12]

In their devotional fervors, the Sufis developed what has been called *fana* (extinction) which means both passing away into God, and dying to the self. Each of these elements are present in the following narrative attributed to Abu Yazid:

Once He raised me up and stationed me before Him, and said to me, 'O Abu Yazid, truly My creation desire to see thee.' I said, 'Adorn me in Thy Unity, and clothe me in Thy Self-hood, and raise me up to Thy Oneness, so that when Thy creation see me they will say, We have seen Thee: and Thou wilt be That, and I shall not be there at all.'[13]

Any authentic intimacy with Allah requires a dying-to-self since, from the Sufis' point of view, it is God who causes one to die from self, and to live in God. Allah then becomes lover, beloved and the act of loving itself.

The best way to prepare for dying is to practice the sacred art of dying while alive. Practicing *fana* is to concentrate one's purpose on loving God everywhere, in everyone, and on maintaining recollection upon God's truth. One's soul begins to enter into intimate conversation with God, while eating, drinking, working, sleeping, in all motions. And when God's nearness possesses one's heart, "it overwhelms all else, both the inward infiltrations of the purposes and the outward motions of the members."[14]

In some forms of Sufism, where *fana* developed into a discipline, a disciple was said to pass through three stages. In the first stage, the disciple asked for forgiveness from God and sought purification. In the second stage, the disciple blessed the Prophet Muhammad and became absorbed in Muhammad's vision of Allah. Finally, neither the disciple nor the Prophet existed. Everything, including the disciples' self-identity, was extinguished into Allah. Al-Ghazali writes: "When the worshiper no longer thinks of his worship or himself but is altogether absorbed in Him whom he worships, that state is called *fana*."[15] As in Zen, the one who practices the process of self-extinction dies before dying, never to die again.

Death Ritual

While there are many different popular Islamic practices, generally the Muslim tradition dictates that a person who shows signs of dying (*muhtader*) should be positioned on his or her back, head facing Mecca. The room is perfumed, and anyone who is unclean or menstruating leaves the room. Some Islamic traditions describe the visit of *Iblis*, the evil one, who tempts the dying person to deny Allah. At the same time, appropriate *suras* from the Qur'an are recited by the dying person or, if he or she is unable, by a relative. Then the basic creed of Islam—"There is no God but Allah and Muhammad is his Prophet"—is recited. The dying person is also expected to repent of all earthly sins. With the holy name of Allah in the heart, the Muslim is ready to pass into the next world.

Once dead, mouth and eyes are closed, feet are tied together, and the body is covered with a sheet. While it is unlawful to recite from the Qur'an near the deceased, a prayer, like the following, would be uttered:

> O Allah, ease upon him his matters, and make light for him whatever comes hereafter, and honour him with Your meeting and make that which he has gone to better than that which he came out from.
> O Allah, forgive me and him, and grant me a good reward after him. And those who are grieved by this demise may read:
> To Allah do we belong, and to him shall we return.
> O Allah, reward me in my affliction, and requite me with something better than this.[16]

The dead body is then gently cleaned, perfumed, and wrapped in white cotton by members of the family. As in Judaism, embalming is not practiced. Prayers for the dead are performed in a disciplined manner by the company present, usually an Imam (teacher) and his followers who say customary prayers for the deceased, some silently and some out loud. Prayers for the dead are recited in a standing position only, for in Islam no bowing or prostrations are allowed, except before Allah.

The deceased is then placed in a plain wooden coffin and carried to the place of burial. As the coffin is carried the bearers repeat the prayer: "God is great, God is merciful." The body is taken from the coffin and lowered into a six-foot-deep grave. All those present cover the body with flowers and dirt, and pour over it blessed rose water. Prayers remind the mourners that the deceased is created from dust and to dust returns, that through death we return to await our fate, and that we will be raised at the Last Judgment.

We have mentioned how the great teachers died (e.g., Buddha, Socrates and Jesus), that they died as they lived because they were able to live the way they died. What about Muhammad? How did he die? We must remember that unlike Jesus and Buddha, he was not an incarnate, or awakened, master, and, unlike Socrates, it was not his wisdom that he taught. Therefore the story of Muhammad's personal life is subordinated to the will of Allah.

Two years after establishing Islam as the faith of the Arab world, while on a pilgrimage in Mecca and surrounded by a multitude of fervent followers, the Prophet delivered what was to be his farewell address. He told the loyal assembly that he bore witness to none but Allah, who wanted all un-Islamic customs and all blood-feuds to be wiped out, who wanted wives treated with utmost respect, who wanted there to be no preference between Arab and non-Arab, between white and dark-skinned, and who wanted the rituals mentioned in Allah's book (the Qur'an) to be rigorously observed. If Allah's authority is observed, Muhammad continued, then you shall be admitted into His paradise.

There was a tremendous response and the people affirmed: "You have discharged in full your obligations as Prophet and Messenger." As soon as he concluded, a revelation came to him: "Today I (Allah) have perfected your religion for you, and I have completed My blessing upon you, and I have approved Islam for your religion" (*Sura* 5:5).

After his return from the Farewell Pilgrimage, he was seized with a violent headache and fever which passed away as quickly as it had come. At this time he received the following revelation:

> Now that Allah's succour has become manifest and victory has been achieved, and thou hast seen people join the religion of Allah in large numbers, then glorify thy Lord, with His praise, and seek forgiveness of Him for their frailties. Surely, He is Oft-Returning with compassion.[17]

He interpreted this to mean that his task had been fulfilled and that his time on earth was drawing to a close. For a day or two he continued to lead prayer services even though his sickness returned upon him with increasing pain. After a fortnight, his fever rose. In the midst of his agony, tradition has it, he said: "Suffering is an expiation for sin. If a believer suffer but the scratch of a thorn, the Lord raiseth his rank thereby, and wipeth away from him a sin."[18]

Finally, exhausted, Muhammad was stretched upon a pallet on the floor of his wife's chamber. Tenderly she raised his head to her bosom. In a whisper she heard: "To the blessed Companionship On High; to the blessed Companionship On High . . . "[19] And then there was silence.

NOTES

[1]*Sura* 23:14–16. This and the following passages are selected from the Qur'an and translated by Abdullah Yushf Ali in his *The Holy Qur'an* (Lahore, Pakistan: Sh. Muhammad Ashraf Publishers, 1934).

[2]*Sura* 22:5–8.

[3]*Sura* 2:34–35.

[4]*Sura* 2:36.

[5]*Sura* 2:38–39.

[6]*Sura* 22:66.

[7]*Sura* 14:28–30.

[8]*Sura* 16:30–31. Elsewhere Allah promised believing men and women "gardens in which rivers flow" and where the greatest of all is "Allah's good pleasure" (*Sura* 9:72).

[9]*Sura* 56:8–10.

[10]*Sura* 56:47–50.

[11]*Sura* 69–18. In *Sura* 75 ("Resurrection") Allah is depicted as the one who gathers the bones of the dead together, even reshaping his fingertips, on "Resurrection Day" when the "sun and moon are brought together."

[12]Quoted in A. J. Arberry's *Sufism* (New York: Harper & Row, 1950), 53.

[13]*Ibid.*, 55.

[14]*Ibid.*, 56.

[15]Quoted in Edward Rice's *Eastern Definitions* (New York: Doubleday, 1980), 135.

[16]A traditional prayer. On Muslim graves centuries old, and today, one finds the words: "We are God's and to Him we return."

[17]*Sura* 110:2–4.

[18]Muhammad Zafrulla Khan, *Muhammad: Seal of the Prophets* (London: Routledge & Kegan Paul, 1980), 255.

[19]*Ibid.,* 257.

JOURNAL EXERCISES

1. What does the Qur'anic version of creation add to the Judaeo-Christian version? Is there finally any difference between the Islamic view of death and (a) the Jewish view? (b) the Christian view?
2. Why does the Qur'an stress the Day of Judgment? Does it resemble the Egyptian "weighing of the Soul"?
3. Compare what Sufi Dhu'l-Nun writes—"I die, yet not die in me"—with the Zen master's dying to the self while still alive. What would a Zen Buddhist say about Allah?
4. In what way do you understand *fana* (extinction)? How does one both pass away into God and, at the same time, die to the self?
5. Reread the final prayer prayed over the dead body. What is the connection mentioned in the prayer between the prayer itself and the one who prays?
6. How might an intelligent spiritually, practicing *Muslim* answer the following question: What does your tradition teach about how to die artfully? That is, what is the most sacred way of dying?

Chapter 12 AMERICAN INDIAN ATTITUDES TOWARD DEATH

Ho Ka Hey
Today's a good day to die.
Chief Crazy Horse

As with each of the traditions studied in this text, when discussing the North American Indian's beliefs about dying, we must remember that we are discussing a great variety of cultural expressions, and that we can only make large generalizations here. For of the multitude of Native American Indian tribes (e.g., the Seminole in Florida, the Cherokee and Powhatan in the southeast; the Chippewa, Oneida and Mohawk in the northeast, the Lakota Sioux, Winnebago, Arapaho and Shoshoni across the northern plains, the Apache, Hopi, and Navajo in the southwest, and the Squamish and Spokane in the northwest), in what follows we will focus largely on the traditions of the Yaqui and the Lakota Sioux.

Indian cultures have been present in the Americas for at least thirty thousand years, and have expressed their attitude toward death in poems, songs, stories, rituals and ceremonies. Furthermore, as with other traditional cultures, Indian language has had a special, evocative potency. Since words share in the power of what they name, and since what is named is made present, when the Lakota recite creation myths, for example, the narrative becomes a reenactment of the creative event. In what follows we will briefly examine Carlos Castaneda's account of what he learned from a Yaqui sorcerer Don Juan.

Concepts of Death

One of the best known death songs was sung by the Sioux warrior Chief Crazy Horse just before he entered into battle:

Hoka hey! Follow me
Today is a good day to fight
Today is a good day to die.[1]

Each morning the Oglala Sioux warrior said *ho ka hey* (it's a good day to die), thus expressing a willingness to surrender to death at any time, fearlessly.

The trained warrior Don Juan Matus, a Yaqui Indian sorcerer, was one who practiced this sacred art of dying. He treated death as if it were a constant companion. In *The Teachings of Don Juan* and *A Separate Reality*, Don Juan teaches the American anthropology student, Carlos Castaneda, how to become a man of knowledge, to explore non-ordinary realities, to contact the power of an ally, and to experience the crack between the worlds. In the third book, *Journey to Ixtlan,* he teaches Carlos that death is waiting for each person and that one must focus on the link between life and death without remorse or anxiety: "Our death is waiting and this very act we're performing now may well be our last battle on earth," Don Juan instructs. "I call it a battle because it is a struggle. Most people move from act to act without any struggle or thought," he continues. Since a hunter "has an intimate knowledge of his death, he proceeds judiciously, as if every act were his last battle."[2]

Early in 1961, Carlos reports visiting Don Juan to ask him about the ritualistic use of peyote. "He looked at me," Carlos says, "as if I were crazy, and then, as we walked, warned me repeatedly about the uselessness of my self-importance and personal history." His words put Carlos in a turmoil, as they usually did, and Carlos became depressed and dejected. Don Juan at that point told Carlos to turn to his left. When he did, he experienced the sensation of a flickering shadow. "Death just gave you a warning," Don Juan said. "Death is our eternal companion. It is always to our left, at arm's length."[3] Don Juan revealed an essential ingredient in the American Indian attitude toward death when he said:

> "The thing to do when you're impatient," he proceeded, "is to turn to your left and ask advice from your death. An immense amount of pettiness is dropped if your death makes a gesture to you, or if you catch a glimpse of it, or if you just have the feeling that your companion is there watching you."[4]

Mother Earth

American Indians practiced a way of life much like the Chinese, in which nature was sacred and life was lived ritualistically. Mother earth was respected as a vehicle through which the Great Spirit (*Wakan tanka*) flowed. By their late thirties and early forties, all persons who treated all of nature as sacred (e.g., the four-leggeds, the trees, the bugs, the winged creatures, the rocks) became themselves sacred (*wakan*). Every day the Sioux Indian expressed gratefulness to *Wakan tanka* for being allowed to walk on the earth, and for the earth's abundance of vegetation and game.

In this worldview, of course, the white Europeans' attempt to buy land from the Indians was considered by the Indians as total foolishness. A letter written in 1855 to President Franklin Pierce by Chief Sealth (Seattle) of the Duwamish Tribe in Washington expresses this view:

> How can you buy or sell the sky—the warmth of the land? The idea is strange to us. Yet we do not own the freshness of the air or the sparkle of the water. How can you buy them from us? We will decide in our time. Every part of this earth is sacred to my people. Every shining pine needle, every sandy shore, every mist in the dark woods, every clearing and humming insect is holy in the memory and experience of my people.[5]

Chief Sealth bemoaned the white man's way of replacing open space with buildings, of replacing the cry of whippoorwills with the clatter of city-life, for the white man does not seem to notice the air that he breathes. "Like a man dying for many days," the Chief writes, "he is numb to the stench." The Indian, on the other hand, true to the ancient ways, preferred to remain connected to the prairies, rivers, woods, and animals in their unaltered nature.

The Sacred Pipe

We have said that for American Indians all of life was lived within the context of rituals and ceremonies. The thread that bound them together was the sacred pipe, the pipe of peace brought by the miraculous coming of White Buffalo Calf Woman. In both *Black Elk Speaks* and the *Sacred Pipe*, Black Elk tells the following story of the gift of the pipe (called cannunpa).

Early one morning many winters ago, two hunters, standing on a hill looking for game, saw coming toward them a very beautiful woman dressed in white buckskin. One of the warriors had bad intentions toward the sacred woman, but she caused a cloud to cover him. When it lifted, he was nothing but bones, and terrible snakes were eating him. Black Elk emphasized the universal truth of this story, explaining that anyone who is attached to the senses is consumed by passion's snakes. The sacred (*wakan*) woman in white then instructed the other warrior to return to his people and to prepare a ceremonial lodge for her coming.

When the lodge was completed she came, took a bundle from her back, held it out with both hands in front of the chief, and said: "Behold this and always love! It is *lela wakan* (very sacred), and you must treat it as such."[6]

After this, the mysterious woman took from the bundle a sacred pipe and presented it to the Chief:

"With this sacred pipe you will walk upon the Earth; for the Earth is your Grandmother and Mother, and She is sacred. Every step that is taken upon Her should be as a prayer. The bowl of this pipe is of red stone; it is the Earth. Carved in the stone and facing the center is this buffalo calf who represents all the four-leggeds who live upon your Mother. The stem of the pipe is of wood, and this represents all that grows upon the Earth. And these twelve feathers which hang here where the stem fits into the bowl are from *Wanbli Gleshka,* the Spotted Eagle, and they represent the eagle and all the wingeds of the air. All these peoples, and all the things of the universe, are joined to you who smoke the pipe—all send their voices to *Wakan tanka,* the Great Spirit. When you pray with this pipe, you pray for and with everything."[7]

From this time on, the people took the holy pipe and sent their voices to *Wakan tanka*. Elders of each tribe, for instance, would sit in the chief tipi in a circle around the central fire. After an invocation, the pipe was lit and passed from hand to hand around the circle.

For the power of the sacred pipe to be efficacious, it had to be handled carefully, as one would hold an egg, for if dropped, that person was no longer worthy to take care of it. As the pipe was filled, prayers and songs were offered to invite the powers of the universe to be present. When the fire (The Great Spirit) was brought to the bowl, heaven, earth and humanity were intimately joined. Mingling one's breath (*ni*) with the tobacco smoke, the Great Spirit was inhaled, and in the process the smoker sacrificed the self who smoked. Inhaling, the smoker drew in all the elements, the powers of the four directions (north, east, south, west), and, exhaling, expanded out into the wholeness of nature. Smoking the pipe shattered the illusion of separation, and increased one's awareness of connectedness to all of nature. As if prayer, as if a sacrament, as if yoga, as if a meditation, the ritual of the pipe reunited the smokers with their Holy origins.

Afterdeath

Like the Chinese, generally the North American Indians believed in the existence of two souls. One soul was the spirit or breath (*ni*) or vital force of the body. The second soul, called the "free" soul or *nagi,* left the body during sickness or dreams. At death, the free soul migrated to the land of the dead.

To be more specific, when a person dies his or her *ni* departs. It is believed that all supernatural beings and powers and all animate and inanimate objects have innate power called *sicun* (shi-cun) which is immortal. At birth a person is given a *sicun* by the supernaturals and guardian spirits. At death the *sicun* returns to the supernaturals. The *sicun* of things makes reincarnation possible; in fact it is believed that sacred men are usually invested with the *sicun* of a deceased sacred man.

When a person physically dies, he or she loses his or her *ni* (life breath) and his or her body decays back to the elements. The *nagi* however lingers on near his or her kinsmen and kinswomen. The Lakota Sioux believe that this is a dangerous time because the soul longs for the company of its loved ones. This beloved soul is kept by the parents or loved ones for one year afterward when it is freed for the last time. It will then depart to the south on the Ghost Road (*wanagi tacanku,*) which is lit by the campfires of traveling spirits or souls.

At the end of their journey he or she is met by an old woman (*winuhcala*) who evaluates actions and deeds during his or her mortal lifetime. Those who are judged as good people continue along to a good place with *ni*, while those who are thought of as bad or evil are pushed over a cliff and their spirits return to the earth. These doomed spirits continue to contribute to the evil forces which threaten the well-being of the living.[8]

Death Ritual

We have already said that the White Buffalo Calf Woman brought the central ritual, that of the sacred pipe. She also brought other ceremonies which functioned as satellites around the nucleus of the sacred pipe. Of the various rites brought by the White Buffalo Calf Woman—the sweat lodge ceremony and the vision quest, the sun dance, the bonding for life, the girl's puberty ceremony, and throwing the ball—we will concentrate here only on one, namely keeping the soul or "Ghost Keeping."

Black Elk explains the meaning and ritual practice of this ceremony in the story of Standing Hollow Horn. When Standing Hollow Horn's child died, he went with the child's body and announced, to his friends, that he was going to keep his child's soul with his family, and that through this the family would be *wakan*. He then took a lock of the child's hair, and as he cut it he prayed:

"O *Wakan tanka*, behold us! It is the first time that we do Thy will in this way, as You have taught us through the sacred woman. We will keep the soul of this child so that our Mother the Earth will bear fruit, and so that our children will walk the path of life in a sacred manner."[9]

He ritualistically blessed and purified his child's hair over the smoke, wrapped it in buckskin, and laid it in a special place within the tipi. The pipe was then lit, smoked and passed (toward the east) around the circle. Prayers were offered, consecrating their intentions to make sacred their family's way.

A bundle was then made of the child's body, and it was taken away from the camp and left on a scaffold with some of the child's possessions (e.g., bow and shield), which would be returned to the agents of heaven (i.e., winds, rains, the wingeds), each of which absorbed a part. Addressing himself in the presence of his family and tribal members Hollow Horn then said: "You are now keeping the soul of your own son who is not dead, but is with you."[10] One can imagine that this ceremony and the keeping of the soul cast a special presence in the family atmosphere while it remained with them.

But the soul was not kept indefinitely. Within six months to a year and a half, a second ceremony was performed called the "Releasing of the Soul." As with the Keeping of the Soul, with the release of the soul the entire community was present. Buffalo were killed, food was prepared, and the tribal leaders were assembled. The sacred pipe was readied and prayers were offered to the four directions. The bowl of the pipe was then placed over the fire in such a way that smoke passed through the stem-end which pointed to heaven. In this way, *Wakan tanka* smoked first, thus purifying the pipe. Also, in this way, the smokers were *wakan* as the soul was released.

Food that was to be given to the soul was then brought in by four virgins. The keeper of the soul dug a small hole at the foot of the "soul post" into which the prepared food was put. It was then covered with dirt as the family prayed that the soul would not forget them on its journey. Then the keeper of the soul took the soul bundle and, after touching it to each of the virgins, carried it outside the lodge and cried: "Behold your people! Look back upon them!"[11] The moment the soul bundle left the lodge, the soul was released and departed on the spirit path.

It was believed that at a fork in the road, an old woman (Maya Winuhcala) sat to judge each soul. Those who passed to the right were united with *Wakan tanka*. Those who passed to the left remained as disembodied souls, until properly purified.

We began by saying that the American Indians expressed their attitudes toward death in poems and songs. And we have seen that one type of death-related song was received in a vision, like the one chanted by Chief Crazy Horse before going into battle. Another type was the song composed at the hour of one's death, and chanted with the dying breath. The following song was written by a member of the Ojibwa tribe in Canada who confronted death far from home:

> If I die here in a strange land,
> If I die in a land not my own,
> Nevertheless the thunder,
> The rolling thunder,
> Will take me home.
> If I die here, the wind,
> The wind rushing over the prairie,
> The wind will take me home.
> The wind and the thunder,
> They are the same everywhere,
> What does it matter, then,
> If I die here in a strange land?[12]

NOTES

[1]James La Pointe, *Legends of the Lakota* (San Francisco: Indian Historical Press, 1976), 160.

[2]Carlos Castaneda, *Journey to Ixtlan* (New York: Simon and Schuster, 1972), 112.

[3]*Ibid.*, 54.

[4]*Ibid.*, 55.

[5]Quoted in "Environmental Action," November 11, 1972.

[6]Black Elk, *The Sacred Pipe*, recorded and edited by Joseph Epes Brown (New York: Penguin Books, 1971), 5.

[7]*Ibid.*, 5–7.

[8]I owe the information in these last two paragraphs to Alan Leventhal of San Jose State University, Department of Anthropology, and to his "father" Urban Timothy White Weasel. For further information see William Powers, *Oglala Religion* (Nebraska: University of Nebraska Press, 1977).

[9]*The Sacred Pipe*, 12.

[10]*Ibid.*, 14.

[11]*Ibid.*, 29.

[12]Thomas E. Sanders and Walter W. Peek, eds., *Literature of the American Indian* (Beverly Hills: Glencoe Press, 1976), 83.

JOURNAL EXERCISES

1. What did it mean for Native Americans to sing each morning: "Today is a good day to die"? How do you think such a discipline would affect a person's life?

2. What does Don Juan teach Carlos Castaneda about death, and how did Carlos respond to it? Can you imagine experiencing the persona of death behind your left shoulder? What would you say to death if you could see death?

3. In what way does death enter the story of the bringing of the sacred pipe by the White Buffalo Calf Woman? Do you agree with Black Elk's interpretation of the story?

4. In what way did smoking the sacred pipe prepare one to die? What was the relationship between smoking the pipe and sacrifice?

5. What psychological effect do you think the keeping of the soul ritual would have on the family who was keeping the deceased's soul? Is there any western practice similar to this one?

6. What might a Native American do just before dying? In what other tradition was this practiced? If you were dying what would your song be?

Chapter 13 DYING ALL DEATHS

> I have already died all deaths,
> And I am going to die all deaths again. . . .
> H. Hesse, *Poems*

From the earliest beginnings of recorded civilization, cultures have developed rituals and beliefs which account for the seeming absurdity of death. In the last eleven chapters we have examined a variety of death related customs and rituals which include the disposal of the corpse (e.g., cremation, burial, scaffolding), the posture and wrapping of the body (e.g., mummification, enshrouding, robing), and funerary rites (e.g., prayers, processions, lamentations).

Along with these variations in ritual practice, each sacred tradition has expressed itself in myths or sacred stories which present the inner significance of death. We have also examined the major symbols in each of the traditions: from the True Self of the Hindus to the no-self of the Buddhists; from the reverence for the dead of the Chinese to the Great Death of Zen Buddhists and the Clear Light of the Tibetans; from societal immortality of the Mesopotamians to the weighing of the soul of the Egyptians; and from the immortality of the soul of the Greeks to the resurrection of the body of Jews, Christians and Muslims. What sense can we make of these varying images, doctrines and rituals? Is there anything they share in common?

There have been many scholarly attempts to draw comparative themes from materials in the preceding chapters. British historian Arnold Toynbee, in an essay entitled "Man's Concern with Life after Death," writes:

> At the present day the belief in a reembodiment of the dead is still officially obligatory for all Zoroastrians, Jews, Christians, Muslims, Hindus, and Buddhists; and these six religions, between them, still command the adherence of a great majority of mankind. The teaching of the first four of these religions is that a human being lives only a single life; that his soul survives his death, disembodied; and that, at some unpredictable future date, every soul will be reembodied in order to undergo the Last Judgment and, according to the verdict, to enjoy physical bliss in Heaven or physical anguish in Hell. The teaching of Hinduism and Buddhism is that a soul (or, a Buddhist would say, a not yet cleared karma-account) is reborn in psychosomatic form not just once but a number of times.[1]

For Toynbee, the comparison of eastern and western attitudes toward death and dying is presented by the image of the body reduced to reincarnation versus the resurrection of the body. In his view, this distinction represents the major difference between the sacred traditions—multiple lives versus one life, one death, one resurrection.

From our point of view, however, when we review the various teachings and texts represented here, a common process emerges: if one wishes to discover what a sacred tradition teaches about death and dying, the source of those teachings can be found in that culture's creation mythology. In fact, it can be said that by and large creation myths implicitly if not explicitly tell a story whose characters outlive the seeming finale of death, and in so doing reveal the destiny of humankind. In this chapter we will compare world religious views on death by focusing on the reciprocal relationship between death attitudes and creation stories.

Hebrew Creation

From time's beginning, two of the most fundamental and perplexing human questions have been: Where do I come from? and Where am I going after death? In what follows we will briefly compare ways in which these questions have been answered in the sacred traditions of India and the Near East. The significance of this comparison becomes evident when we realize that explanations of death seem to be contained in, and determined by, stories of creation. That is, each culture's creation story contains, at the same time, its deepest response to the problem of dying. Here we will examine and compare Jewish, Christian, Hindu and Buddhist stories of creation and death.

In the beginning, the Hebrew God created everything from a "formless void," from chaos or nothingness. After separating the dark from the light, and the land from the waters, God created the sun, the moon and the stars, the plants, the fowl of the air, the fish of the sea, and the beasts of the earth. Finally, God created Adam in his own image. God breathed life into a human body made from the dust of the ground. Then from Adam's rib God brought forth the female, Eve. Placed in the Garden of Eden, Adam and Eve were told that they could eat of any tree except the tree of the Knowledge of Good and Evil. God warned them, "You must not eat of it lest you die." However, the serpent, the most subtle of all God's creations, tempted them to eat. "You will not die!" the serpent assured them. "In fact you will be like gods, knowing good and evil." They did eat, and as a result of this disobedience, Adam and Eve were banished from the Garden forever. Angels with flaming swords were posted at the gate to guard the way back to the tree of Immortal Life, lest they eat from it in the fallen state. The fall of the first parents had two major results: human beings had to enter a world in which death is inevitable. Thus, for the Hebrews, creation is *separation*.

Hindu Creation

Death also plays an important role in the Hindu accounts of creation found in the Vedas. In one, the world was created by the sacrificial dismembering of the cosmic giant, Purusa, the man of a thousand heads, a thousand eyes, and a thousand feet. From his dismemberment, all things came into existence. In another, and perhaps the most famous Hindu creation story, in the beginningless beginning, before sky or signs, before death and immortality, "That One" breathed breathlessly. From desire, which arises in "That One," "everything comes to be . . . " AUM signified the soundless sound of "That One." But, as the story further relates, the sages and priests of the Vedic sacrifice were perplexed. They asked themselves and each other about the source of this emanation. Who can possibly know? Even "That One," perhaps, does not know. But through profound meditation and yoga they realized that the mystery of creation is beyond human knowing.

For the Hindu, human beings are emanations of the Divine Force, and they contain the Divine within themselves. In recognition of this indwelling divinity, for example, Hindus greet each other with "Namas Te"—"I bow to the Divine in you." In the Hindu view of creation as emanation, humans are ignorant of their True Self, their original nature. There is only one True Self and each individual is a unique expression of It.

If the beginning is beginningless, what happens at death? Hindus believe that when a person dies the gross physical body separates from the subtle body, *jiva* or soul. Rebirth, or redeath as Buddhists call it, is the transmigration of the psychic sub-stratum of the individual person from one body to another. Thus, when a person dies the old body is no longer of any use. An elaborate set of death ceremonies includes the cremation of the corpse and sacrificial offerings made to the astral or ghostly body as it progresses to its next life-form. At death, the soul is purged of its earthly or karmic cravings and experiences heaven, symbolized in various paintings by a divine garden. The length of this experience of bliss is in direct proportion to the *jiva's* accumulation of life-merits. After the appropriate interval, the purified *jiva* takes on a fresh body, one whose dignity is determined by past-life choices, and is reborn. Until one wakes up and realizes True Self, he or she is condemned to be reborn, at death, into another life-form.

Search for Immortality

The continuous cycle of life through various reincarnations does not play a significant role in western attempts to comprehend death. Instead it is the fearful awareness of death's finality that is characteristic of western thought.

The *Epic of Gilgamesh* tells of a hero's unsuccessful search for immortality. At the beginning of the epic, Gilgamesh, the hero, is weeping bitterly over the body of his friend Enkidu who had been killed. Gilgamesh laments: "When I die, shall I not be like Enkidu?" Filled with grief and resolve, Gilgamesh immediately resolves to search for the meaning of death, convinced that something must survive it. He seeks Utnapishtim, the only mortal known to have achieved immortality. He crosses the sea of death finally and finally meets Utnapishtim, who tells him that death is final, a natural part of the human process and that "While the gods determine life and death, the number of life's days are not revealed."

When Utnapishtim is about to send Gilgamesh back home, his wife urges him to send Gilgamesh away with a gift. "I will disclose a hidden thing to you," he says to Gilgamesh. Utnapishtim tells him of a plant "whereby one may regain life's breath," a plant which rejuvenates the eater. Gilgamesh dives into a pool of water, brings it back and so happily begins his boat ride back across the sea of death to his home. However, a serpent emerges from the sea and carries it off. At the story's end, Gilgamesh realizes that human fate and mortality are in the hands of the gods, that human society is the only immortality that can be achieved, and that the possibility for rejuvenation cannot be retained.

The Hindu *Upanishads* offer a contrast in the story of Nachiketas. One day Nachiketas observes his father performing the fire sacrifice with an impure heart. In an attempt to understand the meaning of sacrifice and death, Nachiketas visits Yama, the God of Death, in his underworld kingdom. Because he waits patiently for three days for Yama to appear, Yama grants him three boons. First, Nachiketas asks that his father will not be worried about his safety. Second, he asks the secret of the fire sacrifice. Third, he asks Yama to explain what happens at death. And Yama answers: "The wise realize through meditation the timeless, divine Self. This Self—*Atman*—is unborn, undying. When the body dies the Self does not die. The one who knows the omnipresent Self puts death to death." While the near eastern story dramatizes human limitation in the face of death, the Hindu account portraits the realization of the deathless Self.

The Eternal Self

Hindu mythology weaves together many figures associated with this realization such as Yama, whom we have seen, and Kali, who wears a garland of skulls and a skirt composed of severed hands, who drinks blood and who presides over destruction and death. Kali's husband, Shiva, is also the god of death and of creative destruction. In later representations, Shiva is depicted as a dancer with four arms ringed with holy flames. The Dancing Shiva destroys evil so that at the same time new beauty can be born. Beneath Shiva's foot is the dwarf, who represents evil forces. Shiva's dance embodies the principle that the world is always in the flux of being created and destroyed.

By far the most popular Hindu story dealing with death is that of the Warrior Arjuna and his charioteer, the Lord Krishna. Krishna is an incarnation of Vishnu (the Preserver), who comes to save his people from the forces of evil. In the beginning of the *Bhagavad Gita,* Arjuna throws down his bow in the midst of battle and refuses to fight. "Why should I fight," he asks, "when if I win, I lose because my kinsmen will be dead!" Krishna tells Arjuna to fight, not only because it is his caste duty, but also because Atman is *birthless* and *deathless:*

> "If the slayer believes that he can slay or the slain believes that he can be slain, neither knows the truth. The eternal self slays not, nor is ever slain."[2]

In a moment of sheer ecstasy, Krishna reveals his cosmic body. Arjuna recognizes Krishna as Vishnu and dies spiritually to his own separate identity. Krishna further says to Arjuna: "If a person is meditating upon me at the moment of death, that person shall come straight to me." Such a person would thus break the repetitive cycle of life and death, and would become eternally present as *Atman.*

Consciousness of Nirvana

Krishna's challenge to meditate on him at the moment of death led to a tradition among some Hindu monks of attempting to transcend death by meditating on it. The practitioner sought to quiet senses and thoughts in order to discover the inner tranquility of True Self by one's own efforts. Such an experience of death through meditation profoundly affected the young prince Siddhartha Gautama, who lived in the sixth century BCE. While in his late thirties, as the texts relate, Siddhartha encountered old age, sickness, and death. Each experience raised questions he could not answer. "If I am only going to die," he wondered, "why live?" His question, like those of Gilgamesh and Arjuna before him, echoes a universal human concern.

For six years Siddhartha followed the teachings of Hindu ascetics, meditating, begging, starving himself in an attempt to answer his questions. Emaciated, weakened, and unenlightened he decided that such excesses would not help him find enlightenment. He resolved to sit under a Bodhi tree, the tree of transcendental Wisdom, and, not moving, to meditate until he was fully awakened. He passed through four watches of the night in which Siddhartha came to realize the source of all previous lives, the omnipotent eye, the overcoming of *karmic* influences, and the complete emptying of self-identity. During that intense period, Siddhartha became the Buddha which means the Awakened or Enlightened One. He died to his old, *karmically* imprisoned self, to any belief in the True Self of the Hindus. He discovered that he had no name, no form, no thoughts, and that no separate existence could identify him. He became the Buddha, the Awakened, *Tathagata,* the Traceless One.

Buddha's entire teaching is summed up by the term *anatta,* a death to the idea of a self. For Buddha there is no permanent self underlying name, form, sensation, feelings and consciousness. Only action exists; there is no one who acts. Death therefore is an illusion. Just as there is no one who dies, for Buddha there is no one who is reborn. This teaching is illumined by another, *nirvana,* which means extinction. Attachments to ideas, including the idea of immortality, die in *nirvana.*

Once a disciple came to the Buddha and asked: "What happens to the soul at death? Does it live on?" The Buddha answered: "You are like a man who has been shot in the back with an arrow and wonders who shot him, from where, with what trajectory? These are stupid questions. The real question is: How can I be liberated from suffering?" Since death was not to be feared, Buddhist monks could be found sitting quietly at burning sites amid bones and the charred remains of bodies, meditating upon death. Death for them was not a physical event, but rather a spiritual method for awakening consciousness of *nirvana.*

Dying Sacramentally

Christians too prepared for death and eternal life through meditation. Meditating on a skull or on the crucified Christ was common practice in the Middle Ages and the Renaissance. Such meditation was intended to make the believer aware of the brevity of life and of the need to be prepared at any instant for death. It was a moral admonition to live piously in order to achieve a state of grace when death struck and so avoid damnation for eternity. Books on how to make a good death were carefully studied by the faithful since the moment of death was so feared. Contemplation of Christ's sacrifice was an important aid at this perilous time, for just as Christ had died and been resurrected, so, too, the believer would be resurrected at the last day. However, this knowledge would not save him or her from the rigors of death or of purgatory.

According to medieval Christian theologians, at death the soul leaves the body. The soul is met by several angels who conduct the soul through its journey into the afterlife. The soul continues striving in the next life for purification. In purgatory the soul suffers for sins committed on earth, whether gluttony, avarice, pride or lust, or any of the other numerous offenses against God and humanity. Prayers of the living, as well as intercession by the saints, are offered to assist and support souls through this difficult journey. It is not until Christ's second coming that the Final Judgment is consummated when bodies are resurrected and rejoin their souls. And at that time, each traveler proceeds to his or her own final destination, either to heaven or to hell.

According to the Catholic and Orthodox tradition, death is viewed liturgically as a sacrament. Just as *The Tibetan Book of the Dead* prepared its hearers for death, just as Krishna urged Arjuna to meditate on him at death, what is variously called "Extreme Unction," "Last Rights," or the "Sacrament of the Sick" prepares the Christian for entrance into afterlife. At the sacrament, the dying person makes his or her last confession, is forgiven for sins and is anointed with olive oil. And since a Catholic's last words form a pathway into the life-death transition, they often will be prayerful. For example, one might repeat over and over, almost like a prayer *mantra:* "Holy Mary, Mother of God, pray for us sinners now, and at the hour of our death!"

Eternal Cycles

We have now seen how answers to questions like "Where do I come from?" influence answers to questions like "What happens at death?" We have visualized the difference between the eastern view of creation as emanation, where all things emerge from and are part of the original creation, and the western view in which the creator creates through separation. And we have seen that each of the creation myths raises, at least implicitly, the problem of death. In the eastern tradition, we are born again and again until we discover our true identities. In the western tradition, because humankind is estranged from God, we must face our own death and seek salvation through it.

Each view, however, can be represented as a significant part of a cosmic circle which symbolizes the dynamic processes of creation, life, death and rebirth. This circle is reflected in an image from a sixteenth century altarpiece, in a twentieth century photograph of earth taken from outerspace, in a medieval Christian manuscript of God creating the world, in a Tibetan mandala, in the dancing images of the destroyers, Kali and Shiva, in the wheel of life from the Hindu chariot temple, in Gandhi's spinning wheel, in the rose window of a Gothic cathedral, and, finally, in the cross-section of a DNA molecule. Each cosmic circle revolves in its eternal cycles of creation, death and re-creation, and beckons the viewer to a deeper understanding of its mysteries. Hidden from full view, the spiritual geometry of each image symbolizes, in its own fashion, the source of human origins and human destiny.

NOTES

[1]See Arnold Toynbee and Arthur Koestler, eds., *Life After Death* (New York: McGraw-Hill, 1976), 29.

[2]Bhagavad Gita 2:19. Among the various death technologies, the eastern traditions have produced a wide variety which include the Hindu *savasana* ("corpse pose"), the Buddhist *vipasana* (mind in breath), and *zazen* (no-self sitting), the Chinese *ch'i kung* (body in breath), and the Tibetan "Ejection of Consciousness" (into the mind of the Buddha).

JOURNAL EXERCISES

1. Reread Arnold Toynbee's assessment of the various sacred traditions' teaching on life after death. Do you agree with his conclusion that the major east-west distinction is between reincarnation and the resurrection of the body?
2. Compare the Hindu myth of creation with the Judaeo-Christian myth. In what way(s) do their differences explain differences in their respective attitudes toward death?
3. Compare the story of Nachiketas to the story of Gilgamesh. Is there anything in the later story which could have happened to make it more comparable to the former one? What might that be?
4. Recall Krishna's admonition to Arjuna to meditate on him at the moment of death. Compare this practice with similar practices in other sacred traditions. What is your response to this comparison?
5. For you, finally, are there fundamental differences between the various sacred teachings in death which present one with a choice, or are these traditions variations on a common teaching?
6. Reflect for a moment on the entire text. Recall those thoughts and insights which stand out most dramatically in your mind. If you had to essentialize what you have gained from *The Sacred Art of Dying* what would it be? Can it be represented by one image or symbol?

Chapter 14   DYING BEFORE DYING: THE EXPERIENCE OF REBIRTH

Those who are dead
and yet fully alive . . .
enter in the city of love
unattached.

Haridas, *Bhattacharya*

No journey is complete without the last step. Ours will be to reanimate a fundamental teaching of the world's sacred traditions, namely that ordinary human consciousness is wounded or divided and that any healing or reunification (of the split of sinful, alienated or dualistic self) occurs as a function of spiritual death and rebirth. Not only is the seeker separated from the transformational source of being (be it God or True Self), but the seeker is also divided from the search itself by internalized anxieties, self-doubts and fears about living and dying. Spiritual death transforms the situation through a spiritual birth of the new self. This is nowhere more trenchantly expressed than in the Zen tradition where sages say that "one who dies before dying never dies again."[1] Our concluding motif will be that it is only by dying before dying, that is, dying spiritually and anticipatorally, that the experience of holistic rebirth occurs.

The Great Death

Of the many Zen stories which dramatize spiritual dying, that of D.T. Suzuki is especially important since he is largely responsible for bringing an initial understanding of Rinzai Zen to the West.[2] As a young teacher and translator of Buddhist materials, Suzuki tells how he struggled intellectually with the koan *Mu* (or "No") which his master had given to him. He remembered that in the *Zenkan Sakushin* he had read that all knowledge of Zen had to be transcended, and that when he became like a dead man, something would start up within him. Finally, knowing he was about to leave Japan for America, he poured all of his spiritual strength into *Mu*. He ate *Mu*, drank *Mu*, meditated on *Mu* and sat with *Mu* until spontaneously, intuitively, naturally, he ceased being conscious of *Mu*. He writes: "I was one with *Mu*, identified with *Mu,* so that there was no longer the separateness implied by being conscious of *Mu.*"[3]

As fascinated as one may be with Suzuki's *samadhi* (emptiness) or spiritual suicide, the real truth of the story, as Suzuki says, is coming out of that void-like state. True *satori* (enlightenment) is the awakening from spiritual death. Suzuki then, walking to his room, saw that the trees in the moonlight looked transparent to him. "And I was transparent too," he concluded.

We should be careful here to distinguish between what Zen calls the "Great Death" experience, which is the "Great Birth" as well, and what might be called "little deaths." Every time I change my ideas or beliefs, each time a relationship changes or dies, whenever I discover a better way to accomplish a task, whenever I have to wait in line, I experience little deaths. A portion of ego-consciousness is rearranged, material discarded, material added, attitudes redirected, but as irritating as they are, these deaths are not to be confused with Suzuki's "Great Death."

Psychologically speaking, Zen's Great Death is a death to or overcoming of one's dualistic, self-reflective awareness. In true self-awakening, "that which awakens is that which is awakened, that by which it is awakened, and that to which it is awakened."[4] Old subject-object, ego-non-ego images are reconciled. Non-dualistically, I am I, and you are you, *and* I am also simul-temporally and simultaneously you, and not-I. This root-self-transformation is the final step, the step of steps, when lover, beloved, and loving are not three.[5]

Having experienced the transformation of his ego, and having awakened to its true source, Suzuki was able to see *Mu,* to hear the sound of one hand clapping, to be fully transparent to mountains, rivers and stars. Koans, for him, became transfigured from conundrums requiring a solution to clarifications of his awakening. And, at the same time, D.T. Suzuki was still the D.T. Suzuki who existed dualistically in the phenomenal world. His ongoing experience of dying, while yet being fully alive, was also the source of his ongoing experience of rebirth.

To better understand this death/rebirth process, in what follows we shall cluster and discuss three integral elements: *confession* (a death to the fear of making public one's psychologically deadening anxieties); *conversion* (a death to one's prior ego-controlled tendencies and a birth to new self-awareness); *confirmation* (a death to the monologue of mistrust and the birth of compassion). While we will discuss these sequentially, their relationship is less one of causality and more one of mutual imminence in which each element expresses an interdependent uniqueness and catalyzes the other. We will conclude with the story of a pilgrimage to the headwaters of the Ganges where, in a eucharistic celebration, confession, conversation and confirmation become one.

Confession

> To whom do I tell these things? Not to
> you, my God, but before you I tell them
> to my own kind, to mankind, or to
> whatever small part of it may come upon
> these books of mine.[6]

If I were suddenly to step away from the established point of view of this essay and to insert here personal materials from my journals, the reader might begin to attend these pages with altered expectations. You might pay closer attention to the scenario. You might identify with parts of the story. You might even be tempted to create your own story, your own confession. I juxtapose "story" with "confession" because it is my conviction that every story is the confession of, or from, a human voice (sometimes called point of view), and that every confession tells part of the confessor's story.

We begin with confession not so much because it is necessarily or sequentially first, but because, as Carl Jung has remarked, every system or interpretation of psychological theory is also a "subjective confession." Even silence speaks. For example, in the same moment a Zen monk sits silently, facing a wall, simply breathing a meditative confession of Buddha-mind, and a Christian nun sits on her prayer stool silently praying the Jesus prayer, a devotional confession of faith in Christ. Each ritual witnesses to the confessor's perception of his or her reunification with the source of being and non-being.

The word confession suggests to some a literary genre, to others a form of psychotherapy or a holy sacrament. Yet in each, there is a common prerequisite, what William James called an "uneasiness," being conscious of a bifurcated, discordant, dualistic perception of the world. A personal confession, no matter what form it takes, usually expresses a sense of imperfection and incompleteness, an awareness of character-flaws and missed opportunities. Passionately called forth, the confession and the confessor recognize each other as if old friends, yet ironically they are separated from the source of the confession itself.

A most self-revealing example of the confessional voice is that of St. Augustine, bishop of Hippo (354–430), one of its creators, Augustine utilized the autobiographical mode to take his hearers into the storyteller's point of view. In this way, Augustine revealed secrets from his past and shared intimate details of his life with an unrelenting "restlessness." He provided at least eight justifications for writing the *Confessions:*

- as a testimony to sin (1:1);
- as purposeful recollection (2:1);

- to convince the teller and reader to realize the necessity of a contrite heart (2:3);
- as a healing catharsis and therapy (5:1);
- as a God-led recollection (9:7);
- as an act of thanksgiving (9:8);
- as a testimony to who he is now, not to who he was (10:4);
- to express both what he knows and does not know about himself (10:5).

When we look closer at the *Confessions,* nothing seems more obvious than Augustine's incessant attitude of guilty self-reproach, "Having turned from you, the One," Augustine laments, "I lost myself in the many." His initial confession, his fundamental disquietude toward self and others, psychologically reflects what William James calls a discordant personality, one melancholy with self-condemnation and a sense of sin.

James describes Augustine as a "divided self," citing passages like the following from the *Confessions:*

A new will, which had begun within me, to wish freely to worship you and find joy in you, O God, the sole sure delight, was not yet able to overcome that prior will, grown strong with age. Thus did my two wills, the one old, the other new, the first carnal, and the second spiritual, contend with one another, and by their conflict they laid waste my soul.[7]

Within Augustine, James recognized a constant movement and countermovement between his desire to conform his life to God's will and his sexual drives, between his strong desire to conform to his mother's wishes and his own need to be free from them. As long as Augustine experienced himself as divided from himself, and from God, he was without access to avenues for reunification. In Zen's understanding, when this point is reached, all seemingly subjective projections and all seemingly objective realities congeal and cease to function. Dualistic or divided consciousness can continue no further. Only when his habitual duplicity could neither be resolved nor sustained could Augustine finally die spiritually and thereby experience rebirth.

Just prior to his conversion experience, Augustine describes himself as torn between the carnal and the spiritual, a habitual inner conflict which became an existential necessity. While for Samuel Becket's characters habit was the great psychological deadener, for Augustine it took an act of dehabituation to transform his psychic conditioning, to trigger his spiritual death and rebirth. Having given full reign to his tears, in a moment of deep reflection, he heard the voice of a child chanting: "Take up and read. Take up and read" (8:12). When he did, he opened to a passage in the New Testament and read: "Not in rioting and drunkenness, not in chambering and impurities, not in strife and envying; but put you on the Lord Jesus Christ, and make not provision for the flesh in it concupiscences" (Rom 13:13-14). Instantly, by the end of Paul's sentence, a peaceful light streamed into his heart, doubt left him, and he resolved to become a sacrifice of praise.

Conversion

> To be converted, to be regenerated, to receive grace, to experience religion, to gain an assurance, are so many phrases which denote the process, gradual or sudden, by which a self hitherto divided, and consciously wrong, inferior and unhappy, becomes unified and consciously right, superior and happy, in consequence of its firmer hold upon religious realities.[8]

That conversion experiences are expressed through the confessional mode is evident in the following accounts. The first happened to Saul at the beginning of the first century on the road to Damascus. As he later described (in Acts 26:12-18), he was knocked to the ground by a light brighter than the sun, and heard a voice say: "Saul, Saul, why are you persecuting me?" Then, Jesus says: "It is hard for you, kicking like this against the goad."[9] Speaking Taoistically and psychotherapeutically, Jesus convinces Saul that he must reverse himself, that to be "righteous" he had to "serve" the Jesus whom he was persecuting. Saul was forced to totally surrender his misdirected, self-righteousness to Christ's goad or prod. For three days he was blinded. It was as if he had died. When Ananias later laid his hands on Saul, scales fell away from his eyes, and he could see again. Saul, who died to his self-divided egocentricism, was reborn as Paul-in-Christ.

At the beginning of the twentieth century a second confessional conversion is told of a young man in Madura, India who was suddenly overcome by a violent fear of death. Instead of resisting it, he had the presence of mind to surrender to the process. As a young man of seventeen, Ramana Maharshi recalls, he was sitting alone in his uncle's house when suddenly a violent fear of death overtook him.

> The shock of the fear of death drove my mind inwards and I said to myself mentally, without actually framing the words: "Now death has come; what does it mean? What is it that is dying? The body dies." And I at once dramatized the occurrence of death. I lay with

my limbs stretched out stiff as though *rigor mortis* had set in and imitated a corpse so as to give greater reality to the enquiry. I held my breath and kept my lips tightly closed so that no sound could escape, so that neither the word "I" nor any other word could be uttered. "Well then," I said to myself, "this body is dead. It will be carried stiff to the burning ground and there burnt and reduced to ashes. But with the death of this body am I dead? Is the body I? It is silent and inert but I feel the full force of my personality and even the voice of the 'I' within me, apart from it. So I am Spirit transcending the body. The body dies but the Spirit that transcends it cannot be touched by death. That means I am the deathless Spirit." All this was not dull thought; it flashed through me vividly as living truth which I perceived directly, almost without thought-process. "I" was something very real, the only real thing about my present state, and all the conscious activity connected with my body was centered on that "I". From that moment onwards the "I" or Self focussed attention on itself by a powerful fascination. Fear of death had vanished once and for all. Absorption in the Self continued unbroken from that time on.[10]

While the source of the conversions differs, a psychological description of the process would, from James' perspective, be similar. James describes the soul as an oscillation of interests and ideas between the center of one's habitual energies and the remoter outskirts of one's mind. To say that a person is converted means "that religious ideas, previously peripheral in consciousness, now take a central place, and that religious aims form the habitual center of energy."[11] What formerly occupied a cold place in consciousness becomes hot (James' terminology), and one's sensations, perceptions and attitudes recrystallize. For James, this occurs when a discordant self is reunified, when inactive memory from the subliminal or transmarginal region (the unconscious) becomes the fountainhead of one's ultimate convictions.

Admitting that psychology can only take us so far toward an understanding of the subconscious region, James describes the locus of conversion as a change of equilibrium in which both "self-surrender" and "a new determinism" simultaneously conspire. In our terms this means that spiritual death is simultaneously the act of spiritual rebirth, and that this death/rebirth process is the transformational core of human reunification.

A last question then arises: What is the result of this transformation? In what ways does this recrystallization of heart/mind or whole-soul influence a person's fundamental life-attitudes?

Confirmation

The human person needs confirmation because man as man needs it. An animal does not need to be confirmed, for it is what it is unquestionably. It is different with man: Sent forth from the natural domain of species into the hazard of the solitary category, surrounded by the air of a chaos which came into being with him, secretly and bashfully he watches for a Yes which allows him to be and which can come to him only from one human person to another.[12]

From Martin Buber's standpoint, the answer to the question is dramatically simple, for it occurs in creative lives of dialogue. Buber distinguished and recognized the relation between three dimensions of dialogue—acceptance, affirmation and confirmation. The three move from a generic acceptance (e.g., I accept you as a person like myself), to a specific affirmation of one's unique personhood (e.g., I affirm you in your difference from myself), and to a confirmation of the other (e.g., I trustingly validate you both now and in the future). Confirmation is mutual when, as Buber says, partners are able to "imagine the real," that is, to imagine what the other person is thinking, feeling and wishing. This is not to be confused with empathy or fusion. Rather, confirming relationships require a distancing as well as an intimacy. A distancing must occur between persons for true dialogue to occur, for in that space each person becomes a self with, for, and within the other. Inner growth is not accomplished through self-exploration alone but, as Buber asserts, in the relationship between persons, in making the other pre-eminently and mutually present. Through making the other fully present, and in knowing that one's own self is made present by the other, there exists together the mutuality of affirmation, of acceptance and of confirmation.

Experiencing the other's side of the relationship is essential to confirmation, since to confirm another person, one must imagine, concretely, what that other person is feeling and thinking. It was, in fact, a non-confirmational event that led Buber to realize this. One afternoon, he reports that while still glowing from a morning of religious enthusiasm, he received a visitor, a young man into his office, but without being fully present in spirit. Buber conversed attentively, but, as he writes, he omitted to guess the questions which the student did not ask. That is, Buber failed to read the young man's deeper concern which had made his life both difficult and tenuous. Afterward, Buber learned through friends that the young man had come not for a chat, but to decide a matter of life and death. Two months later he was killed in war. This event converted Buber from one who sought other-worldly mystery in isolation to one who sought the mystery imbued in each "mortal hour's fullness of claim and responsibility."[13]

The Death/Rebirth Process

> To express the same point somewhat differently: one's death (or rather the internalized anxiety of one's physical death) can be metamorphosized into axiological death from which one is resurrected or transformed into a new being, living a life transcending previous illusions and banal or destructive practice.[14]

We have said that confession (or self-reflective revelations), conversion (or a shift at the core of consciousness), and confirmation (or existential trust and genuine dialogue) are mutually imminent elements of an ever-recurring death/rebirth process. We have also proposed that this death/rebirth experience prepares one to die in an anticipatory way, and therefore to conquer the fear of dying. To put it differently, though their symbols and rituals pertaining to death differ, the variety of the world's sacred stories have encouraged both the de-repression of death-anxieties (dread and fear in the face of dying) and the cultivation of methods of transformation. Bringing the experience of one's own death from the future into the present initiates a new, death-transcending, attitude toward life. Death is now experienced each day, but in a way which overcomes anxieties about the process itself.

Here I will conclude with a story of two Christian pilgrims, one a priest born in India of a Catholic mother and a Hindu father, and the other, Abhishiktananda, a monk. Together they travel to the headwaters of the Ganges to celebrate the eucharist. Each has in his own way experienced a spiritual death to false phenomenological and numenological separations, and each has confirmed the other's unique pilgrimage.

It was in the month of June, and along with their Hindu brothers and sisters, Abhishiktananda and the priest climbed toward the mysterious peaks of the Himalayan mountains. As they walked, they shared and affirmed the devotion and faith of their Hindu counterparts. Each was aware of the Hindu myth in which the Ganges was said to flow from the crown *chakra* of Lord Shiva who sat in meditation on that same Himalayan peak. They were also traveling in the height of the pilgrimage season, and all over India men and women journeyed silently chanting the ineffable sound of OM. They climbed further inspired by the realization that mother India and the holy church were meeting in a place where each felt most deeply himself. The Himalayan mountains became like Mount Sinai and Mount Zion, the ascent like the ascent to the top of Mount Moriah in Jerusalem.

Crossing numerous streams which flow into the Ganges, they finally arrived at its source. Finding an appropriate place, where their privacy would be insured, they threw off their clothes and plunged into the icy water. Then, taking water from the river, and using unleavened *chapatti,* they prepared to celebrate the eucharist. Sitting cross-legged, they first sang verses from the Upanishads and then verses from a Sanskrit hymn in praise of Christ. But it was in vain that they tried to hear each other over the accompaniment of the roaring waters. Together they were caught up in the Voice of the one Spirit. Together they sang the "Our Father." Together they divided the bread. Together they drank from the cup.[15]

In effect, with this confirmational co-celebration of the eucharist, we come full circle. We began by facing dualistic anxieties and fears about death. We noticed how we tend, as Ernest Becker writes in *The Denial of Death,* to repress our fundamental concern about the inevitability of our own mortality. We now see, paradoxically speaking, that to de-repress death-anxiety, to experience death in an anticipatory way, to die spiritually before dying, is to experience a dying from which one resurrects in a new, holistic mode of being. Instead of the termination of human creativity, the axiological presence of death in life restores the original interpenetration of life and death. Dying before dying, to paraphrase the American poet Wallace Stevens, becomes then the mother of the beauty of rebirth.

NOTES

[1]This non-dualistic approach to life and death could be said to paraphrase the Zen teacher Bunan who says: "When you're both alive and dead, thoroughly dead to yourself, how superb the smallest pleasure": Lucien Stryk and Takushi Ikemoto, ed. and trans., *Zen: Poems, Prayers, Sermons, Anecdotes, Interviews* (New York: Doubleday, 1963), 15.

[2]According to the Zen school, as distinguished from other schools of Buddhism, the following four principles, attributed to Bodhidharma, accentuate the core of Zen teaching: outside scriptures; not dependent on words; a direct transmission; from heart/mind to heart/mind.

[3]D.T. Suzuki, *The Field of Zen* (New York: Harper, 1970), 10.

[4]D.T. Suzuki, Erich Fromm, and Richard De Martino, *Zen Buddhism and Psychoanalysis* (New York: Evergreen, 1963), 168. In his chapter "The Human Situation and Zen Buddhism," De Martino comprehensively elucidates the "as if dead" state which becomes the great awakening.

[5]It should be noted that in the larger Zen tradition a distinction is made

between the gradual school (those Buddhists who claim that one must move step-by-step toward awakening), and the sudden school (those Buddhists who say that awakening happens all at once). In other words, dualistically speaking there is always another step to take, steps after steps. Non-dualistically, Zen's understanding of spiritual death is the last or stepless step in which the real value and total miracle of every other step is also realized.

[6]Augustine, *The Confessions of St. Augustine,* trans. John K. Rayan (New York: Doubleday, 1960), 67.

[7]Augustine 189.

[8]William James, *Varieties of Religious Experience* (New York: Random House, 1902), 186.

[9]A goad was a prod used by shepherds to move sheep, and thus kicking against the goad was a Greek expression for useless resistance.

[10]Ramana Maharshi, *The Teachings of Ramana Maharshi,* ed., Arthur Osborne (London: Rider, 1962), 10. In yogic practice this exercise is called *savasana* or the "corpse pose," in which the practitioner lies flat on his or her back, eyes closed, allowing the body to become completely limp.

[11]James 193.

[12]Martin Buber, *The Knowledge of Man,* trans. Maurice Friedman (New York: Harper, 1965), 71.

[13]Buber 14.

[14]Antonio R. Gualtieri, *The Vulture and the Bull* (New York: University Press of America, 1984), 164.

[15]This story is found in Brother David Steindl-Rast, "Christian Confrontation with Buddhism and Hinduism," an unpublished manuscript.

JOURNAL EXERCISES

1. Imagine that you could meet D.T. Suzuki. What would you want to ask him about his experience with *Mu*?
2. Do you agree with Jung's remark that every psychological theory is a "subjective confession"? In what sense are your journal writings subjective confessions?
3. What does William James mean by divided self? What does James mean by conversion? And what connection is there between these two understandings, if any, in your life?
4. According to Martin Buber, why does the human person need confirmation? Describe a relationship, either personal or fictional, that evidences the confirmational process.
5. What did Martin Buber learn from the student who visited him just prior to committing suicide? How would you have felt in that situation if you had been Buber and it had happened to you?
6. Imagine that you are dying. What would you want your last words to be and whom would you especially want to hear or read them? Perhaps you might wish to write your last words in a letter.

ENDING: LAST WORDS

You die exactly the way you live!
Sogyal Rinpoche

As we have seen, the experience of death and dying cannot be objecti-
fied, kept abstract or denied, for it is inevitable, irreversible, anxiety-producing, and question-raising. Therefore it had originally occurred to me to
conclude with a section on "being with" the grieving and dying, but lack of
theoretical background, professional training and practice convinced me
otherwise. Yet, at the close of each semester students continue to ask questions like:

1. What do I say to someone who is dying?
2. When I am with a very close friend who talks about suicide,
   what should I say or do?
3. How do you tactfully discuss a person's imminent death
   when you are not sure if that person is acknowledging the
   fact that he or she is dying?
4. When an acquaintance (not a close friend) has experienced a
   loss of friend or relative, and I feel that he or she needs to
   talk, what should I ask or talk about without being too
   invasive?
5. How do you comfort a person who has just been told that he
   or she is dying?
6. When I'm with someone who is dying, how can I alleviate his
   or her fear of dying?
7. Should I have a lot of physical contact with a dying person,
   such as holding, kissing, or some type of physical support?

Questions like these arise because either we have been or we will be asked
to speak humanly and meaningfully to a person who is dying or grieving a
death. In such a situation: What can I say? What should I do?

Trained grief counselors from hospices and hospitals alike who have
spoken in my classes emphasize two themes: first, that it is necessary to listen carefully to the dying or grieving person's feelings; second, that it is
equally necessary to listen deeply to your own. Carefully and caringly listening to a dying person includes doing whatever you can to alleviate suffering
(physical, emotional, spiritual), behaving compassionately and treating the
person as a *living* being, respecting the patient's wishes for information

about his or her condition, encouraging the patient to talk about his or her illness, dying and death, and allowing the patient as much control as possible.

Finally, however, there are no sure and certain words to say to someone who is dying, nothing that can be planned out ahead of time. As long as the counselor is grounded in a desire to respond compassionately, the right words will come, the right silences will be heard.

At the same time, it is equally important to listen to one's own denials, fears, angers. To be an effective counselor one must acknowledge and at times even express whatever feelings the situation may evoke. In fact, such expression of the counselor's feelings, when appropriately timed, may catalyze a change in the dying person's attitudes.

As is well known in her book *On Death and Dying* Elisabeth Kübler-Ross notes that the dying person (and the counselor) experience at least five stages (or coping mechanisms) in response to terminal illness:

1. Denial ("No, not me, it can't be true!")
2. Anger ("Why me?")
3. Bargaining ("Yes me, but . . . ")
4. Depression ("What's the use!")
5. Acceptance ("I can't fight it any longer.")

A graphic illustration of this sequence follows:

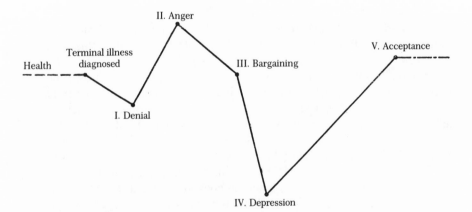

While these defense mechanisms may last for different periods of time, exist in any order, or side by side, and are components also to all experiences of loss, the one thing that persists throughout, according to Kübler-Ross, is hope—hope for a miracle, hope for a new drug, or hope for a new diagnosis.

To the extent that these five stages are viewed sequentially or consequentially and thereby establish a direction of movement from life unto death, from the world religious perspective a sixth should be added—the stage of transformation. As we have seen, the world's sacred traditions teach that the person who is able to appropriate death from the future into life, who is able to die anticipationally and spiritually, and thereby to be reborn or awakened, is able to face death with a transformed attitude. Like Ivan in *The Death of Ivan Ilych,* the experience of death can be transforming not only to the dying person but also to those who work with the dying.

Accordingly, an effective way to be with a dying person is to be aware of the transformational possibilities within the dying experience. He or she would be the person who:

- becomes a "caring presence" (present at whatever level is possible)
- listens as an equal from the heart
- touches gently when appropriate
- avoids psychological or religious jargon
- finds out where a person hurts
- offers to call in a professional practitioner of the dying person's practice (if appropriate) to hear any final confession and to offer the sacred community's final blessings
- offers to help with any final business

Last Words

If I had only one lecture to give, one chapter to write, one more journal entry to make before dying, what would I say? Having reached this point the reader may wish to consider this question especially in light of the ensuing quotations. Convinced that knowing how a person lived is to know how that person died, that the manner of one's dying encapsulates the essential qualities of a person's life, and that to speak of the dead in some special sense allows them to live again, we end with these quintessential last words:

LORD KRISHNA   1. "He who utters the single syllable AUM (which is) BRAHMAN, remembering ME as he departs, giving up his body, he goes to the highest goal."

BUDDHA   2. "Decay (Change) is inherent in all component things, but the Truth will remain forever! Work out your Awakening with diligence."

CONFUCIUS   3. "The great mountain must crumble; The strong beam must break: And the wise man withers away like a plant."

LAO TZU   4. "For Heaven's way is to sharpen without cutting, And the Sage's way is to act without striving."

CHUANG TZU   5. "The heavens and the earth will serve me as a coffin and a coffin shell. The sun and moon and stars will decorate my bier. All creation will be at hand to witness the event. What more need I than these?"

HUI NENG   6. "When I am gone, just practice correctly according to the Teaching, just as you did during my days with you. Remember, even were I to remain in this world, if you disobeyed my teaching my presence among you would be pointless."

JESUS   7. Seven Last Words from the Cross
— "Eloi, Eloi, lama sabachthani (My God, my God, why have you forsaken me)";
— "Father, forgive them, for they know not what they do";
— "This day you will be with me in paradise";
— "Father, into your hands I commit my spirit";
— "I am thirsty";
— "Woman, behold your son; son, behold your mother";
— "It is finished."

SOCRATES   8. "Criton, we owe a cock to Asclepios; pay it without fail."

MUHAMMAD   9. "To the blessed Companionship on High; to the blessed Companionship on High."

TOLSTOY   10. "Seek, keep seeking" . . . "So this is the end! And it's nothing . . . "

BIBLIOGRAPHY: GENERAL ANTHOLOGIES

Carse, James P. and Dallery, Arlene B. *Death and Society: Book of Readings and Sources*. New York: Harcourt Brace Jovanovich, 1977.

Eliade, Mircea. *Death, Afterlife, and Eschatology*. New York: Harper & Row, 1967.

Feifel, Herman (ed.). *The Meaning of Death*. New York: McGraw-Hill, 1959.

Feifel, Herman (ed.). *New Meanings of Death*. New York: McGraw-Hill, 1977.

Fulton, Robert; Markusen, Eric; Owens, Greg; Scheiber, Jane L. (eds.). *Death and Dying: Challenge and Change*. Reading, MA: Addison-Wesley, 1978.

Fulton, Robert L. (ed.). *Death and Identity*. New York: John Wiley and Sons, 1965.

Kübler-Ross, Elisabeth (ed.). *Death: The Final Stage of Growth*. Englewood Cliffs, NJ: Prentice-Hall, 1975.

Reynolds, Frank and Wangh, Earle (eds.). *Religious Encounters with Death*. University Park, PA: Pennsylvania State U. Press, 1977.

Shneidman, Edwin S. (ed.). *Death: Current Perspectives*. Palo Alto, CA: Mayfield Publishing, 1976.

Stannard, David E. (ed.). *Death in America*. Philadelphia: University of Pennsylvania Press, 1975.

Toynbee, Arnold (ed.). *Man's Concern with Death*. St. Louis, MO: McGraw-Hill, 1968.

Wass, Hannelore (ed.). *Dying: Facing the Facts*. New York: Hemisphere Publishing (McGraw-Hill), 1979.

Wilcox, Sandra Galdieri and Sutton, Marilyn (eds.). *Understanding Death and Dying: An Interdisciplinary Approach*. Port Washington, NY: Alfred Publishing, 1977.

GENERAL REFERENCE WORKS

Aries, Philippe. *Western Attitudes Toward Death*. Baltimore: The Johns Hopkins University Press.

Bugen, Larry A. *Death and Dying: Theory/Research/Practice*. Dubuque, IA: William C. Brown, 1979.

Davis, Richard H. (ed.). *Dealing with Death*. Los Angeles: Ethel Percy Andrus Gerontology Center, University of Southern California, 1973.

Dempsey, David. *The Way We Die: An Investigaion of Death and Dying in America Today*. New York: McGraw-Hill, 1975.

DeSpelder, Lynne and Stuckland, Albert. *The Last Dance: Encountering Death and Dying*. Palo Alto, CA: Mayfield Publishing Co., 1983.

Garrison, Webb. *Strange Facts about Death*. Nashville: Abingdon, 1978.

Grollman, Earl A. *Concerning Death: A Practical Guide for the Living*. Boston: Beacon Press, 1974.

Hardt, Dale V. *Death: The Final Frontier*. Englewood Cliffs, NJ: Prentice-Hall, 1979.

Hinton, John. *Dying*. Baltimore, MD: Penguin Books, 1972.

Kübler-Ross, Elisabeth. *On Death and Dying*. New York: Macmillan, 1969.

Kübler-Ross, Elisabeth. *Questions and Answers on Death and Dying*. New York: Collier (Macmillan), 1974.

Largone, John. *Vital Signs: The Way We Die in America*. Boston: Little Brown, 1974.

Largone, John. *Death is a Noun: A View of the End of Life*. New York: Dell, 1972.

Lifton, Robert Jay and Olson, Eric. *Living and Dying*. New York: Bantam, 1975.

Matson, Archie. *Afterlife: Reports from the Threshold of Death*. New York: Harper & Row, 1975.

Moody, Raymond. *Life Afterlife*. Harrisburg, PA: Stackpole Books, 1976.

Shneidman, Edwin. *Voices of Death*. New York: Harper and Row, 1980.

Shneidman, Edwin. *Deaths of Man*. New York: Quadrangle Books, 1973.

Simpson, Michael A. *The Facts of Death*. Englewood Cliffs, NJ: Prentice-Hall, 1979.

DEATH AND LITERATURE

Agee, James. *A Death in the Family*. New York: Bantam, 1969.

Beckett, Samuel. *Waiting for Godot*. New York: Grove Press, 1964.

Camus, Albert. *The Stranger*. New York: Vintage Books, 1958.

Camus, Albert. *The Plague*. New York: Alfred A. Knopf, 1957.

Crichton, Michael. *The Terminal Man*. New York: Alfred A. Knopf, 1974.

Langer, Lawrence L. *The Age of Atrocity: Death in Modern Literature*. Boston: Beacon Press, 1978.

Lewis, C.S. *A Grief Observed*. London: Faber & Faber, 1961.

Lewis, Oscar. *A Death in the Sanchez Family*. New York: Vintage Books, 1970.

Malz, Betty. *My Glimpse of Eternity*. Waco, TX: Chosen Books, 1977.

Miller, Arthur. *Death of a Salesman*. New York: Macmillan, 1948.

Olsen, Tillie. *Tell Me A Riddle*. Philadelphia: J.B. Lippincott, 1961.

Plath, Sylvia. *The Bell Jar*. New York: Harper & Row, 1971.

Tolstoy, Leo. *The Death of Ivan Ilych*. New York: Signet, 1960.

Wiesel, Elie. *Night*. New York: Avon Books, 1958.

DEATH AND PHILOSOPHY

Bataille, Georges. *Death and Sensuality: A Study of Eroticism and the Taboo*. New York: Walker and Company, 1962.

Becker, Ernest. *The Denial of Death*. New York: The Free Press, 1973.

Becker, Ernest. *Escape from Evil*. New York: The Free Press, 1975.

Boros, Ladislaus. *The Mystery of Death*. New York: The Seabury Press, 1965.

Choron, Jacques. *Death and Western Thought*. New York: Macmillan, 1963.

Choron, Jacques. *Death and Modern Man*. New York: Collier Books, 1972.

Frankl, Viktor. *Man's Search for Meaning*. Boston: Beacon Press, 1959.

Hick, John. *Death and Eternal Life*. San Francisco: Harper & Row, 1976.

Kamath, M.V. *Philosophy of Death and Dying*. Honesdale, PA: Himalayan International Institute of Yoga Science and Philosophy, 1978.

Koestenbaum, Peter. *Is There an Answer to Death?* Englewood Cliffs, NJ: Prentice-Hall, 1976.

Selzer, Richard. *Mortal Lessons: Notes on the Art of Surgery*. New York: Simon and Schuster, 1976.

Sontag, Susan. *Illness as Metaphor*. New York: Farrar, Straus and Giroux, 1978.

Unamuno, Miguel de. *The Tragic Sense of Life*. New York: Dover Publishing, 1954.

DEATH AND RELIGION

Aries, Philippe. *The Hour of Our Death*. New York: Alfred A. Knopf, 1981.

Bailey, Lloyd. *Biblical Perspectives on Death*. Philadelphia: Fortress Press, 1979.

Bermejo, Luis M. *Light Beyond Death*. Chicago: Loyola University Press, 1987.

Brandon, G.G.F. *The Judgment of the Dead: The Idea of Life After Death in the Major Religions*. New York: Charles Scribner's Sons, 1967.

Budge, E.A. Wallis. *The Egyptian Book of the Dead*. New York: Dover Publications, 1967/1985.

Choron, Jacques. *Death and Western Thought*. New York: Macmillan, 1963.

Cullmann, Oscar. *Immortality of the Soul or Resurrection of the Dead?* London: Epworth Press, 1958.

Doss, Richard W. *The Last Enemy: A Christian Understanding of Death*. New York: Harper and Row, 1974.

Dunne, John S. *Time and Myth*. Notre Dame: University of Notre Dame Press, 1973.

Easwaran, Eknath. *Dialogue with Death*. Petaluma, CA: Nilgiri Press, 1981.

Ebon, Martin. *Reincarnation in the Twentieth Century*. New York: New American Library, 1969.

Evans-Wentz, W.Y. *The Tibetan Book of the Dead*. New York: Oxford University Press, 1960.

Flore, Charles and Landsburg, Alan. *Death Encounters*. New York: Bantam, 1979.

Ford, Arthur. *The Life Beyond Death*. New York: G.P. Putnam's Sons, 1971.

Ghose, Sri Aurobindo. *The Problem of Rebirth*. Pondicherry: Aurobindo Ashram Press, 1969.

Grof, Stanislav and Halifax, Joan. *The Human Encounter with Death*. New York: E.P. Dutton, 1977.

Gualtieri, Antonio. *The Vulture and the Bull: Religious Responses to Death*. New York: University Press of America, 1984.

Head, Joseph and S.L. Cranston (eds.). *Reincarnation: An East-West Anthology*. Wheaton, IL: Theosophical Publishing House, 1968.

Herbert, Albert. *Raised from the Dead*. Rockford, IL: Tan Books, 1986.

Holck, Frederick H. (ed.). *Death and Eastern Thought: Understanding Death in Eastern Religions and Philosophies*. Nashville, TN: Abingdon, 1974.

Humphry, Derek and Wickett, Ann. *The Right To Die: Understanding Euthanasia*. New York: Harper & Row, 1987.

Johnson, Jay and McGee, Marsha (eds.). *Encounters with Eternity: Religious Views of Death and Life After Death*. New York: Philosophical Library, 1986.

Kapleau, Philip (ed.). *The Wheel of Death: A Collection of Writings from Zen Buddhist, and Other Sources on Death–Rebirth–Dying*. New York: Harper and Row, 1971.

Küng, Hans. *Eternal Life?* New York: Doubleday & Co., 1984.

Larue, Gerald. *Euthanasia and Religion: Survey of the Attitudes of World Religions to the Right-to-Die.* Los Angeles: The Hemlock Society, 1985.

Levine, Stephen. *Who Dies?* New York: Anchor Press, 1982.

Lewis, C.S. *A Grief Observed.* New York: Bantam Books, 1961.

Moltmann, Jürgen. *Theology of Hope.* New York: Harper and Row, 1967.

Mullin, Glenn. *Death and Dying: The Tibetan Tradition.* Boston: Arkana Paperbacks, 1986.

Rahner, Karl. *On the Theology of Death.* New York: Herder & Herder, 1961.

Rahner, Karl. *Theological Investigations,* Vol. XIII. New York: Seabury Press, 1975.

Rose, Seraphim. *The Soul after Death.* Platina, CA: The Saint Herman of Alaska Brotherhood, 1980.

Scott, Nathan. *The Modern Vision of Death.* Richmond, VA: John Knox Press, 1967.

Stendahl, Krister (ed.). *Immortality and Resurrection.* New York: Macmillan, 1965.

Szekely, Edmond Bordeaux. *The Conquest of Death.* San Diego: Academy Books, 1973.

Watts, Alan. *Death.* Millbrae, CA: Celestial Arts, 1975.

Weldon, J. and Levitt, Z. *Is There Life After Death?* Irvine, CA: Mayfield, 1977.

Wolff, Richard. *The Last Enemy.* Washington, DC: Canon Press, 1974.

APPENDIX: SELECTED
JOURNAL WRITINGS

The following journal selections are included to complement the more literary, conceptual and ritual dimensions of the sacred traditions studied in the text. They were written before the journal writing suggestions (provided at the end of the various chapters) were developed. They will provide readers who plan to keep, or who are keeping, a journal with examples of what others have written in response to the themes of the text.

I

When I was in the seventh grade in Middle School, I underwent a drastic shift in consciousness for the worse. One night, I was dreaming about a samurai scenario; I was in a tree looking around, when all of a sudden [my mind] went haywire—the continuity of the dream was interrupted by a massive shock of something . . . then, everything went black. I didn't feel my heart beating so I started to squirm and think "inhale, exhale, inhale, exhale. . . . " After about twenty seconds (I think), I came to. My heart was pounding away as if it needed to make up for what it had forgotten to do. I was in a cold sweat, shivering and scared out of my wits, because I had never experienced anything like this before in my life. I couldn't go back to sleep, so I stayed awake for the rest of the evening. The next morning, I felt very different. I felt as if [my body] was drained away of all its energy and spirit; I felt like a husk with nothing inside. My vision (20/20) was not impaired or blurred but things didn't look or feel the same to me. Life was (and still is) just a three dimensional movie to me. I became severely depressed because I felt as if *I lost something quite dear to me*. Perhaps I am insane but calling me insane will not change the way I feel. Perhaps it is a common disease, or perhaps everyone goes through it at some point in his or her life.

(Michael M. Masuda)

II

As far as illustrating how my anxiety goes, I thought about one of the training sessions for doing phone work at the Suicide and Crisis hotline.

"Mark, the psychologist who facilitated last night's discussion, asked us all to repeat after him . . . 'I want to kill myself.' We were again hesitant, myself almost unwilling. In the moment before I spoke those words I quickly looked around the room to catch a supporting glance while snickering. I couldn't catch anyone's eyes and before I knew it I had to say, 'I want to kill myself.' This was a revealing moment for me, because I recognized my anxiety about death, and what's my method of dealing with it, to laugh it off."

I repeatedly avoided the confrontation of death as a reality and I now recognize one of the many ways I have evaded this issue of issues.

(David Brandt)

III:
Act Three

Next Day. Same time, same place.
The Tree has four large balls hanging from the branches.
Estragon is asleep under the Tree.
Vladimir enters dragging a short rope.

VLADIMIR: (Shaking Estragon) Look, look, I brought a rope!
ESTRAGON: (Strirring) What . . . what . . .
VLADIMIR: So this is where you sleep.
ESTRAGON: You again! (Pointing at the rope) What's that?
VLADIMIR: (Proudly) I said I would bring a rope and I have.
ESTRAGON: My God! A man of scruples. Embrace me!
             (Rising)
VLADIMIR: (Backing away) What! Wait . . . why now?
ESTRAGON: (Pushing closer, arms open) Why, a man of your stature is
             so rare! Better now than never.
VLADIMIR: (Contemplating) Just so.
             (They embrace and quickly separate)
ESTRAGON: (Throwing up his hands) What now?
VLADIMIR: Why, we wait.
ESTRAGON: (Looking around) What of the rope?
VLADIMIR: (Shuffling) A trifle. Forget it.
ESTRAGON: No, let me see . . . (He grabs the rope and runs to the tree)
ESTRAGON: (Screaming, Estragon recoils from the tree and drops the
             rope)
             Eeahh! Horrible! (He turns and falls to the ground)
VLADIMIR: (Crossing slowly to Estragon) You are hopeless. (Helping
             him up) You can't even stand alone.
ESTRAGON: But LOOK! (Pointing at the Tree) It's US!

VLADIMIR: What foolishness? Let me see . . . (Leaning close to the Tree)
What is the matter?

ESTRAGON: My God, don't you see? (Screaming) THE HEADS! OUR HEADS ON THE TREE!

VLADIMIR: (Trying to calm Estragon) No. No. Easy, it's just a grapefruit.

ESTRAGON: (Still upset) No! No! That's a Willow tree.
(There is a noise off stage and they both turn in expectation.)

VLADIMIR: Wait! It's Godot. He's come at last.
(Two boys enter in elaborate Harness. One boy is Fair, golden haired and healthy, the other dark, thin and in ragged clothes. The Harness is connected to a Black wooden cart with high sides and open back gate. The driver is a white bearded man in a long fur coat. He reins in the boys as the cart passes Vladimir and Estragon.)
(Vladimir and Estragon huddle together. The cart driver motions to the men to get into the cart)

VLADIMIR: (Stammering) Are . . . are you Mr. Godot?
(No answer)
(The driver beckons again, pointing to the back of the cart where legs are dangling out. Vladimir and Estragon approach the cart and peer in)

ESTRAGON: (Holding his nose) Agh! What a stench!

VLADIMIR: (Retching from the cart) Good Lord! Bodies!

ESTRAGON: What? What?

VLADIMIR: (Retching) Bodies and Parts! Butchery! Disease!
(Vladimir and Estragon turn to run)

VLADIMIR: Run, Estragon, run!

ESTRAGON: I am! (He does not move)
(Neither man moves. They gasp and fall breathless.)

VLADIMIR: (Sitting up) What a scare! Did you see?

ESTRAGON: (Rolling over) See what?

VLADIMIR: (Incredulous) Why, the cart? The Bodies!

ESTRAGON: (Irritated) What game is this? Where's the rope? (He gropes around the floor for the rope)

VLADIMIR: (Vladimir grabs Estragon and shakes him) The cart! What of the cart? (They turn together and look at the driver who beckons them to get in) (Light fades to darkness. Voices in the darkness)

VLADIMIR: You again.

ESTRAGON: What are you doing now?
VLADIMIR: Waiting . . .
             (Darkness fades and Light returns. Vladimir and Estragon
             are in the Harness in place of the boys. The driver, now in a
             Black coat, lifts the reins. The men move forward.)
ESTRAGON: You again. What do we do now?
VLADIMIR: Pull! Pull . . . pull.

(William J. Neven)

IV

I need to make a conscious effort, during a funeral, not to hide my emotions. It is too easy for me to "lose myself" in the funeral ceremony and ignore my feelings. Sometimes it is easier to concentrate on the ceremony instead of what it represents. When I do this, I commit psychological suicide. I react to a situation very methodically and lose touch with my emotions. Psychological death occurs at this time.

The lack of traumatic and gut wrenching emotions associated with psychological death may feel comfortable. However, I believe it is unhealthy for people not to acknowledge their emotions when something traumatic, such as death, happens in their life. Unfortunately, I feel that a lot of people subject themselves to psychological death when a family member or friend dies. These people may become so engrossed with the habitual behavior associated with funeral rituals that they lose track of their feelings altogether. Grief is not a pleasant emotion for anyone to experience. However, I believe that a person, who habitually restricts his or her emotions, may create a pattern that denies himself or herself the opportunity to experience enjoyable emotions as well. A person may lock himself or herself into this unhealthy pattern until a point is reached where he or she is no longer in touch with his or her feelings. (This happened to me. I reached a point where I was no longer in touch with my feelings and had, in a sense, committed psychological suicide.)

Habitual behavior is dangerous when it limits one's feelings. Different cultures have many types of rituals associated with death. I believe that there is nothing self-destructive about a funeral ritual, or habitual behavior, except when it is used as a means to hide and not acknowledge one's feelings. I believe that people would be healthier, especially those who are prone to hiding their emotions, if they became familiar with Lao Tzu. This belief emphasizes how important it is for an individual to recognize and act on one's feelings irregardless of how it may look to others. I believe that if a person used this philosophy to look at life, the individual would know more about himself or herself and be more comfortable with who he or she is.

I believe that people should allow themselves the opportunity to express their feelings when someone dies. People should be careful not to use a funeral ritual as a scapegoat to confronting their feelings about death. I used to ignore my feelings about subjects, such as death, that I felt uncomfortable with. This made it difficult to realize who I was. I went through an identity crisis. It took me almost a full year to learn how to identify my feelings. I had always looked to others and tried to react the way I thought I should. The subject of psychological death was important to me because it helped me identify some of the unhealthy thinking patterns I had developed in my life. When I was at the funeral services, I saw some of these "patterns" in others by the way they described their reactions to death. At this time, I realized that it is not the event but one's reactions to ritualistic or habitual actions that cause psychological death. I believe it is important for an individual to identify his or her feelings and react accordingly instead of acting a certain way because he or she thinks it is how others expect him or her to act.)

(I have never felt comfortable with my feelings toward death. This class has helped me become more aware of my feelings about this subject.

(Kimberly L. Hanesworth)

V

I still remember the night. It was wet and dark. It had been raining all day and continued into the night. Pete, Tony, and I were going on a winter camping trip to Yosemite. The three of us had all been very good friends through high school, but had seen little of each other since graduation. The trip seemed as though it would be a wonderful time to share our lives with each other again. Something seemed wrong, though. I kept thinking that this road was not a place to be tonight.

The drive to Yosemite had been very enjoyable and quiet, until about three miles from the park entrance the car hit something very slick on the road and slid toward the guard rail. We did not stop, but instead jumped over the railing and rolled 270 feet into the canyon below. I remember thinking very quietly that I was probably going to die; I would not live through this accident.

My sense of time was very distorted; it seemed as if the car continued to roll down the hill forever. Yet after it came to rest the hours that passed seemed measured only in minutes. The first thing I did was begin calling for Pete and Tony to make sure they were okay. Pete answered, but we could not find Tony. We decided that one of us should go back up to the road and the other should look for Tony. Pete climbed up to get help, and I began to look for our friend.

I found him. He was pinned under the car from his chest up, his lower torso and legs protruding. I felt his chest and stomach to see if he were still breathing. He seemed to still be alive. I thought, "If I can push the car back over I can set Tony free and he will be okay." I tried, but I was too tired, and the car was too heavy.

I reached down again to touch my friend, to try to tell him I was sorry. As I knelt down I heard Tony draw in a very sharp breath, and then let it out very slowly. And then he breathed no more. Tony was dead, and there was nothing more I could do for him. I stood up crying, and called to Pete. I heard someone above call down that everything would be all right, for the police were coming.

"No," I yelled, "Tony is dead." Everything was not all right. My friend, a man I loved, had died, and I had killed him.

At eighteen years of age, when people begin to gain responsibility as adults, I became responsible for a friend's life. The one question that haunted me then, and continues to do so now, is, "Why Tony and not me?" If there is an answer to that, I have yet to find it. I may never find my answer, but I continue to ask the question.

I cried for Tony. I did not grieve so much his death as I did the fact that I had taken his life. If anyone's life had to be taken, it should have been my own. I offered in any manner I could think of to trade my life for my friend's. But no deals were struck. There was no God or Satan to come to my aid. I continue to cry for Tony. And I shall probably do so for the rest of my life.

(Bruce Horn)

VI

Dear Death,

Why am I so afraid of you? Who are you? Why do you hide in the back of my mind? Never fully revealing yourself? Are you afraid of life? What do you look like? A monster? A mist of green? What . . . ? Are you painful? Are you a figment of my imagination?

As I sat in class today, I sat wondering about you. Why cause so much pain for Ivan Ilych? No one deserves that much pain in order to learn a lesson. Is that who you are, a teacher? Do you teach me the meaning of life in the last breath of my life? Are you supposed to show us to appreciate each other?

What ever your purpose in life is, I hate you for it. I don't want my friends, family, and lovers to leave me. I don't want to die. That is the bottom line. I hate you because I want to sail the oceans, find new friends, and live new experiences. No matter how routine life gets, I want to live. Yes, I really do hate you. Isn't that odd? I want to kill death itself. I want to kill you.

(Georgann Raeth)

VII

The Hindu concepts of karma and reincarnation help me face death in a different way. My karma is not something predestined; it is something I have control over. I needed to know this. It is somehow comforting to know that I am in total control of my own fate, that death, when it comes for me, will come because I am ready—not ready to die, but ready to take the next step and be reborn only if I choose to. This endless cycle of reincarnation will only happen to me again if I choose to be born again.

When I had my first baby in the winter of 1968 it was a difficult delivery. At the time I did not know how difficult it was, for I almost died. Quote from journal, "All of a sudden or in specks of sensation I started to feel myself come out or up from a long black entry way and it was like I was coming up into my body." On the surface of my body, there was a nice nurse frantically pushing and rubbing my legs and arms and packing hot blankets around me. Every life gesture seemed hard to perform. It took a month to recover from just having a baby by natural childbirth. Upon reflection, I think they had given me too much ether as the baby's head showed and I was on my way out of my body. I really don't know what turned me around. I do believe the desire to stay at this pinpoint existence has some effect on life and also the death process need not be painful. This semester has reaffirmed what I have known and felt all along. "Pain is created by the struggle to go against the stream of events." I also feel we can understand the forces that bring about life and death. There is nothing sacrilegious about it and nothing wrong with knowing. It doesn't make life any less wonderful.

(Linda Repke)

VIII:
Funeral Customs of India

Being raised in America by Indian parents has given me the opportunity to become familiar with customs of my own country and those of my adopted country. I want to share the funeral customs of my Sikh religion and my native country. I have not experienced these customs personally but these are things I have learned through my parents who grew up in a small village in India.

When a person dies nothing is done with the remains for about two hours. I assume this is done so the rest of the village and relatives in other villages or cities can be notified.

After several hours the body is then bathed and dressed in new clothing by family members. Then a ladder is constructed of wood and rope to bear the body to the funeral pyre. The funeral pyre is a combustible pile of dry wood that is used in the funeral rites.

The body then is placed on the ladder to be carried by four members of the family to the funeral pyre. The procession is begun with the men following directly behind the remains and the women following the men. This is typical because the men are considered to be the supreme being while the women are considered worthless.

In the beginning the head is directed toward the funeral pyre. When the body is halfway to the pyre, it is then turned around and the feet are directed toward the pyre. The symbol of this is: Please do not come back to our house. It is considered extremely bad luck when the dead comes back in the form of a dream. At this point, a vase that has been filled with water is thrown to the ground. This is a symbolic gesture. This is done to release the brain from the body. The pieces of the vase are picked up to be carried to the pyre. The body is then turned around again so that the head is again directed toward the funeral pyre. The procession is begun again with the men following directly behind the remains and the women following the men. It usually takes them ten to fifteen minutes to reach the cremation site. As the ladder is placed on the pyre the men are chanting a silent prayer saying "Wahaguru" meaning true God. The women show their emotions by hitting themselves and crying. They chant questions such as "Why have you left?" or "Why did it have to be you?"

The pieces of the vase are placed on top of the remains. It is then torched completely around the pyre so that the fire will be very hot in order to disintegrate the remains. The fingernails will pop and do not burn. The same thing happens with the eyes. After the fire has ceased to burn, the family members look for these remains so that they can be carried to the river and thrown in.

(Kulvi K. Purewal)

IX:

Hinduism in Top Gun

I saw Top Gun this weekend and I noticed something I've never noticed before. If you have never seen the movie before, the major scene shows a hot shot pilot lose control of his F-14, and he needs to eject himself and his RIO (Radar Intercept Officer) from the cockpit. After the ejection the RIO smashes into the canopy, causing death. The pilot feels mortally wounded by the death of his close friend and, after trying to fight, realizes he can't and nearly gives up. This may seem like just another movie plot where the main actor feels responsible for the supporting actor's death. However, it is much more complex than that. The head instructor of the flight school tells the pilot that, even though his RIO and friend has died, there will be more deaths. The pilot tries to fight again but realizes that he has lost the will, and he is scared to kill anyone else. Finally, at the end of the movie, when he is in a situation of kill or be killed, he asks his dead friend to talk to him. (The dead friend never says anything because the movie would then seem kooky, but the idea is still there.) The pilot realizes that fighting is his fate and goes on to win.

Now we come to the Hinduism in Top Gun. I remembered the story of Krishna and Arjuna in Hinduism while the movie was being played. Arjuna was a warrior; so was the pilot. Arjuna became scared of killing his brothers; so did the pilot. Krishna told Arjuna that there was no such thing as death and that, in this lifetime, he must fight because of this caste, much as the RIO told the pilot in the imaginary conversation! Arjuna realized that fighting was his way of life and that death was irrelevant; so did the pilot. Do you see the parable?

Anyhow, I wonder if the writer of the movie ever read the story of Arjuna. The script seemed to be, to me at least, a modern day telling of the story.

(Kevin Wood and Galen Maclorrie)

X:
Buddhist Journal Exercise

There is no fire like passion
no capturer like hatred;
There is no net (snare) like delusion,
no torrent like craving
Dhammapada (18:17)

Commentary:

No it does not address the relationship between sexuality and spirituality. I think it points out that human emotions are the strongest influences over our actions, that our minds alone hold the key to peace and fulfillment; that our thinking and our focus (mind) will determine whether or not we find ourselves caught in the whirlpool of craving, the blindness of delusion, the terrible all-consuming intensity of hatred, the raging driving force of passion. *BE REMINDED,* EACH OF US IS SUBJECT TO THESE FORCES WITHIN OURSELVES.

(Hal Foraker)

XI

I've just been reading about Zen Buddhism, and although on some levels I understand, on others I don't. For instance, if the answer is nothing/emptiness, then why bother being alive at all?

Dualistic consciousness—I understand, when I feel separate I feel weakest, I feel strongest when I let myself join in with those non-tangible feelings of oneness.

Non-dualistic consciousness—I am I, I am you, I am not-I—for me means oneness, that blissful feeling that's been coming in more and more lately. Apparently this is achieved through spiritual death—rebirth. Departure of self from context/problem; focus on non-dualistic awareness; crisis—give up, I've tried it all, surrender; duality block—gears jam—breakthrough.

I feel like I'm in the Duality Block but have been for some time because I've not made a decision and feel like my wheels are spinning. I feel like I can break through at any time. I don't know what the catalyst will be. I identify with and understand these stages so well, am I just human or am I going through some sort of spiritual death?

(Karen Ehrenfeldt)

XII:
Zen Stink

These realizations dawned on me at a time when, being quite young, my mind was a blank slate, very near a Taoist pre-cognitive clarity, and I, of course, had very few words which could adequately explain my experiences. I did get the feeling though that nobody knew what was really going on, and that people were perpetrating a colossal lie rather than gathering to themselves the vast "unreality" that existed all around them. These were my feelings at an early age and after I began to approach puberty I occasionally would find myself "returning" from my experiences "in the void" very shaken and with an intuitive sense that what I was experiencing was probably death or something very near to it. The unsettling sensation this created in me, as well as the memories of how pleasant that space was, gave birth in me to a spiritual faith and curiosity that remains strong and compelling to this day. And lest you think me too pompous; I know that this is a bunch of pucky, but thanks for the opportunity to unburden myself of it anyway.

(Steve Farmer)

XIII:
Journal Inquiries into Eden
Creation

The feminist upset over Adam being the first creation in the garden of Eden story in Genesis would be calmed if Adam were seen, just like all the men since him, as being born out of a woman. This would be an obvious thought for a Hindu who always considers that the aspect of God that creates or births is the Mother, that is the Ad Shakti, primal creative feminine power. This shows up symbolically in the Eden story inasmuch as Adam is formed out of the earth. The earth is, of course, the Divine Mother.

The creation of Eve second could be seen as the compassion of the Creatress who lovingly provides a womb or context into which Adam can plant his seed. The seed (or idea) is received by Eve, incubated and then birthed into the physical world. Thus creation continues to unfold, context birthing content, context birthing content, eternally.

The Snake

The Serpent is perhaps one of the only symbols that is a fully empowered feminine symbol and a fully empowered male symbol. Clearly it is a phallic symbol in shape and in the way it comes into erection to strike. The snake is also the animal that transforms itself and it is associated with the cycles of the moon and therefore with the lunar (menstrual) cycles of women. No wonder the snake shows up as the universal symbol of power whether judged evil or divine.

The Tree of Knowledge

I think of the Tree of Knowledge of Good and Evil as actually the Tree of Knowledge of not only Good and Bad but also Light and Dark, Up and Down, Out and In and all other polarities. If this is true then clearly humankind needed to eat of the fruit of this tree in order to become the self-aware thinking and distinguishing beings that we are. It is fitting that Eve would eat of this fruit as she is the Mother of humankind, the transmitter of the qualities of humaness.

The Punishment

Adam and Eve were given the same eternal punishment for their apple snitching. Eve was given pain and suffering in her creative process of birthing and Adam was given pain and suffering in his creative process of work in the world.

This idea that pain and suffering are connected to the creative process in humans creates some interesting areas for exploration. When Buddha says that life is suffering is he implying that life *is* creation and creation is suffering? When Christ suffered on the cross was he in a creative process, a birthing? If so, what was born of his labor?

(Kamlapati K. Khalsa)

XIV

The gripping passage of Abraham and Isaac brought back memories of the first time I heard it told as a small child. It made me aware of the differences in how I absorbed its importance between the two instances. The first time the building suspense was most prominent, from God's requesting voice directed at Abraham to the thrust of the knife. Fear became the moral of this historical account. The ending was never resolved either. I was told that all of a sudden Isaac was A-OK, but how or why remained a mystery; such an anticlimactic ending to a powerful and scary tale, I never fathomed. This time, as an adult, the story takes on a completely new meaning. The notion of resurrection/reincarnation by a mortal is taken into account. The sacrifice becomes ultimate expression of faith and alignment with the Creator who is especially present for us in times of extreme fear.

(Elizabeth Brand)

XV

O.K. we have a midterm, this could be sudden death, I mean a few wrong answers and oh no, you get a "C." Death from the university not to mention mom and dad; they'll call and wonder why I'm not more like they were in college—perfect. I'm going to die. Do I know this stuff? No. I'm going to die. After the midterm, I will die. I will know that I didn't know the answers and I will have failed. A slow psychological death for me during the forty-five minutes of test-taking.

Well hey, maybe I should just relax and then maybe I'll do well . . .

No, I'm going to die.

(Anonymous)

XVI:
Before Death

The process of dying has been removed from the everyday ordinary experience in the Western Culture. This creates a distance between the dying person and others.

It is important to think about and talk about one's own death. To decide the environment and atmosphere of one's own choosing. So, the death process can occur without distractions. The awakening should be experienced "in dignity and calmness." An individual needs to make decisions such as, "Do I want to be cremated? Do I want an open or closed casket? What funeral home do I want for the service? What Scripture readings do I want?"

(Joan M. Loher)

XVII

"Once you have accepted death, then you have accepted life." Those people who cannot accept the fact that death is necessary and that they themselves must eventually die cannot fully accept life as we know it. Life without death is not possible; of course, the reciprocal is true also—death without life is not possible. The relationship between life and death is a tautology. The two go hand-in-hand and cannot be separated. If one or the other is accepted into one's way of thinking, then the other is accepted automatically.

"Death is the ultimate escape from life as we know it." This statement, which is also a way of thinking, only applies when things go wrong for a person. When the pressures of life and its sufferings become too great for a person to handle, then death becomes a viable means to escape all the hurt and misery. Such is the nature of suicide. Whether a person has lost a loved one, is intensely lonely, is unhappy in his or her job or with his or her family, is handicapped or old, or simply feels that he or she is being treated unfairly with no apparent solution in the near or even distant future, that person stands a very good chance of developing this way of thinking—that death is the only solution for such seemingly insurmountable problems.

(Richard Sims)

XVIII

I saw a television show on Amazing Stories about a family and their experience in coping with the death of a loved one. The mother and father had an only child, a daughter about twelve years old. All three were involved in a summer scouting activity, as the parents were active as counselors.

Their curious daughter had managed to lose herself in the woods when her attention was diverted from the other hikers by the sighting of a deer. In a frantic desperation she wondered aimlessly further away. Her presence was soon missed and they all searched until dusk when the authorities joined in. After about two days without any clue they reported back with the conclusion that she most probably fell victim to an area that is abundant with quicksand.

The parents, especially the mother, took it very hard. They were so devastated that for the next forty years they devoted their time and home to run a school for the young in memory of their daughter. But they kept her bedroom just as it was when she was with them.

As they grew old the mother became bedridden and sick apparently near death. While constantly at her side, the father begged her not to go, that he needed her and so did the school and the kids. She said nothing and died quietly before him. Then there was a knock at the front door. He got up slowly and answered it to find it was his own little girl perfectly the way she was the day she departed in the woods forty years ago. He was shocked, and while not able to fully understand she assured him that it really was she and that she was fine. Although he didn't understand her mysterious return he hugged her. She asked about her mother and his face grew grim as he explained.

He led her to the room to see her mother. They looked at her body, and as the little girl touched her the old woman was transformed into the beautiful young woman she once was (probably forty years ago). Then the both of them disappeared before his eyes, and when he looked up there they were standing in the doorway ready to say goodbye. He wanted to go with them, but the mother said not yet, for it wasn't his time and he still had work to do. They told him they would be waiting for him and again they vanished.

The story reflects a great point of discussion about death and what happens after. From the living viewpoint it seems that generally people are fearful of losing themselves as well as others to death and there is a basic ignorance as to what will happen thereafter. All they can know for certain is that life is where its at and nobody really wants to go away. Also human attachments give us a security about life. The loss of the little girl, especially not knowing how it happened or where she is (a mystery in itself), might have been meant to portray the mystery of death and what is beyond. Then when his wife died I think it really might have given him an insecurity about life.

But it seems we don't really lose anybody through death as was shown by the little girl returning just as she was remembered, perhaps to show her dad that it wasn't a loss after all and that she is still around somewhere. Also I think she came to him to ease his grieving pain of his wife's death and to offer him hope and relief and understanding of the transformation. I think as they left he realized as we all should that it is not the end but rather a new beginning.

(James J. Candelaria)

XIX

In a sleeping bag, alone on the desert with a million stars all around, I lay, thinking of death. How is it going to be, and where and when, are the simple, obvious questions. It's the only definite event, the only event that I know will happen. Everything else is only a dream . . .

The most frustrating part is there's no way to answer the questions. No book in the world is going to tell us. No professor.

The information's just not in existence.

And so the only alternative is to imagine it for ourselves. What seems sensible? Which way would we construct life and death if it were up to us? Do we want to recycle souls? If not, do we have a place to deposit them when they're done? Should we judge them or let them judge themselves? Or can we just let them expire peacefully no matter how awful they were on earth? Let the civilization work itself out? Let it evolve so it produces good souls?

Ultimately it seems the question of death is wrapped up into the question of purpose: Why is there a world at all? What is its reason?

If I could create my own after-death experience I'd hope to be no more. Complete nonexistence.

No past evils to torment me because the pain is too great.

And it doesn't make me stop committing bad deeds. They still come out.

Being reincarnated doesn't offer much hope because I won't remember who I am. The me right now doesn't remember any past lives. I only associate myself with this time and space. So it doesn't matter if I get reborn a million times—I won't know those other people.

Just this me is all I know.

The idea of heaven would be nice, of course, but it seems like wishful thinking; it doesn't matter to me who dreamed it up.

Why should we expect something good to happen? Who are we to expect to be rewarded? Do tortoises dream of heaven. I don't think we should expect anything different.

So death is an enigmatic certainty. Something to be curious about, a little afraid of, and always something lurking.

But now the sun is rising and Life is more important. Death thoughts turn to live ones as the birds start to chirp, furry animals scurry around, dew melts. And I wonder how to live life so that I can truly Live. Really be Alive.

Life is the only thing I can be certain of.

I am living.

Or at least having a dream that I'm living.

(Debby Beard)

XX:
Working

Doing data entry for a small company and talking with the woman sitting behind me. I couldn't see her, but we were talking about this and that. Out of the blue she mentioned she was going to put flowers on her brother's grave.

I asked when he had died, and she said when he was ten months old and she was three. I said it must be awfully hard to lose a baby and she said yes, especially for her mother, because he died in their mother's arms.

I immediately perked up my ears and got very excited. I said that must have been wonderful for both of them, and I thought how great it would be to be cradled in a loved-one's arms when I die.

She said yes, and added that her family was hard-hit, especially their father, who is a pastor, because the baby at 8 months was already walking and talking, a huge red-haired baby. It turns out he had muscular dystrophy—the reason he was so so big was that with M.D. you grow/develop very rapidly and then your body wastes away while your brain remains active.

But this was particularly important to this story, because, she said, her brother knew, was conscious of what was happening to him. She said he knew he was dying because he was so developed, and added that just before he died, his mother was holding him. He looked up and held out his arms, as if someone were reaching down to him to pick him up, and he said, "Jesus." The next moment he was dead.

I was so excited! I had goose-bumps all over my body and I felt so happy. I said how wonderful, what a great death, and how it must have been a great comfort for both of them to be so near each other and to God in that moment.

It was such a happy story, it didn't seem sad or tragic. We all have to die, and, yes, it is hard to lose a child, but this death seemed so right, so good, and I thought, felt, how wonderful it must have been, and I felt good just listening to it.

(Maria Mendenhall)

INDEX